Lecture Notes in Computer Science 9669

Commenced Publication in 1973
Founding and Former Series Editors:
Gerhard Goos, Juris Hartmanis, and Jan van Leeuwen

More information about this series at http://www.springer.com/series/7411

Jaizki Mendizabal · Marion Berbineau
Alexey Vinel · Stephan Pfletschinger
Hervé Bonneville · Alain Pirovano
Simon Plass · Riccardo Scopigno
Hasnaa Aniss (Eds.)

Communication Technologies for Vehicles

10th International Workshop Nets4Cars/Nets4Trains/Nets4Aircraft 2016 San Sebastián, Spain, June 6–7, 2016 Proceedings

Springer

Editors
Jaizki Mendizabal
Ceit and tecnun
University of Navarra
San Sebastián
Spain

Marion Berbineau
IFSTTAR
Villeneuve d'Ascq
France

Alexey Vinel
Halmstad University
Halmstad
Sweden

Stephan Pfletschinger
Dtsch. Zentrum für Luft- und Raumfahrt
Oberpfaffenhofen
Germany

Hervé Bonneville
Mitsubishi Electric R&D Centre Europe
Rennes
France

Alain Pirovano
Ecole Nationale de l'Aviation Civile
Toulouse
France

Simon Plass
Dtsch. Zentrum für Luft- und Raumfahrt
Oberpfaffenhofen
Germany

Riccardo Scopigno
Istituto Superiore Mario Boella
Turin
Italy

Hasnaa Aniss
IFSTTAR
Versailles
France

ISSN 0302-9743 ISSN 1611-3349 (electronic)
Lecture Notes in Computer Science
ISBN 978-3-319-38920-2 ISBN 978-3-319-38921-9 (eBook)
DOI 10.1007/978-3-319-38921-9

Library of Congress Control Number: 2016939057

LNCS Sublibrary: SL5 – Computer Communication Networks and Telecommunications

Printed on acid-free paper

This Springer imprint is published by Springer Nature
The registered company is Springer International Publishing AG Switzerland

Preface

The Communication Technologies for Vehicles Workshop series provides an international forum on the latest technologies and research in the field of intra- and inter-vehicles communications and is organized annually to present original research results in all areas related to physical layer, communication protocols and standards, mobility and traffic models, experimental and field operational testing, and performance analysis among others.

First launched by Tsutomu Tsuboi, Alexey Vinel, and Fei Liu in Saint Petersburg, Russia (2009), Nets4Workshops series (Nets4Cars/Nets4Trains/Nets4Aircraft) have been held in Newcastle-upon-Tyne, UK (2010), Oberpfaffenhofen, Germany (2011), Vilnius, Lithuania (2012), Villeneuve d'Ascq, France (2013), Offenburg, Germany (2014, Spring), Saint Petersburg, Russia (2014, Fall), Sousse, Tunisia (2015, Spring), and Munich, Germany (2015, Fall).

These proceedings contain the papers presented at the 10th International Workshop on Communication Technologies for Vehicles Nets4Workshops series (Nets4Cars/ Nets4Trains/ Nets4Aircraft 2016), which took place in San Sebastián (European capital of culture 2016), Spain, in June 2016, organized by Ceit and tecnun (University of Navarra), Spain, with the technical support of IFSTTAR, France, and Halmstad University, Sweden.

The call for papers resulted in 17 submissions: eight for Nets4Cars, eight for Nets4Trains, and one for Nets4Aircraft. Each of them was assigned to the international Technical Program Committee members in order to be reviewed by at least three independent reviews. The co-chairs of the three Technical Program Committees (Nets4Cars, Nets4Trains, and Nets4Aircraft) selected 13 full papers for publication in these proceedings and presentation at the workshop, five of them for Nets4Cars, seven for Nets4Trains, and one for Nets4Aircraft. In addition, two invited papers, one demonstration paper, and two keynote papers were also accepted. The order of the papers presented in these proceedings was aligned with the workshop program.

The general co-chairs and the Technical Program Committee co-chairs extend a sincere "thank you" to all the authors who submitted the results of their recent research as well as to all the members of the hard-working comprehensive Technical Program Committee who worked on the reviews.

April 2016

Jaizki Mendizabal
Marion Berbineau
Alexey Vinel
Stephan Pfletschinger
Hervé Bonneville
Alain Pirovano
Simon Plass
Riccardo Scopigno
Hasnaa Aniss

Organization

General Co-chairs

Jaizki Mendizabal	Ceit and tecnun (University of Navarra), Spain
Marion Berbineau	IFSTTAR, France
Alexey Vinel	Halmstad University, Sweden

TPC Co-chairs (Nets4trains)

Stephan Pfletschinger	DLR, Germany
Hervé Bonneville	Mitsubishi Electric R&D Centre Europe, France

TPC Co-chairs (Nets4aircraft)

Alain Pirovano	ENAC, France
Simon Plass	DLR, Germany

TPC Co-chairs (Nets4cars)

Riccardo Scopigno	ISMB, Italy
Hasnaa Aniss	IFSTTAR, France

Steering Committee

Alexey Vinel	Halmstad University, Sweden
Antonella Molinaro	University Mediterranea of Reggio Calabria, Italy
Jaizki Mendizabal	Ceit and tecnun (University of Navarra), Spain
Joel Rodrigues	Instituto de Telecomunicações, University of Beira Interior, Portugal
Kishor Trivedi	Duke University, USA
Marion Berbineau	IFSTTAR, France
Mohamed Kassab	HanaLab, Tunisia
Thomas Strang	DLR, Germany
Tsutomu Tsuboi	Nagoya Electric Works Co., Ltd., Japan
Yan Zhang	Simula Research Lab, Norway

Technical Program Committee

Aitor Arriola	IK4-IKERLAN, Spain
Alexey Vinel	Halmstad University, Sweden
Amine Dhraief	HANA Lab, Tunisia

Anis Laouiti	Telecom SudParis, France
Benoit Hilt	University of Haute Alsace, France
Brian Park	University of Virginia, USA
Christophe Couturier	Télécom Bretagne, France
Christophe Gransart	IFSTTAR, France
Claudia Campolo	University Mediterranea of Reggio Calabria, Italy
David Mottier	Mitsubishi Electric R&D Centre Europe, France
Dorian Petit	LAMIH-University of Valenciennes and Hainaut-Cambresis, France
Fabien Garcia	ENAC, France
Francesca Martelli	IIT-CNR, Italy
Ghofrane Fersi	University of Sfax, Tunisia
Hacene Fouchal	University of Reims, France
Hasnaâ Aniss	IFSTTAR, France
Hervé Bonneville	Mitsubishi Electric R&D Centre Europe, France
Ibrahim Rashdan	German Aerospace Center (DLR), Germany
Iñigo Adin	Ceit and tecnun (University of Navarra), Spain
Iyad Dayoub	IEMN-DOAE, France
Jaizki Mendizabal	Ceit and tecnun (University of Navarra), Spain
Javier Goikoetxea	CAF, Spain
Jose Soler	DTU Fotonik, Denmark
Jouni Tervonen	University of Oulu, Oulu Southern Institute, Finland
Juan Moreno	Metro de Madrid/Universidad Politécnica de Madrid, Spain
Konrad Doll	University of Applied Sciences Aschaffenburg, Germany
Marion Berbineau	IFSTTAR, France
Mohamed Kassab	IFSTTAR, France
Nicolas Gresset	Mitsubishi Electric R&D Centre Europe, France
Paolo Santi	IIT-CNR, Italy
Paula Fraga-Lamas	University of A Coruña, Spain
Saioa Arrizabalaga	Ceit and tecnun (University of Navarra), Spain
Sebastien Simoens	Alstom, France
Simon Plass	German Aerospace Center (DLR), Germany
Subha P Eswaran	International Institute of Information Technology, India
Unai Alvarado	Ceit and tecnun (University of Navarra), Spain
Vasco N.G.J. Soares	Instituto de Telecomunicações/Instituto Politécnico de Castelo Branco, Portugal

Hosting Institutions

Ceit, San Sebastián Spain
Tecnun (University of Navarra), San Sebastián Spain

Organizing Committee

Iñigo Adin	Ceit and tecnun (University of Navarra), Spain
Saioa Arrizabalaga	Ceit and tecnun (University of Navarra), Spain
Juan Melendez	Ceit and tecnun (University of Navarra), Spain

Co-organizers and Sponsoring Institutions

Ceit, Spain
Tecnun (University of Navarra), Spain
IFSTTAR, France
Halmstad University, Sweden
Turismo & Convention Bureau, San Sebastián, Spain
European capital of culture, San Sebastián, Spain

DSS2016.EU

Contents

Nets4trains

Nets4cars

Nets4aircraft

Nets4trains

Roadmap Towards the Wireless Virtual Coupling of Trains

Javier Goikoetxea(✉)

Construcciones y Auxiliar de Ferrocarriles, S.A. (CAF),
José Miguel Iturrioz 26, 20200 Beasain, Spain
jgoikoetxea@caf.net

Abstract. Today coupled trains have become an important bottleneck in terms of performance. Transmission through the auto-coupler is notably impaired by the contact nature and the performance of train communication backbone is much lower. Many times applications on both sides of the coupling point are incompatible, due to different implementations, versions, or retrofitting statuses. Solution comes by providing the so called virtual coupling, where the consists run together, as coupled, but without any physical connection, thus trains manufactured by different companies and with different interfaces could be virtually coupled, driven together by the leading cabin and sharing the same traffic slot. In this paper the virtual coupling is introduced together with the technologies required for its implementation which will be developed within the Shift2Rail initiative.

Keywords: Virtual coupling · Wireless · Shift2Rail

1 Introduction

Today coupled trains have become an important bottleneck in terms of performance. Transmission through the auto-coupler is notably impaired by the contact nature and the performance of train communication backbone is much lower. Coupling trains is time consuming and must be performed during a stop in a station or in the depot before starting the journey.

Wireless communications are already a reality, but there are no onboard applications in railways (except internet connection for passengers). Many uncertainties concerning technology, and safety and security aspects block any attempt to use them.

Even if the communication is possible, applications on both sides of the coupling point are many times incompatible, due to different implementations, versions, or retrofitting statuses.

Self-configuring adaptive solutions providing plug-and-play features through a functional open coupling may solve this issue.

However, the final step is providing the so called virtual coupling, where the consists run together, as coupled, but without any physical connection, thus trains manufactured by different companies and with different interfaces could be virtually coupled, driven together by the leading cabin and sharing the same traffic slot.

J. Mendizabal et al. (Eds.): Nets4Cars/Nets4Trains/Nets4Aircraft 2016, LNCS 9669, pp. 3–9, 2016.
DOI: 10.1007/978-3-319-38921-9_1

Pushing the concept to its limit, it would be possible to couple and uncouple trains on-the-fly (i.e. both consists moving or even cruising) and increase significantly the capacity of the line by making long chains or convoys of virtually coupled trains. This concept will change dramatically the way trains will be controlled in the future because trains will monitor and keep themselves the distance between them with little or none intervention from the infrastructure (i.e. signalling).

In order to develop this breakthrough concept, crucial technical solutions should be available. First the radio communication between trains will require performance equivalent to the current wired Ethernet train backbone in terms of safety, security, throughput, network dynamics and availability. And on the other hand the functional open coupling will have to be implemented to become the needed abstraction layer between applications of the virtually coupled trains.

In that sense, the European initiative Shift2Rail [1] will lead the definition and development of the virtual coupling concept and the required technologies, as it is described in its Master Plan [2]. First activities are currently ongoing within the initiative's lighthouse project Roll2Rail [3].

The following chapters introduce the virtual coupling mechanisms and technologies, and details the planned steps to achieve its development by 2022.

2 The Virtual Coupling

2.1 The Need

Flexibility and modularity are aspects much demanded by the railway undertakings in order to adapt the assets to the real traffic, passenger and pay loads at any time. While airlines allocate their different size airplanes to their more or less demanded routes, railway undertakings count on coupling and uncoupling consists and passenger coaches.

Coupling consists is becoming today a real challenge due to the increased performance of the train functions and due to compatibility issues:

- Consists must be electromechanically compatible at the auto-coupler (type, size, position of the auto-coupler, pin and pipe layout, etc.)
- Communication technology and protocols must be the same (e.g. WTB and UIC 556)
- Consists must implement the same functions
- Implemented functions must be compatible

This leads in fact to the need of having consists of the same train manufacturer, of the same model/series and implementing the same software versions. Even when the said conditions are fulfilled the contact nature of the auto-coupler constraints the real achievable communication throughput and brings reliability issues. Consist must be coupled or uncoupled in a station, extending the dwell time by 3–5 min and affecting the line capacity [4].

As an example the third generation of TGV operated by SNCF is composed of more than 10 different types of configurations able to couple, meaning that there are over 100 different possible coupling combinations. This has led to having to perform a daily average in excess of 2000 functional verifications to check that there is no regression in each possible combination. This is a significant constraint in terms of lack of flexibility of the fleet, operational cost, homologation cost and loss of potential revenue by failing to create suitable trains of TGV consists[1].

2.2 The Concept

A new radical approach is needed to overcome the lack of flexibility and poor performance of the actual coupling mechanism. Taking advantage of the preparatory phase of the Shift2Rail initiative the European TCMS experts from the industry and from the main railway undertakings proposed already in 2011 a number of technical developments to shape the next generation of TCMS, whose innovative flagship was the virtual coupling concept. The solution goes through coupling consists of any manufacturer or generation without any physical connection (i.e. not depending on the auto-coupler) but still commanding the formed convoy from the leading cab as it is being done today.

The first question that immediately comes up is about the distance between consists (i.e. headway). The answer is as simple as the minimum necessary to guarantee safety. It must be noted that the virtual coupling does not derive from the moving block signalling concept. It goes beyond. In fact, the virtual coupling will allow trains to run so close to each other as to be inside their absolute braking distance. Other key feature will be the ability to dynamically modify the convoy composition on-the-fly. The concept relies on the assumption that each consist has a breaking curve and needs some distance to stop, so the headway corresponds to the distance equivalent to the reaction time (plus safety factors) of the following consist. Similar behaviour is present when driving cars on the motorway, where the actual headway is less than the required for the complete braking distance [5].

Coupling and uncoupling on-the-fly, without stopping the train, brings an enormous potential for building convoys dynamically. In other words, consists will be able to dynamically join and leave when needed. Sharing a traffic slot within a convoy, detaching for serving a train station and reattaching to a next passing convoy would be a normal operational procedure.

That of course must be achieved while ensuring at least the same level of safety currently provided by the railway system based on standards and well known basic criteria.

2.3 High Level Architecture

The virtual coupling mechanism will be based on two functional layers.

- First, a dependable wireless communication system to command and monitor all virtually coupled consists from the leading cab will be required. On top of this, an

[1] Example for Alstom's TGV type "Réseau" for the compatibility with other TGV types (i.e. Paris-Brussels-Amsterdam, Paris-Brussels-Koln-Amsterdam, Duplex or POS).

abstraction layer allowing different consists to understand each other will be implement (i.e. functional translation). This wireless communication system should, at least, support SIL2 functions.
- Second, the mechanical coupling will be replaced by a safe mechanism to guarantee the distance between consists in the convoy regardless if the first layer fails. This independent system will be based on proximity radars or similar aeronautical technologies, and accurate train positioning.

Technologies supporting this architecture are currently being developed by Shift2Rail projects and are described in the next chapter.

3 Technological Pillars

The virtual coupling mechanism is based on new technologies been developed or adapted for railways, which will mean a breakthrough in the TCMS field.

3.1 Dependable Wireless Communication for the Train Backbone

If following consists are commanded and monitored from the leading cab, the TCMS must reach each of them. Not having physical connection the solution goes through deploying a wireless train backbone.

The consecution of a deep knowledge of the state of the art of wireless technologies used for onboard communications together with a proper understanding of the channel characteristics will be essential for proposing adequate solutions. Communication protocols will be defined then, including safety and security aspects, and hardware and software components developed to validate the solutions in laboratory and vehicle tests.

Strong requirements on full availability and security will probably lead to architectures with several channels in parallel, one of those, having ground components as a relay station. Technologies like cognitive radio are also being into account.

It will be also desirable to allocate specific frequencies to this application. Knowing how challenging this is, lobbying initiatives have started with the European Railway Agency.

Wireless communications for train command and monitoring and other relevant applications have been studied in the last years showing the relevance of this research domain by individuals [6–8] or through collaborative projects [9].

Within the Roll2Rail project, before summer 2016 measurements to characterise channels and radio behaviours will be taken in two different rail environments: High speed lines in Italy (Trenitalia) and metro service in Spain (Metro de Madrid). Later on, in 2017 it is expected to carry out some validation tests in the laboratory.

Shift2Rail will take the results of Roll2Rail over. In 2018 first tests are planned on real vehicles prior to the implementation of prototypes and full scale testing from 2020.

3.2 Functional Open Coupling

The objective of the long awaited functional open coupling is to make possible the coupling of two or more consists supplied by different manufacturers and which could have different train functions or software versions. It will allow the control command and monitoring of the whole virtually coupled convoy, made of different consists supplied by different manufacturers.

The core activity of this technical pillar will be the study of a train functional communication concept that could be assigned to a Function Reference Module (FRM). In each consist, this FRM shall ensure the communication of the function with the same function of other consists or with the external functions (infrastructure or maintenance for instance). Depending on the function, a FRM could be elected as communication master at train level for this function. As a result its location will migrate from the leading consist or vehicle of the train to the consist that has the newest definition or the richest definition for the train function services allowing the communication of the function at train level with all the other consists. The distinction between the master of the function and the master of the communication must be ensured by innovative design.

The innovative functional open coupling design will provide:

- A high reliable dynamic behaviour on:
  - Coupling/decoupling consist in operation from a functional point of view
  - Authorized activating/de-activating of functions
  - Management of transients in the presence of hosting target equipment
- Functional ascending compatibility of consists, ensured by a consolidated list of services per function and the object oriented syntax of functions services on the network
- Interface with the function of the consist

To illustrate the FRM concept and applied to the virtual coupling paradigm the following simple example is clarifying:

Brake function of consist "A" is commanded through five discrete braking efforts, being "1" pure electric brake and "5" full emergency brake. However, the brake function of consist "B" is commanded through an analogue lever providing inputs from 0 % to 100 % of braking effort. Homogeneous braking is crucial for a proper performance of the virtual coupling concept, thus the FRM would translate both functions into a common model and semantics, for example, into deceleration in m/s^2.

The functional open coupling is intended to supersede the UIC 556 leaflet even for current mechanical coupling.

This technology will be developed within the first projects of Shift2Rail and a preliminary proof of concept is planned for the end of 2018.

3.3 The Safe Anti-collision Mechanism

Regardless any potential loss of the radio link or any other failure or incident, including cyber-attacks the concept must remain safe, as safe as having physically coupled consists. With that respect the mechanical coupler must be replaced by safe (i.e. SIL4 function) virtual coupler.

In the railway domain certain proposals have already been presented based on train to train communications and positioning [10]. While this approach should be further explored taking advantage of the research activities on safe positioning within the Shift2Rail initiative, it must be not forgotten the new developments coming from the car industry, where the rail virtual coupling concept is known as car platooning [11, 12]. However, first adaptive cruise controls based on radar were already introduced in 1996 [13] and since then many developments have been successfully carried out up to reaching the almost autonomous car like the new Mercedes E-Class 2016, which integrates radar devices and stereoscopic cameras for its Drive Pilot system [14].

Most probably the technical solution for the rail anti-collision system will follow the same approach and will integrate information coming from different sources such as a precise positioning, the communication between consists or artificial vision.

First research activities should start within Shift2Rail in 2018.

4 Virtual Coupling Concept as New Train Control Technique

The concept overlaps in its fundamentals the actual train control system (i.e. signalling), therefore it has also been understood as a new way for controlling trains.

Besides the flexibility the main impact of the virtual coupling concept is the reduction of the line headway and line capacity increase. The new required function could be seen as the extreme limit of the moving block on relative braking in order to compact trains dynamically on the fly, up to have logical coupling (i.e. virtual coupling) of trains while they are moving. The function is not only limited to the on board environment but, in order to work properly, it needs new features and to upgrade functionalities in the wayside signalling and supervision systems as well.

The approach of virtually coupled consists is a new paradigm of the train control as it will overcome the current limitations of the signalling and, as said, it is in contrast with the basic train separation principles. In fact theoretically the new train control system should be able to:

- Manage dynamically convoy joining/splitting also during normal traffic and running time
- Manage new train separation systems overcoming the limitation of the brick wall concept (i.e. the minimum distance considers absolute distances)
- Manage train convoys and dynamic route setting/releasing through updated interlocking systems
- Accomplish traffic regulation through updated supervision system in order to manage dynamic train consists and timetables for multiple trains joined in a single convoy
- Guarantee, through updated on board ATP/ATO systems, the safety and the automatic driving according to the new physical constraints and scenario.

Such signalling related modifications and adaptations will be studied from 2018 in the Shift2Rail initiative.

5 Conclusions

The virtual coupling breakthrough concept will revolutionise the paradigm of railways. The never seen before flexibility and capacity will change the way railways is operated.

Today emerging technologies from the telecommunication and computing worlds make it feasible to introduce such concept in railways, while the leverage effect coming from the car industry and their large scale sales will smooth the acceptance of the concept and moderate the costs.

The Shift2Rail initiative gathers, through its members and open consortia, a tremendous task force of experts, that will research and implement the technical pillars to achieve the virtual coupling of trains and that will lead to real demonstrators from 2020.

References

1. Shift2Rail. The Rail Joint Undertaking. http://www.shift2rail.org
2. Shift2Rail Strategic Master Plan, Version 1.0, March 2015. http://ec.europa.eu/transport/modes/rail/doc/2015-03-31-decisionn4-2015-adoption-s2r-masterplan.pdf
3. Peris, E., Goikoetxea, J.: Developing the rolling stock of the future. European Railway Review **21**(5) (2015)
4. Transportation Research Board: Transit Capacity and Quality of Service Manual. Third Edition (2013). ISBN: 978-0-309-28344-1
5. Filzek, B., Breuer, B.: Distance behavior on motorways with regard the active safety. SAE International. Paper# 2001-06-0066 (2001)
6. Meyer zu Hörste, M.: Use of broadband communication for information and control purposes in railways. In: 7th International Conference on ITS Telecommunications, ITST 2007, Sophia Antipolis, France (2007)
7. Rico Garcia, C., Lehner, A., Strang, T.: Channel model for train to train communication using the 400 MHz band. In: Srinivasan, V. (ed.) IEEE Vehicular Technology Conference, VTC 2008 - Spring, pp. 3082–3086. eXpress Publishing (2008)
8. Lehner, A., Rico Garcia, C., Strang, T.: On the performance of TETRA DMO short data service in railway VANETs. Wirel. Pers. Commun. **69**(4), 1647–1669 (2013)
9. Toubol, A., Castagnetti, F.: Marathon project for long trains with distributed traction. Transport Research Arena, Paris (2014)
10. Rico Garcia, C., Lehner, A., Strang, T., Rockl, M.: Comparison of collision avoidance systems and applicability to rail transport. In: 7th International Conference on ITS Telecommunications, ITST 2007, Sophia Antipolis, France (2007)
11. Bergenhem, C., Hedin, E., Skarin, E.: Vehicle-to-vehicle communication for a platooning system. Procedia Soc. Behav. Sci. **48**, 1222–1233 (2012)
12. Robinson, T., Chan, E., Coelingh, E.: Operating platoons on public motorways: an introduction to the sartre platooning programme. In: Proceedings of the 17th ITS World Congress, Busan, Korea, 25–29 October (2010)
13. Ronald, J.: Adaptive Cruise Control. SAE International (2006). ISBN: 978-0-7680-1792-2
14. Intelligent Drive next Level as part of Driving Assistance package. Mercedes-Benz. https://www.mercedes-benz.com/en/mercedes-benz/innovation/with-intelligent-drive-more-comfort-in-road-traffic/

Rail2X: Demonstration of Vehicle2X Technologies for Rail-Related Applications

Michael Meyer zu Hörste(✉), Andreas Kluge, and Tobias Frankiewicz

DLR, Institute of Transportation Systems,
Lilienthalplatz 7, 38108 Braunschweig, Germany
{Michael.MeyerzuHoerste,Andreas.Kluge,Tobias.Frankiewicz}@dlr.de
http://www.dlr.de/ts

Abstract. Transportation vehicles are more and more communicating with their system environment. In the Road Transport Domain the Vehicle2Vehicle communication standard is developed and components are commercially available. Those technologies are suitable to be used for road-rail interactive uses cases (e.g. level crossings) as well as for pure railway use cases (e.g. information at platforms). To show this potential a demonstration has been done at a level crossing in the area of the dock railway in Braunschweig, Germany. This contribution presents the approach, the demonstration and some results.

Keywords: Vehicle2X · Car2X · Rail2X · IEEE 801.11p · Level crossing

1 Introduction

The communication standard IEEE 802.11p has been set together with a specific purely software-defined protocol for the information exchange between road vehicles [1,2]. Hence it is called Vehicle2Vehicle (V2V) or sometimes Car2Car (C2C) communication standard. Nevertheless it can be used to communicate to the infrastructure as well and is than called Vehicle2X (V2X) communication or Car2X (C2X), respectively. Broader use in the automotive environment will lead to a high market penetration and availability as well as extremely low cost for the technology.

For the rail transport a broader distribution of information and a more intensive exchange with other traffic participants as well as with rail users is an increasing demand. One possible idea to solve this demand could be to use common-off-the-shelf technologies as even Vehicle2X. The V2X communication is fitted with an adopted software protocol for railway purposes while leaving the hardware unmodified. This can be used to distribute additional information inside the railway system as well as to other interested users. Nevertheless the automation and protection systems of the railways need to ensure the safety and performance of the operation. Hence they will stay unchanged and the Rail2X systems will either give additional information without safety requirements or act as an overlay.

J. Mendizabal et al. (Eds.): Nets4Cars/Nets4Trains/Nets4Aircraft 2016, LNCS 9669, pp. 10–14, 2016.
DOI: 10.1007/978-3-319-38921-9_2

2 Application Use Cases

The Rail2X technology opens many possibilities in the rail domain. The different application use cases can be classified by many characteristics as e.g. safety-relevance, internal or external, train control, maintenance or informative. Some examples are given in Table 1.

Table 1. Example use cases

Nr.	Use case	Type	Safety relevance
1	Level Crossing Information Broadcast	Broadcast	no
2	Passenger platform stop demand	unidirectional	no
3	Actual arrival time information	unidirectional	no
4	Level Crossing Activation	bidirectional	yes
5	Maintenance status and data information transport	unidirectional	no

Many use cases are possible, which are different with respect to their communication type as e.g. broadcast, uni- or bidirectional peer-to-peer communication. Safety relevance is another important aspect of the use cases. This aspects need to be analyzed in each individual use case. For the demonstration only one should be discussed here in further detail: Broadcasting traffic information at a level crossing.

2.1 Traffic Information Broadcast at Level Crossing

The selected one for the demonstration is the distribution of dynamic information at a level crossing (LX). The train sends an activation message to the road-side unit (RSU) located at the LX. The LX broadcasts the closing information to the road users. For the first demonstration it is easier to implement use cases without safety relevance. Hence the selected use case demonstrates an information overlay system to inform road users about the status of the LX and - if closed - about the expected remaining closing time. It is not foreseen to replace the regular LX activation system.

2.2 Idea

The global idea is shown in Fig. 1. On the railway track, the rail vehicle - in this case the DLR-operated Road-Rail vehicle RailDriVE® approaches the level crossing coming from the upper side [3]. At the same time, the road vehicle approaches from the right side. Whenever a rail vehicle passes the make contact, the light signals at the railway crossing are activated, indicating road vehicles to leave the crossing. According to German regulations, the rail vehicle would have the right of way and would be prioritized to road vehicles. The lights signals on the road indicate road vehicles to leave the crossing, or to stop in front of the crossing, respectively.

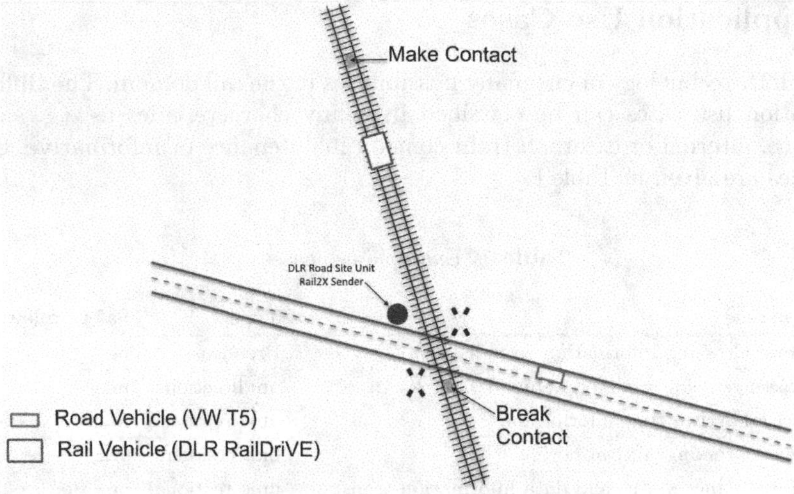

Fig. 1. Demo topology layout

At the same position the V2X Unit of the train identifies by geo-fencing that the LX has to be activated and sends via Rail2X the activation message to the RSU located at the level crossing.

For the road side of the demo scenario the RSU uses the regular V2V standard. After receiving the activation trigger the RSU broadcasts the information to the road users. It will now start to send "signal, phase and timing messages" (SPAT messages), which has been modified to reflect the operational rules for LX.

The demonstration shows both communication domains: The V2X communication between RSU and car as well as the railway part between RSU and train. So it can be seen that the hardware and radio layer are interoperable while the communication protocol software is specific for each domain.

2.3 Implementation

The demonstration was presented at a level crossing of the port railway of Braunschweig, Germany. The minimalistic demo implementation consisted out of the following three elements:

- **Train:** The Road-Rail-Vehicle RailDriVE® of the DLR was equipped with an OBU and a experimental user interface. It was equipped in addition with a high precision digital map of the railway track and a suitable localization unit [4]. They were used for the geo-fencing-based triggering of the RSU. The OBU is fulfilling the current standard and was modified for the demo purpose. A further automotive PC was used for the application itself.
- **Car:** A Volkswagen T5 van was equipped with an OBU and an experimental user interface. The OBU is fulfilling the standard.

- **Infrastructure:** The level crossing at the local road was equipped with the RSU to communicate with the train as well as with road vehicles. The RSU was equipped with a digital map representing the road and rail topography. A RSU according to the current standard was used.

Bounding conditions for the demo were defined as e.g.:

- No modification or interaction with the regular LX.
- Only experimental displays were used without integration in the vehicles.
- Only the regular scenario was demonstrated. No failure scenarios were examined.
- Standard hardware was used as far as possible.

2.4 Demonstration

The demonstration was done at the end of 2015. The Fig. 2 show the perspective of the road and rail vehicles in almost the same moment.

Fig. 2. User Interface in the train (left) and car (right) at Demo Situation with LX activated.

The demonstration was executed successfully and showed that the Vehicle2X technologies can be used for Rail2X applications as well. The user interfaces used in the demo are not designed as usable products, but as demonstrator units to show the data exchange and the current system states. The user interfaces can be seen in Fig. 3.

2.5 Main Findings

The Demonstration showed the functional feasibility as well as the suitability of the communication properties. Further detailed tests have to be done to check the robustness and other requirements of the Rail2X technology.

Fig. 3. User Interface design in the train (left) and the car (right) at Demo Situation with LX activated

3 Conclusion and Perspective

A simple and easy-to-demonstrate application showing an overlay system for LX using Rail2X communication technology has been developed and demonstrated in a "real life" scenario on a public road and a private railroad segment. Because of the passive system design, safety at level crossings can be improved by warning the road drivers without the need of modifications to the rail systems at the level crossing. In future work, a nonreactive way of interaction with the level crossing systems will be designed and implemented, and dedicated messages for interaction between railway and road vehicles shall be specified.

References

1. IEEE: IEEE 802.11p wireless access in vehicular environments (WAVE) (2013)
2. ETSI: ETSI EN 302 663. Intelligent Transport Systems (ITS); Access layer specification for Intelligent Transport Systems operating in the 5 GHz frequency band. ETSI (2013)
3. Lüddecke, K., Kluge, A.: Mobiles Labor RailDriVE - Synchrone Erfassung von Sensordaten. Der Eisenbahningenieur EI **65**, 46–49 (2014). (in German)
4. Gerlach, K., Meyer zu Hörste, M.: Precision and availability evaluation for road and rail localisation platforms. In: NAVAGE 2008, Prague (2008)

The Viability of TETRA for ETCS Railway Signalling System

Amanda Esteban(✉) and Sonia Solanas

Teltronic S.A.U., Zaragoza, Spain
aesteban@teltronic.es

Abstract. The advanced maturity of the ERTMS standard and the obsolescence of GSM-R, the communications technology that supports it, means that transport operators in certain environments are seeking new means of communication that provide an equivalent level of service quality. This study, mainly based on an experimental setup, looks at TETRA technology and its positive correlation to the seven quality of service parameters required of GSM-R as defined in the EIRENE specification – a document that outlines the ERTMS standard – and also helps increase operational safety and reduce costs; demonstrating that TETRA is a real alternative to GSM-R.

Keywords: TETRA · GSM-R · Signalling · Railway · ERTMS · ETCS · EIRENE · Subset 093 · Alternative · QoS · Quality of Service · Finland · Communication

1 Introduction

The three main objectives of transport operators are to improve passenger service, increase operational safety and reduce overall operating costs. Achieving these objectives involves a high degree of information management and processing, particularly in established railway signalling systems. These systems are based on radio communications networks that facilitate end-to-end transmission of the data generated – vital data, since it contains information relating to operation of the trains and, therefore, to the safety of the passengers.

2 Railway Signalling Applications Used Within Europe

Each European country organises its rail transport network in a particular way. However, incompatibility between signalling systems that perform control and protection functions poses a serious problem for the movement of people and goods within the European Community.

The Fig. 1 shows the diversity of signalling systems used throughout Europe in 2003. The majority of these systems are based on information being punctually transmitted to the train via beacons along the route, and may be inadequate and insufficient for the correct operation of current control systems.

J. Mendizabal et al. (Eds.): Nets4Cars/Nets4Trains/Nets4Aircraft 2016, LNCS 9669, pp. 15–26, 2016.
DOI: 10.1007/978-3-319-38921-9_3

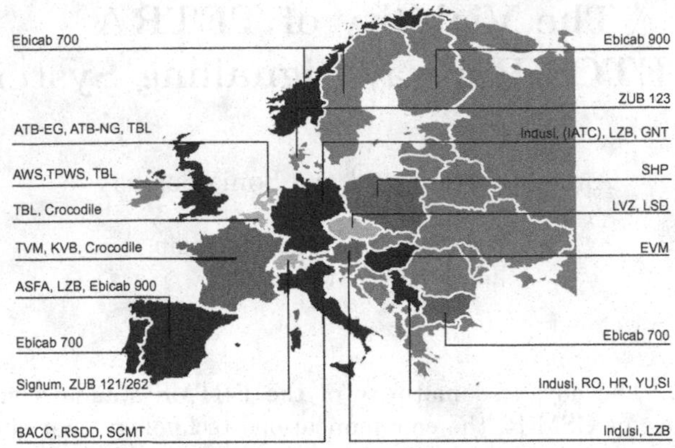

Fig. 1. Railway signalling and security systems used throughout Europe in 2003.

This situation has led the European Union to design a unified ERTMS (European Rail Traffic Management System) system that attempts to achieve medium-term Europe-wide homogenization of railway signalling, control functions and radio communications, via ETCS (European Train Control System) and GSM-R (Global system for Mobile communications - Railway).

3 The ERTMS Standard

The ERTMS standard is basically divided into two main blocks.

On the one hand, the ETCS (European Train Control System), which provides up to three levels of protection depending on the equipment installed. Level 1 provides in-cabin signalling; Level 2 provides radio-based operation, although it is supported by the track's signals; Level 3 operates almost exclusively on radio communications and incorporates moving block feature.

On the other hand, the GSM-R communication system, a variant of GSM cellular technology, based on circuit switching operating in the 800–900 MHz frequency band. This technology provides simultaneous voice and data and incorporates functionality specifically tailored to the rail market.

The GSM-R network must be considered, from a safety point of view, as an open communication system. Consequently, additional functionality is required to ensure adequate integrity. For this, ETCS has defined a secure communication protocol, called EURORADIO, based on an open communication network as GSM-R, as shown in the Fig. 2 [2,3].

Several EU countries currently have Levels 1 and 2 ERTMS systems deployed and running; such as Switzerland, Italy, Germany, Spain and the Netherlands. This system is considered one of the safest and most efficient in existence – hence its implementation beyond Europe, in countries such as China, India, Taiwan, Saudi Arabia and South Africa.

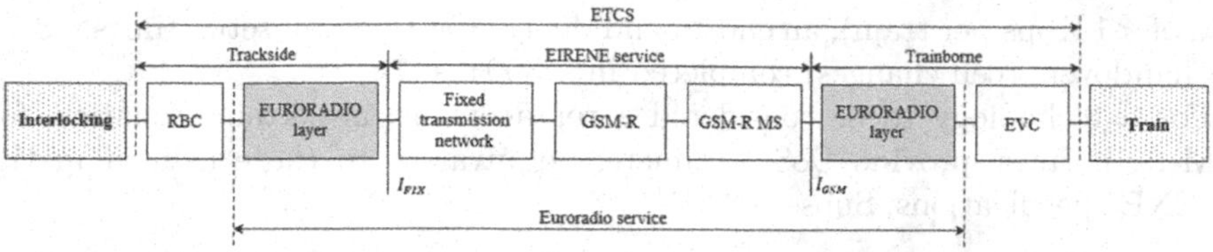

Fig. 2. Architecture of the ETCS signalling system

4 Past, Present and Future of Communications for ETCS Railway Signalling

The obsolescence of GSM-R, together with the emergence of new technologies, has led to major European bodies to lead the search for a substitute, with a proposed deadline of 2022. The intention is, however, to protect any investment hitherto made in this technology.

Regardless of these developments, there are currently many circumstances – among national, regional, metropolitan European lines and even international lines outside Europe – where the use of GSM-R is not mandatory. Here, other technologies that meet today's safety and cost requirements are emerging to manage the data traffic generated by this kind of application, such as TETRA (TErrestrial Trunked RAdio).

The TETRA standard operates in different frequency bands between 300 and 800 MHz and was developed to meet the communication demands of professional users: rapid and secure communications, data transmission services, direct mode communications, quality of service, priority management, group calls, etc.

This leading critical communications technology has been extensively field-tested in hundreds of transportation projects worldwide. In fact, a major initiative of the Finnish railways aims to migrate its GSM-R system for ETCS Level 1 signalling and move to the Government's national TETRA network (VIRVE) since the cost of deployment and maintenance of a TETRA system is lower than that of GSM-R (about half) and, furthermore, TETRA perfectly meets the service quality parameters for communication systems described by the EIRENE specifications (see below). Hence, TETRA covers both present and future needs of Finnish railways: Voice for current ETCS Level 1 and data when the decision to migrate to ETCS Level 2 arrives.

5 Examination of the Quality of Service (QoS) Parameters

Levels 2 and 3 of the ERTMS rely heavily on communication provided by GSM-R: the train regularly reports its position and fixed equipment sends movement authorities, continuously informing how far and how fast the vehicle can move. This requires the constant exchange of small messages (generally <100 bytes, a total of <1 Kbps per train), an end-to-end delay <500 ms, call setup times <8,5 s and handovers (cell changes) completed in <300 ms [7].

For a technology to be considered a replacement, in certain scenarios, for GSM-R, it must provide QoS parameters equivalent to those defined in the EIRENE specifications, Subset 093 [1].

Table 1. QoS requirements for GSM-R, EIRENE specifications, Subset 093

QoS Parameter	Value
Connection establishment delay of mobile originated calls	<8 s (95 %), ≤ 10 s (100 %)
Connection establishment error ratio	$< 10^{-2}$
Maximum end-to-end transfer delay (of 30 bytes data block)	≤ 0,5 s (99 %)
Connection loss rate	$< 10^{-2}$/h
Transmission interference period	<0,8 s (95 %), <1 s (99 %)
Error-free period	>20 s (95 %), >7 s (99 %)
Network registration delay	≤ 30 s (95 %), ≤ 35 s (99 %), ≤ 40 s (100 %)

The QoS comparison made between TETRA and GSM-R uses the Circuit Mode Data (CMD) service offered by the TETRA standard, since it is the natural alternative to the circuit switching service offered by GSM-R[1] (Table 1).

5.1 TETRA Circuit Mode Data Service

TETRA's CMD data service allows an external application (fixed part) to establish a connection with a TETRA radio (onboard unit) for simultaneous data transfer in both directions. This data is transferred transparently between the two ends via the air interface – that is, the TETRA radio does not modify the data during transmission.

A CMD communication consists of the same phases as a voice call – i.e. it is based on a call set-up phase, distribution and allocation of the traffic channel (TCH), data transfer and release of resources. Once the connection is established, the channel remains busy until the transmission is complete.

These calls can be set at different speeds with different levels of protection to overcome possible eventualities caused by the radio channel. There are three types of CMD calls supported by the TETRA standard [5]:

[1] Although both TETRA and GSM-R offer voice and data services, this study only looks at the data side by comparing the response to the Quality of Service parameters established by EIRENE specification.

- 7,2 kbps, unprotected data. This type of call offers no protection during the transmission of data, so any data corruption is accepted by the receiver or a higher-level protocol must be implemented to request retransmission.
- Protection 4,8 kbps short interleaving depth (N = 1). In this type of call, bits of redundancy are used for error detection and correction, increasing security of communications in exchange for a reduction in bandwidth.
- Protection 2,4 kbps short interleaving depth (N = 1). Like 4.8 kbps calls, these calls include additional bits for error detection and correction. These CRC mechanisms require a greater number of additional bits, which increases the security notably, at the expense of a significant reduction in bandwidth.

5.2 Parameter Definition for the TETRA Laboratory Environment

This study was carried out by making a CMD duplex call at 4,8 kbps between an onboard application (OBC) connected to TETRA mobile data radio equipment via RS-232 (serial interface); and an external application (RBC), connected via IP to the infrastructure (fixed part).

The TETRA infrastructure has two base stations (SBS), each with a carrier to enable cell change (handover) testing. All traffic exchanged between the fixed and onboard unit is observed and captured at a single point – a computer known as the Traffic Sniffer, connected to the switch port mirroring and set to simultaneously observe the traffic from both ends. This allows the testing of parameters such as end-to-end delay without requiring the synchronisation of the fixed and onboard units (Fig. 3).

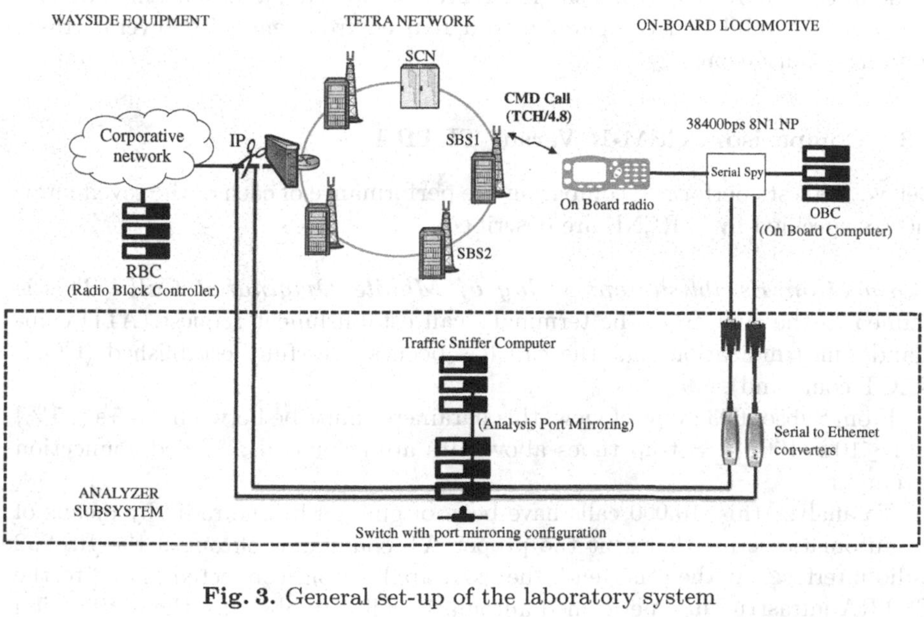

Fig. 3. General set-up of the laboratory system

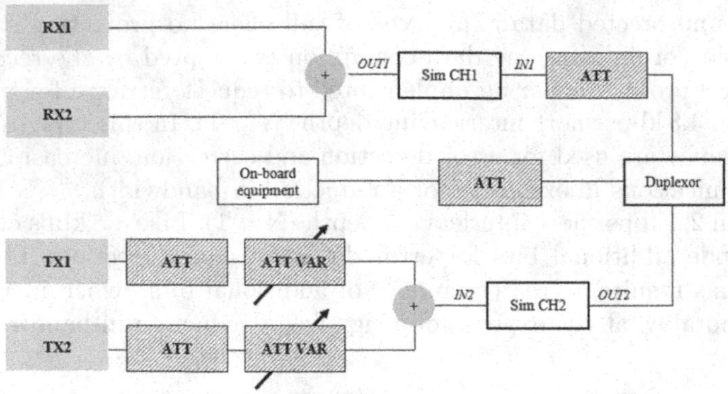

Fig. 4. RF set-up to simulate handover in the laboratory environment

To make conditions as realistic as possible, the laboratory set-up used a channel simulator baseband, simulating a propagation environment HT100 (mountainous environment with the train traveling at 100 km/h) at the limit of dynamic sensitivity, −99 dBm radio and −102 dBm at the carrier (Fig. 4).

As indicated in Subset 093, the QoS criteria must be guaranteed regardless of the number of trains simultaneously registered in the same base station coverage area, so that in situations of high density os users like stations or depots as well as in the whole tracks, this analysis has considered the use of an own data channel per train to ensure availability at all times. Thus, the measurements made in the laboratory with a single TETRA radio using a data channel (TCH) are perfectly valid and comparable to a real environment with several trains running simultaneously.

5.3 Comparison: GSM-R Versus TETRA

Below, the tests performed comparing the performance of each of the seven parameters specified by EIRENE are described:

Connection Establishment Delay of Mobile Originated Call. This is defined as the time from the terminal's call establishment request (ATD command) until indication that the call has been successfully established (CONNECT command).

From Subset 093 point of view, this parameter must be between <8,5 s (95 %) and ≤10 s (100 %). Set-up times above 10 s are evaluated as failed connection attempts.

To analyze this, 10.000 calls have been originated by the radio by means of an automatic script that sent the proper AT commands througth the RS-232 radio interface. At the other end, the fixed application, connected via IP to the TETRA infrastructure, performed automatic call pick-ups once the notification was received. Once the CMD duplex call was established, both ends transmitted a message of 30 bytes, after which time the call was released from the fixed end. Six seconds after establishing the previous call, the TETRA radio repeated the process.

In the described environment, taking into account the methodology of the tests, the establishment time of a CMD call was <1 s (100 %) with no failed attempts – a time that exceeds the performance required by EIRENE.

Connection Establishment Error Ratio. This value must be $< 10^{-2}$, considering as errors all failed call attempts and established calls >10 s. Therefore, considering the results above, TETRA technology must be considered competitive, as far as call set-up times are concerned.

Maximum End-to-End Transfer Delay. This is defined as the time between the first byte (of a user data block of 30 bytes) being sent by the transmitter and the last bit of the block being received by the receiver. According to EIRENE especifications, this should be ≤0,5 s (99 %).

To study this, once the CMD call between the TETRA radio and the fixed part has been established, both ends begin to transmit packets of 30 bytes every 1 s. This makes possible to analyse the maximum end-to-end delay in both uplink (onboard unit to fixed part) and downlink (fixed part to onboard unit). Packet transfer is maintained for one hour four times. Each packet sent is identified by a number in consecutive sequence. Since the same packet, sent from one end and received by the other, is captured in a single point, end-to-end delay can be accurately measured.

As shown in the table below, the maximum end-to-end delay is <0,5 s (100 %), so, in terms of this criterion – a vital parameter in a transportation system – TETRA complies with the standard (Table 2).

Table 2. TETRA end-to-end transfer delay

Iteration	Link	Maximum delay (s)	Average delay (s)
1	Uplink	0.402	0.218
	Downlin	0.360	0.194
2	Uplink	0.377	0.219
	Downlink	0.372	0.195
3	Uplink	0.449	0.214
	Downlink	0.402	0.196
4	Uplink	0.433	0.215
	Downlink	0.372	0.194

Transmission Interference Period (TTI) and Error Free Period. The TTI is defined as the period of time in which there may be loss of information or information received with errors. The maximum value of the TTI should cover all transmission errors from the train's journey, since cell changes (handovers) are a critical moment of communication.

Regarding Subset 093 QoS parameters, this value must be between <0,8 s (95 %) and <1 s (100 %).

The cell change in GSM-R is caused by the infrastructure. This parameter assumes the worst case scenario, known as "cell radius handover with preemption" – i.e. a lower priority call has to be disconnected before performing the handover. In this case, the TTI = time it takes to disconnect the call (around 600 ms) + time of handover in GSM-R (about 300 ms) (Fig. 5).

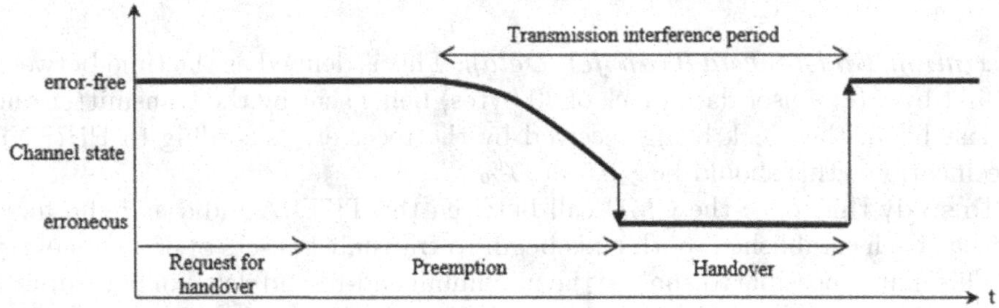

Fig. 5. GSM-R transmission interference period

In view of the above, the TTI is clearly linked to the time of handover. The typical time of handover in GSM-R is about 300 ms. In TETRA technology, this time depends on the type of handover used. The most common is handover type 3, which requires for synchronisation of the TDMA frame when moving from one cell to another. In a type 1 handover, the mobile unit engaged in a call and occupying a traffic slot informs the carrier that it has detected another cell with better coverage. The carrier then tells the radio which slot to occupy within the other cell.

When changing cell, the call is not interrupted and goes directly to the traffic channel of the target cell, without the need to achieve synchronization on the TDMA frame, be registered in the new cell and reconnect the call. The effect of this is a reduction of handover time compared to a type 3 handover, where the call is interrupted. The mobile unit must search for synchronisation of the TDMA frame and, then, register in the new cell to establish the call again.

This analysis utilised the same set of tests as described for maximum end-to-end transfer delay – that is, four sessions 1 h each where both ends begin to transmit packets of 30 bytes every 1 s while causing the handover of the TETRA radio by modifying the RSSI level it received through the use of variable and programmable attenuators every minute. The tests were performed with both handovers types with the following results:

- Handover type 1: TTI <0,8 s (95 %) and <1 s (100 %)
- Handover type 3: TTI <1 s (95 %) and <3 s (100 %)

Therefore, we can conclude that TETRA technology offers a performance within the limits set by EIRENE especifications in terms of the value of TTI when using handover type 1.

Each interference period should be followed by a criterion called an Error-Free Period, which allows the transmission of information that has not been received or has been received with errors, along with the new information waiting to be transmitted. By definition, in Subset 093, this must be between >20 s (95 %), and >7 s (99 %). Taken into account a minimum distance of 14 km between TETRA base stations and assuming a train traveling at 200 km/h, the handover will happen every 250 s approximately; for which the error free period (free time of error that must follow every TTI) in TETRA meets with the requirements demanded by EIRENE. Additionally, the distance of 14 Km between TETRA base stations (determined by the coverage study realized in this type of environment) is necessary to guarantee, statistically, a coverage level of 99.99 % in the perimeter of the cell.

Network Registration Delay. This is defined as the time from requested registration of the radio network to the receipt of an ACK.

According to Subset 093, this must be between <30 s (95 %) and ≤35 s (99 %); values of >40 s are considered to be errors.

To carry out this test, the time elapsed between power being provided to the TETRA radio and the +CREG command being received was measured 200 times – obtaining a result of <15 s (100 %). This is a great improvement over EIRENE requirements.

All these results show that, in terms of QoS parameters, TETRA technology can be a viable alternative to GSM-R.

However, in addition to the Subset 093 criteria, there are other fundamental aspects that endorse TETRA usage:

Bit Error Rate (BER). This parameter is defined as the number of erroneously received bits compared to the total number of bits sent in a given time interval. In this area, both TETRA and GSM-R provide figures around $< 10^{-4}$.

Maximum Speed. A maximum speed of up to 200 km/h must be guaranteed without affecting the QoS parameters. To this end, it has been empirically verified that with a more restrictive propagation model (HT300, mountainous environment with the train traveling at 300 km/h), increasing the speed results in an improvement in the error message rate (%MER) of the TETRA receiver. This coincides with the results shown in the Technical Report ETSI ETR 300- 2 [4]. In addition, it has been proven that even with a 1 KHz frequency deviation between transmitter and receiver, all receivers are able to synchronise with the transmitter and receive without appreciable loss in dynamic sensitivity.

The next step is to calculate the speed at which the deviation of frequency due to the Doppler Effect is 500 Hz. This limit is given, since a mobile terminal moving from the base at $\pm V$ (V being the speed at which the Doppler shift is

500 Hz) will transmit at ±500 Hz frequency from the base, the total frequency error of the signal received by the base being ±1000 Hz.

$$f_{Doppler} = \frac{c \cdot f}{c + V} \tag{1}$$

where c is the speed of transmission of light in a vacuum; f the operating frequency; and V the relative speed of the mobile terminal - base station.

$$|\triangle f| = |f_{Doppler} - f| = |\frac{c}{c+V} - 1| \cdot f \leq 500\,Hz; \tag{2}$$

$$V \leq \frac{500 \cdot c}{f - 500}; \tag{3}$$

For example, for $f = 470$ Mhz ⇒V≤ 1148, 9 km/h; and for the maximum frequency currently used in TETRA systems, 870 Mhz, V≤ 620, 7 km/h.

Thus, it can be concluded that speed does not affect either symbol synchronization or the calculation of the optimum sampling time. The algorithms used are independent of the frequency error that could cause the Doppler effect; the first measurement supports this, as does ETSI's Technical Report ETR 300-2.

With the frequencies used in TETRA systems today, the speed limit is around 620,7 km/h at a frequency of 870 MHz. Thus, the tests performed within the HT100 simulation environment can be considered equally valid for a train traveling at 200 km/h.

6 Additional Advantages of TETRA Technology

Besides the aforementioned quality of service factors, TETRA technology provides a number of additional features that make it an even more attractive proposition:

Operational Frequency Bands. TETRA is especified to operate in a wide range of frequencies within the lower part of UHF band, while GSM-R operates in the upper part of the band, concretely in 800–900 MHz. Since radio propagation loss is directly proportional to the frequency, GSM-R requires many more repeater stations than TETRA to achieve the same coverage (approximately twice). This translates into savings – not only in terms of radio equipment, but also in terms of associated civil works (shelters, towers, buildings, electrical installations, antenna mounts, power systems, etc.).

Spectrum Access. Nowadays, spectrum is a limited resource. In fact, spectrum availability often limits the choice of technology. With regard to this, the range of frequencies included in the TETRA standard is wider than GSM-R ones and hence, this facilitates the access to the spectrum.

Spectral Efficiency. In this respect, TETRA is four times more efficient than GSM-R, providing four channels on a bandwidth of 25 KHz, compared to GSM's eight channels of 200 KHz. Thus, in the same frequency space, TETRA can offer more channels to the user – 32 – supporting much higher levels of traffic and facilitating the implementation of future data applications.

IP Technology. As shown in Fig. 2, the interface between the fixed part and the GSM-R (I_{FIX}) network is, in an ETCS system, a Primary Rate ISDN (PRI) type and must be provided in compliance with ETS300011 [6]. In addition to this interface, the V.110 adaptation scheme is used in the user data channel. The reality is that today, in certain countries, it is practically impossible to have links of this type or the cost is prohibitive – making even more expensive the deployment of an ETCS signalling system on GSM-R. However, over the years, TETRA manufacturers have tended to 100 % IP-based systems, providing certain services to third parties such as CMD calls, via an IP connection with the central node of the infrastructure. Thus, along with an adaptation of the elements along the tracks, the E1 links could be replaced by IP connections, eliminating the cost and maintenance that those links require.

Profile of Technology Use. GSM is an ETSI standard designed for mobile telephony: frequency reuse is of paramount importance, and the cost of the infrastructure becomes less relevant, since there are tens of millions of subscribers to support it. Obviously, this system is not cost-efficient for use low user-density circumstances such as rail where, in the best case, there are hundreds – rather than millions – of users.

TETRA technology is an ETSI standard as well, but designed for a usage profile significantly closer to that of a rail network. The sizing of a TETRA system is precisely based on the number of network users. This is complemented by priorities management where, if the system is congested, the highest priority calls can be given precedence. Furthermore, careful design of the coverage area ensures the high levels of system availability required in transportation environments – in most cases, exceeding 99,9 %.

Standard TETRA Functionality. Some of the features natively included in the TETRA standard are particularly suited to the railway environment (group calls and emergency call priorities, group dynamics assignment, called ambient listening, direct and various data services mode, etc.). This is in contrast to GSM-R, where the basic technology GSM must be significantly adapted to meet functional requirements.

7 Conclusions

The diversity of signalling systems within Europe leads to difficulties on international railway lines. The ERTMS standard attempts to solve this problem using GSM-R as communication support.

However, there are currently many circumstances – among national, regional, metropolitan European lines and even international lines outside Europe – where the use of GSM-R is not mandatory, and other technologies, such as TETRA, can be used to meet both safety and cost requirements.

TETRA technology naturally meets the requirements defined by the EIRENE specifications for communication systems. Furthermore, thanks to the advantages in terms of spectral efficiency, coverage, functionality and cost; TETRA is a viable alternative to GSM-R.

References

1. Alcatel, Alstom, Ansaldo Signal, Bombardier, Invensys Rail, Siemenes: GSM-R Interfaces Class 1 requirements. B37-Subset-093. v2.3.0 (2005)
2. EuroRadio Interface Group approved by UNISIG Steering Committee: Radio Transmission FFFIS for EuroRadio. A11T6001_FFFIS_for_EuroRadio_v124_revmarks (2003)
3. Fisher, D.G., Ole Kaslund, J., Schoper, D.: Boundaries between ETCS and the GSM-R Network. Service and interface definition (2008)
4. ETSI (European Telecommunications Standards Institute): Technical report: Terrestrial Trunked Radio (TETRA); Voice plus Data (V+D); Designers' guide; Part 2: Radio channels, network protocols and service. Performance. ETR 300–2 (1997)
5. ETSI (European Telecommunications Standards Institute): Terrestrial Trunked Radio (TETRA); Voice plus Data (V+D) and Direct Mode Operation (DMO); Part 5: Peripheral Equipment Interface (PEI). ETSI TS 100 392–5 V2.3.1 (2012)
6. ETS (European Telecommunications Standard): Integrated Services Digital Network (ISDN); User-network interface data link layer specification; Application of CCITT Recommendations Q.920/I.440 and Q.921/I.441. ETS 300 125 (1991)
7. Moreno, J., Rodrguez, C., de Haro, L., Rivera, J.M.: Metro Madrid and Universidad Politcnica de Madrid (UPM): A survey on future Railway Radio Communications Services: Challenges and Opportunities. IEEE Communications Magazine (2015)

ETCS's Eurobalise-BTM and Euroloop-LTM Airgap Noise and Interferences Review

Jaizki Mendizabal(✉), Gonzalo Solas, Leonardo J. Valdivia, Gorka de Miguel, Julen Uranga, and Iñigo Adin

CEIT and Tecnun, University of Navarra, Manuel de Lardizabal 15, 20018 San Sebastián, Spain
{jmendizabal,gsolas,lvaldivia,gdemiguel,juranga,iadin}@ceit.es

Abstract. Wireless communications interfaces are vulnerable to interferers and noise. The effect of interferers and noise in the system will depend on the robustness of the communication system and the criticality of the system. ETCS (European Train Control System) is a safety-critical system responsible for the train control and command. There are two ETCS constituents installed on the track with a wireless communication to the train, namely Eurobalises and Euroloops that communicate with Balise Transmission Module (BTM) and Loop Transmission Module (LTM). This paper includes an analysis of the state of the art of noise and interferers and proposes the worst case scenarios to be used in the laboratory to measure the robustness of the systems against noise and interferers.

Keywords: Wireless link · EMC · Noise · Interferer · ETCS · Eurobalise · Euroloop · BTM · LTM

1 Introduction

European Train Control System (ETCS) is de-facto world standard for railway signaling. It was developed by the European railway community and included three different main levels. ETCS level 1, 2 and 3.

- ETCS Level 1 is a cab signalling system that can be superimposed on existing signalling infrastructures. Balise radio beacons are deployed at fixed intervals. These detect signal aspects at trackside and transmit them as a movement authority to any vehicle passing over that section of track. On-board systems monitor the signals and use it to calculate maximum speed/braking requirements. Additionally, a radiating cable Euroloop can be installed on the track for the on-board equipment to receive in-fill information.
- ETCS Level 2 relies on digital radio communications to implement train protection with advanced displays for the driver to remove/reduce the need for track side signalling. A Radio Block Centre (RBC) uses radio signals to monitor the location of trains at regular intervals. Movement authority is transmitted continuously via GSM-R together with balises acting as positioning beacons. On-board sensors help to locate the vehicle between balises by integrating data from braking and propulsion systems.

J. Mendizabal et al. (Eds.): Nets4Cars/Nets4Trains/Nets4Aircraft 2016, LNCS 9669, pp. 27–39, 2016.
DOI: 10.1007/978-3-319-38921-9_4

- ETCS Level 3 provides dynamic spacing between vehicles using radio signals. The RBC can detect when a train has left a track location and can, therefore, grant movement authority to any following train up to that point. There is, therefore, no notion of track sections being locked and released. Separation must preserve absolute braking distances between vehicles, taking into account terrain features, meteorological conditions, legacy rolling stock etc. Data from balises, from on-board systems and potentially from GNSS sources is integrated and monitored to assess the integrity of the positioning information and of the supporting on-board systems.

This paper is arranged as follows: in Sect. 1 an introduction to ETCS is included, the in Sects. 2 and 3 Eurobalise-BTM and Euroloop-LTM subsystems are described and the reported noise and interferers are presented, then Sect. 4 draws the conclusions of the research work.

2 BTM Air-Gap

BTM is the responsible for the communication between Balises on the track and the train equipped with BTM. In order to establish the communication, BTM energizes the Balises installed on the track by means of the Tele-powering signal at 27,095 MHz and receives and processes the Up-link signal in the 3,9 MHz–4,5 MHz band in order to send this information to the on-board EVC (European Vital Computer) kernel. Additionally, BTM is responsible for determining the presence of a Balise and locate it when the train passes over it.

In presence of noise or interferers the BTM functionality might be disturbed affecting to the behaviour of the on-board ETCS system. An analysis of the air-gap is here presented in order to determine the influence in the overall performance of the on-board ETCS system.

This section deals with the BTM-balise air-gap communication. It first describes briefly the functionality of this communication together with the air-gap environment. Then, a case in which problems exist, nowadays, is presented. The EMC harmonized norms and standards are presented. Finally, the candidate models for the BTM testing are identified.

2.1 BTM Physical Functionality

The following paragraphs explain the reasonable principles of the main blocks found in a BTM system, elements of both: balise and on-board BTM transmission equipment (OBBTE). Figure 1 shows a functional block diagram of the elements involved in the delivery of a telegram to the EVC Kernel during a balise passage.

In order to read telegrams from balises, the OBBTE generates a Tele-powering signal using the OBBTE Tele-powering source (OBPowSrc) that is sent to the balise by means of the OBBTE transmission antenna (OBPowAn). When the flux crossing the balise antenna (BaPowAn) exceeds ϕ_{d1}, the balise powers up. Then, the balise starts to transmit the telegram into the Up-link signal using the balise Up-link antenna (BaUpAn). The telegram is

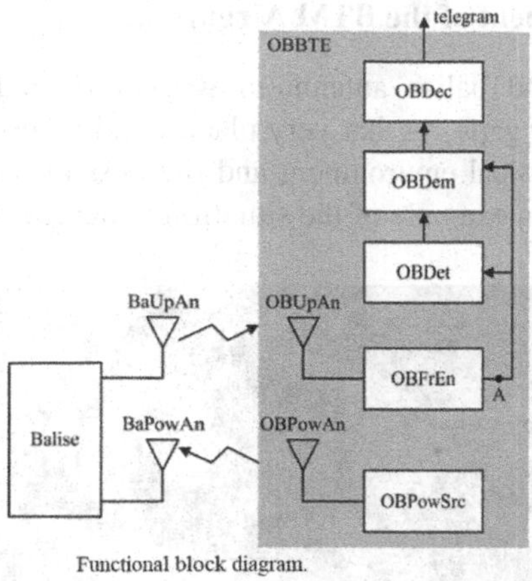

Fig. 1. Functional block diagram of the BTM function [1]

repeated continuously until the balise powers down, when OBPowAn moves away from BaPowAn and the flux crossing the balise antenna (BaPowAn) decreases.

The OBBTE receives the Up-link signal using the OBBTE Up-link antenna (OBUpAn). The OBBTE front-end (OBFrEn) performs signal conditioning. The output of OBFrEn is fed to a demodulator (OBDem), which extracts the received telegram bits from the received signal. The received telegram bits are processed by the decoder (OBDec), to check for errors and extract the user information from the received telegram. The user information is the information required by the EVC kernel to complete its tasks.

The architecture considers an additional element: OBDet, which determines the presence of a balise transmitting an Up-link signal. OBDet controls the activation of OBDem, so that OBDem only works when a balise has been detected, that is to say, when an Up-link signal whose field strength is above threshold voltage (Vth) during a minimum time of detection time (tDet) as stated in [2]. OBDem will be demodulating continuously bit streams in the balise contact zone, i.e. when the Up-link signal received by BTM is above Vth. OBDec only works when OBDem is producing reliable bits. In order to perform the decoding process, OBDec shifts a window over the bits produced by OBDem. For each of these windows, OBDec performs a set of checks as defined in [2]. This check ensures a safety proof for an upper bound of 10^{-18} for the probability, per Balise passage, of accepting a corrupt telegram considering the following hazards: random bit errors; burst errors; bit slips and bit insertions, and all combinations thereof; potential problems with telegram change and format misinterpretation (long versus short telegrams); and some further special error modes.

If the checks defined in [2] are all positive, OBDec can extract the telegram sent by the balise to be transmitted to the EVC kernel. Thus, an error free telegram will be delivered to the EVC kernel in a balise passage, only if OBDec is able to build a window of the required number of error free bits within that balise passage.

2.2 Physical Environment of the BTM Airgap

Physically, the BTM and balise antenna(s) work on the BaUpAn-OBUpAn and BaPowAn-OBPowAn air gaps. At that very place is it interesting to identify the main characteristics of the physical environment and the possible origin of the interference signals. Figure 2 shows an example of the situation under the train.

Fig. 2. BTM test antenna installed under a train

The antenna has a metal frame situated above and parallel to it under the train body. It is placed at the range 15,5 cm to 25 cm. from the top of the rail according to the distance allowed by the standard (Fig. 3) [2]. Restrictions related to distance between BTM antennas and distance from the front of the head of the train are defined in [3].

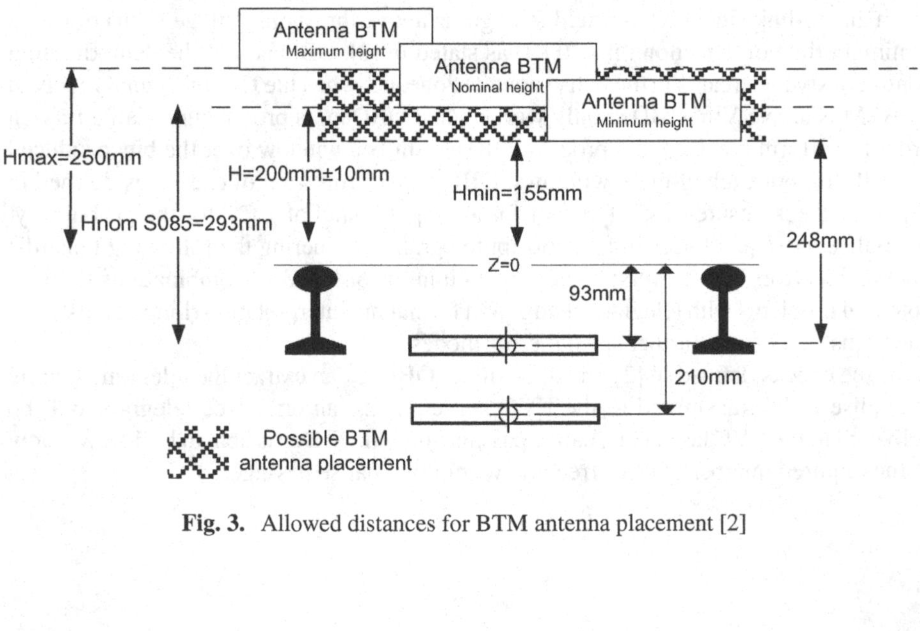

Fig. 3. Allowed distances for BTM antenna placement [2]

Depending on the location of the antenna under the train, the EMIs to be received might differ. Therefore, an optimal installation of the antenna is required.

2.3 Current EMC Norms and Standards

The complete set of standards and norms published from the European Union in the 2011/C214/02 directive affecting the interoperability of the rail system is published by CENELEC as shown in the Appendix 1. All these norms are EMC generic norms for Railways and do not cover BTM and LTM specifically, for that specific ETCS's subsets are available.

2.4 Reported Noise and Interferers

The problem that the European Railway Agency (ERA) is facing is that the tests that the signalling systems, such as BTM and LTM, have to pass before the integration on the rolling stock and the entry of service are not completely avoiding the errors in the BTM and LTM, as seen in the case reported in [4]. A fault in balise group identification was reported in a commercial line near Rome and therefore the emergency brake was caused by a "lost balise". The maintenance intervention did not solve the problem but detected the existence of an external interference affecting the data uplink modulation. This problem illustrates the worries related to balise communication mostly due to transient signals. Moreover it also illustrates the need for a deeper analysis on the BTM air gap understanding.

Two European projects funded by the FP6 and FP7 programmes dealt with BTM air-gap, namely, RAILCOM and TREND.

RAILCOM Project. Electromagnetic Compatibility between Rolling Stock and Rail Infrastructure encouraging European interoperability. Funded by the FP6 programme, it started in 2005 and finished in 2009. The project implementation contributed to the CENELEC standards by defining EMC limiting values. Specifically for BTM air gap, Fig. 4. Shape of the Damped Interference Signal [2] has been showed in the project final presentations, but no changes have been made to the standards, directly (Subset036: transient signals to consider for the BTM air gap).

Finally, from the BTM on-board equipment point of view, two items have been detected: Tele-powering reflections and external bothering on the 27,095 MHz frequency. This point is ruled by the subset036 [2] and the subset085 [6] which sets the applicable Eurobalise test procedure. It defines, among other configurations, the debris conditions that have to be tested. However, punctual problems could be found for that Tele-powering signal for special conditions.

As stated by its foreword, the subset036 [2] is the FFFIS (Functional Form Fit Interface Specification) for Eurobalise and constitutes the mandatory requirements for achieving air-gap interoperability between any possible combination of wayside and train-borne equipment. Its Annexes could be "normative" or "informative".

Last version of Subset036 [2] has an updated immunity section for BTM, which defines that the Eurobalise on-board Transmission equipment (BTM) shall be able to

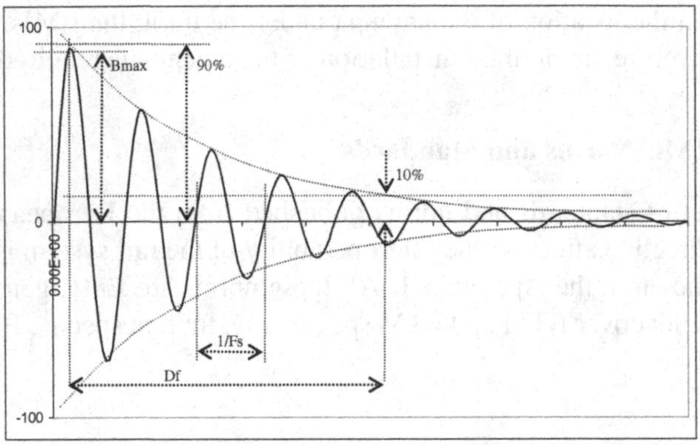

Fig. 4. Shape of the damped interference signal [2]

operate when being exposed to a pure sinusoidal constant wave disturbance radiated noise and a dumped transient signal defined in Fig. 4 and by the following parameters including their range:

- Self-Frequency, Fs [1 MHz – 6 MHz]
- Decaying Factor, Df [5 cycles – 30 cycles]
- Repetition Rate [1.5 kHz – 15 kHz]
- Magnetic field strength, Bmax – different depending on the class.

The Subset085 Test specification for Eurobalise FFFIS [6] does not define any electromagnetic characteristic for the test procedure on this signalling system. Moreover, in the introduction of the test of the Up-link balise (Sect. 4), the first table shows the generic conditions that should be applied for the majority of the tests. Note that the last line sets that the EMC noise is negligible. A new subset, namely Subset116, to be published yet, defines the test procedure to test the system in front of the dumped and CW interferences.

TREND Project. Test of Rolling Stock Electromagnetic Compatibility for Cross Domain Interoperability [5]. Funded by the FP7 program, it started in 2011 and finished in 2014. Its objectives for the BTM air gap issue are to delimit the reasonable worst case scenarios and to define the adequate test setup, test procedure and test site. TREND project [5] summarizes the electromagnetic threats for the BTM communication. The conclusions of the study are that the main threats for the BTM communication are the following:

- Transients due to pantograph arcing or slicing pickup shoe and breaker operation
- Transients due to return current discontinuities
- Radiation in the 9 kHz to 30 MHz frequency band
- Reflections due to debris
- Citizen Band networks affecting the 27 MHz frequency band of the BTM

The assessment of each of these points is performed in relationship with the most common EMC and rolling stock related standards associated in each case.

The transients (the voltage peaks with very high amplitude levels and very short time duration that affect a broadband spectrum), as seen in the case studies in [5] are an issue that are not covered by the current BTM/LTM test specifications [6, 7]. Figure 5 shows a configuration where the Balise-BTM on-board equipment communication is bothered by transients circulating along the rails. The culprits of these transients are diverse but their effects are real and recognized by the ERA and UNISIG official documents. However, no tests are focused on them and no standard proposes a normalization of its shape, yet.

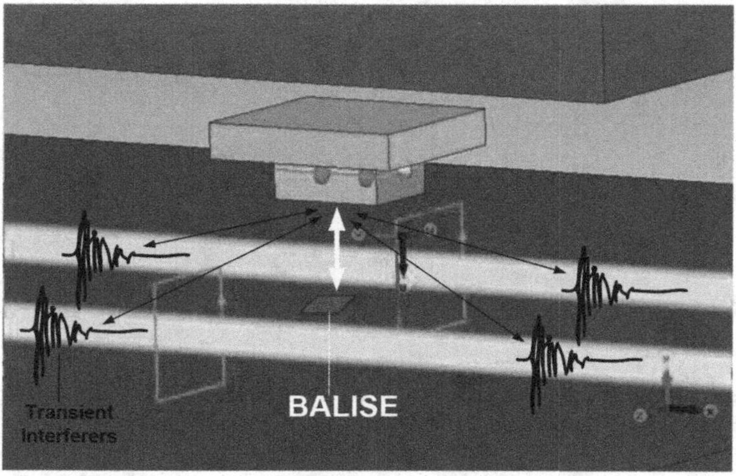

Fig. 5. Balise-BTM and rail interferers model

Moreover, the test setup defined for the current approval tests, e.g. EN 50121-3-1 [8], tries to minimize the effects of the transients by placing the radiated emissions measurement set-up in zones free from potential arcing (no sliding zones, far away from the substations, etc.). This is a drawback that should be amended in the revisions of the current approval standards.

From the radiation point of view, only the frequencies above 80 MHz have been taken into consideration in the EN50121-3-2 [9] approval tests. This point should be improved, as the real electromagnetic environment for the spot signalling systems contains noise and interferences below 80 MHz, and more specifically, from 9 kHz to 30 MHz, which is the band of interest of most of the known spot signalling systems. Noise and interfefreer at these band of interest are not blocked due to the fact that any antenna has a non-metallic radome that is transparent to EM waves in the 9 kHz to 30 MHz band (needed to work at BTM's 4 MHz uplink signal to be received and the 27 MHz telepowering signal to be transmitted), moreover, the metallic defence used by the antenna is connected to the ground of the rolling stock and is not completely stopping any kind of radiation occurring in the focused frequency band.

2.5 Analysis

Taking into account changes in the latest version of the subset-036 [2] that are exclusively focused on the eurobalise air gap, this section investigates how the reported signal has a strong effect on the BTM frequency band. The following figure shows an example of disturbance captured by the BTM antenna [5], with a decaying factor of 18 cycles (inside the 5 to 30 cycles range) and a self-frequency of 2 MHz (inside the 1 MHz to 6 MHz range). With a sliding windowed FFT analysis of a 120 μs long signal which starts with this transient signal the results of Fig. 6 are found.

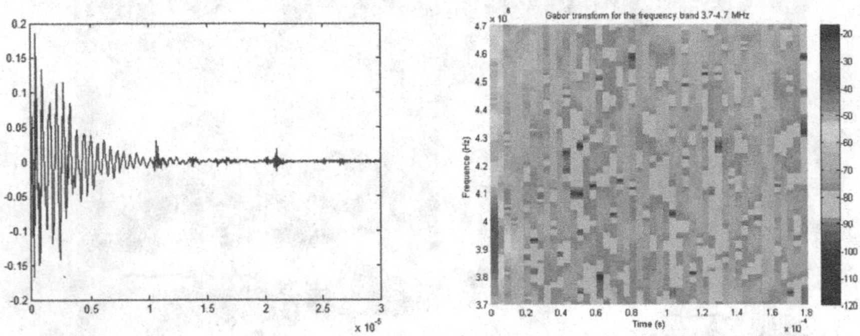

Fig. 6. Real damped interference signal captured by a BTM antenna [Volts] (left); Sliding window FFT analysis of the transient in the BTM frequency band (right) [5]

Eurobalise transmission employs a binary CPFSK (Continuous Phase Frequency Shift Keying) modulation where the logical '0' nominal frequency tone is at 3,951 MHz and the logical '1' nominal frequency tone is at 4,516 MHz [2]. The transient specific analysis shows that mostly the '0' frequency tone and slightly the '1' frequency tone are bothered by the disturbance. Approximately 50 dB of difference is found to be captured by the BTM antenna when this transient is added to the balise signal.

From this short analysis, it is clear that the test specifications of a new version of the BTM air gap subset could be a key project deliverable that should be studied and proposed.

3 LTM Air-Gap

LTM is the responsible for the communication between Euroloops on the track and the train. In order to establish the communication, the on-board equipment activates the Euroloops installed on the track by means of the Tele-powering signal at 27,095 MHz and receives and processes the Up-link signal in the 9 MHz to 18 MHz band.

In presence of noise or interferers, the LTM functionality might be disturbed affecting the behaviour of the on-board ETCS system. An analysis of the air-gap is required in order to determine the influence in the overall performance of the on-board ETCS system.

This sections deals with the LTM-euroloop air-gap communication. It first describes, briefly, the functionality of this communications together with the air-gap environment. Then, a list of the reported interferers and noises is included. Finally, the candidate models are identified.

3.1 LTM Physical Functionality

The following paragraphs explain the reasonable principles of the main blocks found in a LTM system, elements of both euroloop and on-board LTM transmission equipment (OBLTE). Figure 7 shows a functional block diagram of the elements involved in the delivery of a telegram to the EVC Kernel when the LTM is located on a euroloop.

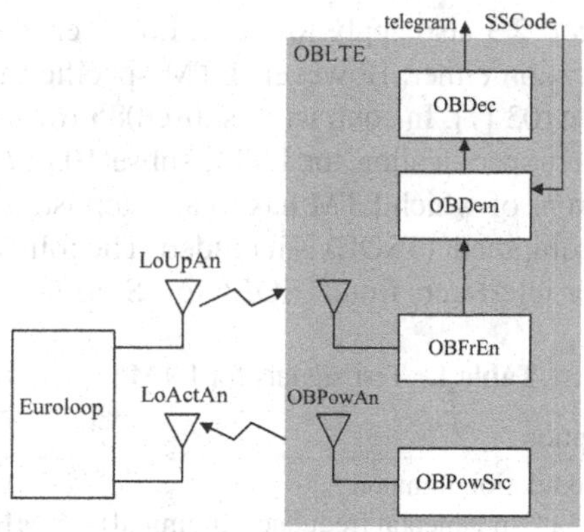

Fig. 7. Functional block diagram of the LTM function [1]

In order to read telegrams from the euroloop, the OBLTE generates a Tele-powering signal using the OBLTE Tele-powering source (OBPowSrc) that is sent to the euroloop by means of the OBLTE transmission antenna (OBPowAn). Usually BTM and LTM share the Tele-powering source and antenna. The euroloop is activated when the flux captured by the euroloop antenna (LoActAn) complies with

$$A = \phi_{TE} \geq \frac{\phi L}{M_\phi} \tag{1}$$

Then, the euroloop starts to transmit the telegram into the Up-link signal using the euroloop Up-link antenna (LoUpAn). The telegram is repeated continuously until the euroloop is deactivated, when OBPowAn moves away from LoPowAn or when the Eurolopop has been transmitting during t_{on}, where $60\text{ s} < t_{on} \leq 90\text{ s}$ (it can be activated again following the same procedure).

The OBLTE receives the Up-link signal using the OBLTE Up-link antenna (OBUpAn). The OBLTE front-end (OBFrEn) performs signal conditioning. The output of OBFrEn is fed to a demodulator (OBDem), which extracts the received telegram bits from the received signal. In order to carry out the demodulation, the demodulator requires the SSCode from the EVC kernel. EVC kernel receives it from a Balise info received by BTM and passes it to the LTM. Then, the received telegram bits are processed by the decoder (OBDec), to check for errors and extract the user information from the received telegram. OBDec process is exactly the same as defined for the BTM. The user information is the information required by the EVC kernel to complete its tasks.

3.2 Physical Environment of the LTM Airgap

The environment of the LTM antenna is the same as the BTM (see Sect. 2.2).

3.3 Reported Noise and Interferers

EMC norms listed in Sect. 2.3 also apply to LTM, however, they do not address the specific LTM communication either. However, LTM specific information is found in subset044 [10] and subset103 [7]. In contrast to subset085 [6] where test specification for BTM was defined, test specification for LTM, subset103 [7] defines a number of expected interferers in front of which LTM has to accomplish its function. A list Test Signal of the On-board Equipment (TSOE) is included. The following table lists the test signals including noise or interferers from TSOE5 to TSOE9.

Table 1. Test signals for LTM [7]

Test signal	Description
TSOE5	Intermodulation immunity TSOE5a Fundamental frequency (nominal) 4.5 MHz (BTM Up-link) TSOE5b Fundamental frequency (nominal) 27.095 MHz (Tele-powering)
TSOE6	Co-Channel Rejection for Narrowband Signal Fundamental frequency fc = 13.54750 MHz ± 30 ppm. Euroloop signal centre frequency
TSOE7	Co-Channel Rejection of Other Euroloop Signal unwanted Euroloop signal, which shall comply with TSOE2 but differing from the wanted Euroloop signal with regard to the Q_SSCODE
TSOE8	Blocking TSOE8a: Nominal frequency for test set-up 27.115 MHz TSOE8b: Nominal frequency for test set-up 28.000 MHz TSOE8c: Nominal frequency for test set-up 29.000 MHz TSOE8d: Nominal frequency for test set-up 30.000 MHz
TSOE9	Dynamic Receiver Performance The Test Signal TSOE9 coincides with the Test Signal TSOE2 except for its amplitude which fluctuates

3.4 Analysis

From the analysis of this section, it is clear that the test specification of the subset103 [7] includes the significant air-gap effects that should be employed to test LTM's immunity. The main reasons for this statement are:

- No problems due to EMIs are currently known for the LTM communication. Due to the robust modulation scheme it is not foreseen to find any negative effect in front of disturbances.
- Standards cover a number of scenarios that are considered to be enough. Moreover, ERTMS baseline 3.0 does not include an update of the standards related to LTM. Therefore it is considered that there is no need to update them.

4 Conclusions

This work shows the characteristics of the air-gap channel of the wireless communications BTM and LTM part of the current ERTMS. The following models have been chosen to be employed as worse case scenarios for BTM and LTM:

- **BTM:** updated specification of the BTM in subset036 [2] states that interferences found in the air-gap has a strong effect on the BTM frequency band. Moreover, this specification introduces interferences and noise that can be found at the air-gap. Currently it is recommended to employ the Damped Interference Signal (Fig. 4) and the CW noise as defined in [2]. Moreover, the way of testing has to be defined and additional test to assess the limits defined have to be carried out.
- **LTM:** Due to the robust modulation scheme and the lack of reported EMI and noise problems for LTM, there is no problem expected. Moreover the test specification of the [7] includes the significant air-gap effects under TSOE5, TSOE6, TSOE7, TSOE8 and TSOE9 signals (Table 1).

Acknowledgment. The research leading to these results has received funding from the European Community's Framework Program FP7/2007-2013 under two grant agreements: no. "285259"–TREND project and no. "314219"–EATS project; and from the Spanish Government's CICyT (Comisión Interministerial de Ciencia y Tecnología) programme through SAREMSIG project.

Appendix 1 Cenelec Railway EMC Norms

The complete set of standards and norms published from the European Union in the 2011/C214/02 directive affecting the interoperability of the rail system can be summarized in the following list:

- Cenelec EN 50121-1: Electromagnetic compatibility – Part 1: General
- Cenelec EN 50121-2: Electromagnetic compatibility – Part 2: Emission of the whole railway system to the outside world.
- Cenelec EN 50121-3-1: Electromagnetic compatibility – Part 3-1: Rolling stock – Train and complete vehicle
- Cenelec EN 50121-3-2: Electromagnetic compatibility – Part 3-1: Rolling stock – Apparatus
- Cenelec EN 50121-4: Electromagnetic compatibility – Part 4: Emission and immunity of the signalling and telecommunications apparatus

- Cenelec EN 50121-5: Electromagnetic compatibility – Part 5: Emission and immunity of fixed power supply installations and apparatus.
- Cenelec EN 50122-1 Railway applications - Fixed installations - Electrical safety, earthing and the return circuit - Part 1: protective provisions against electric shock
- Cenelec EN 50122-2: Railway applications Fixed installations - Electrical safety, earthing and the return circuit - Part 2: provisions against the effects of stray currents caused by d.c. traction systems
- Cenelec EN 50122-3: Railway applications Fixed installations - Electrical safety, earthing and the return circuit - Part 3: mutual interaction of a.c. and d.c. traction systems
- Cenelec EN 50125-1:1999 Railway applications - Environmental conditions for equipment - Part 1: Equipment on board rolling stock (EN 50125-1:1999/AC: 2010)
- Cenelec EN 50125-3:2003 Railway applications - Environmental conditions for equipment - Part 3: Equipment for signalling and telecommunications (EN 50125-3:2003/AC: 2010)
- Cenelec EN 50155:2007 Railway applications - Electronic equipment used on rolling stock (EN 50155:2007/AC: 2010)
- Cenelec EN 50159-1:2001 Railway applications - Communication, signalling and processing systems - Part 1: Safety-related communication in closed transmission systems (EN 50159-1:2001/AC: 2010)
- Cenelec EN 50215:2010 Railway applications - Rolling stock - Testing of rolling stock on completion of construction and before entry into service
- Cenelec EN 50238: Railway applications - Compatibility between rolling stock and train detection systems

Cenelec EN 50388: Railway applications - Power supply and rolling stock - Technical criteria for the coordination between power supply (substation) and rolling stock to achieve interoperability.

References

1. Sevillano, J.F., Mendizábal, J., Sancho, I., Martín, J.R., Meléndez, J.: Reliability Analysis of the On-Board Transmission Equipment of an ERTMS Compliant Balise Location and Transmission System. In: ESREL (2009)
2. UNISIG: SUBSET-036: FFFIS for Eurobalise v3.0.0. ERTMS/ETCS—Class 1 Subset 036: FFFIS for Eurobalise, 24 February 2012
3. UNISIG: SUBSET-040: Dimensioning and Engineering Rules v3.2.0. ERTMS/ETCS—Class 1 Subset 036: FFFIS for Eurobalise, 3 March 2012
4. Caliandro, Vito., Mermec Group: ERTMS line certification using mobile diagnostic solutions. In: 10th ERTMS World Conference, Stockholm (2012)
5. CEIT, et al.: TREND Project, 2.1 – Collection of Experiences and Establishment of Qualitative Relationships (2013)
6. UNISIG: SUBSET-085: Test Specification for Eurobalise FFFIS v3.0.0. ERTMS/ETCS—Class 1 Subset 036: FFFIS for Eurobalise, 24 February 2012
7. UNISIG: SUBSET-103: Test Specification for Euroloop FFFIS v1.0.0. ERTMS/ETCS—Class 1 Subset 036: FFFIS for Eurobalise, 5 February 2008

8. CENELEC: EN 50121-3-1 Railway Applications-Electromagnetic Compatibility
9. CENELEC: EN 50121-3-2 Railway Applications-Electromagnetic Compatibility - Part 2: Emission of the Whole Railway System to the Outside World
10. UNISIG: SUBSET-044: FFFIS for Euroloop v2.3.0. ERTMS/ETCS—Class 1 Subset 036: FFFIS for Eurobalise, 5 February 2008

Wireless Communication Emulator Device and Methodology for the ETCS BTM Subsystem

Gonzalo Solas(✉), Iñigo Adin, Leonardo J. Valdivia, Saioa Arrizabalaga, and Jaizki Mendizabal

CEIT and Tecnun, University of Navarra, Manuel de Lardizbal 15, 20018 San Sebastian, Spain
{gsolas, iadin, lvaldivia, sarrizabalaga, jmendizabal}@ceit.es

Abstract. Currently European Train Control System (ETCS) rollout is a major concern for train manufacturers and railway infrastructure managers. But available laboratory certification procedures do not completely address all the needs of the system, which leads to long and expensive field-testing. This research work proposes a new tool that reduces the required on-site testing amount. The BTM Wireless Communication Emulator (WCE) reproduces the potential interferers that can be found in the air-gap of the BTM wireless communication channel. That way, the laboratory testing procedures can emulate the behavior of the wireless channel in a more realistic way. The identification of the potential interferers to be included in the emulator has been done first, and the design and implementation has been carried out afterwards. Finally, the testing and validation of the tool has been completed.

Keywords: Emulation · BTM · ETCS · Railway · Zero on-site testing

1 Introduction

The European Rail Traffic Management System (ERTMS) is an initiative created by the European Union to improve the interoperability of railway signaling equipment across national borders within the European Union that has been achieved by creating a Europe-wide standard for train control and command systems. It is composed of four elements:

- **European Train Control System (ETCS)**. This is the train-control element and includes Automatic Train Protection (ATP). There are five Application Levels (0, STM, 1, 2 and 3), each offering different degrees of signaling protection and control, and sixteen different Operating Modes. Not all Operating Modes are available in all Application Levels.
- **Global System for Mobile communications – Railways (GSM-R)**. This is the telecommunications element of ERTMS which, in some applications, carries ETCS data between trains and the trackside infrastructure. It also provides for voice

J. Mendizabal et al. (Eds.): Nets4Cars/Nets4Trains/Nets4Aircraft 2016, LNCS 9669, pp. 40–50, 2016.
DOI: 10.1007/978-3-319-38921-9_5

communications. It is based on standard mobile telephone technology, but with a set of railway-reserved frequencies.

ETCS is divided into two parts.

(a) The ETCS on-board equipment.
(b) The ETCS trackside equipment.

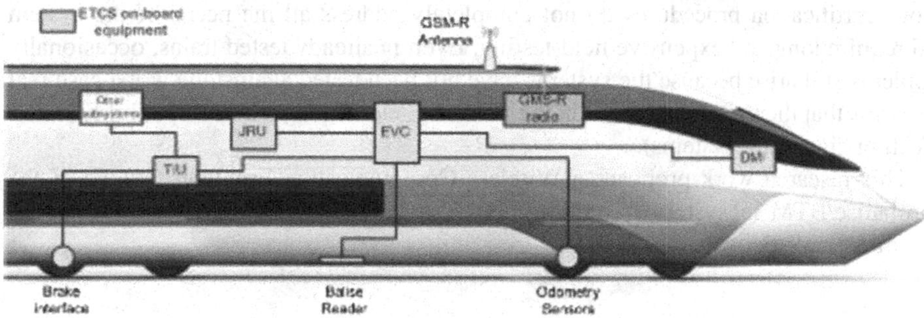

Fig. 1. ETCS on-board equipment [1]

Figure 1 shows the subsystems that compose the ETCS on-board equipment. This research work has been focused on the subsystem formed by the Eurobalise and the Balise reader or BTM.

The Eurobalise/BTM subsystem is the ETCS part devoted to provide the data transmission capabilities between the trackside and on-board equipment. For that, it relies on two devices, each of which belongs to one of the two parts in which ETCS is divided (see Fig. 2).

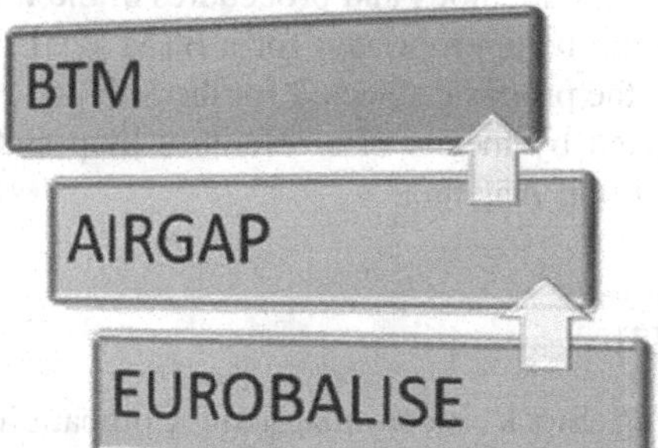

Fig. 2. Eurobalise/BTM subsystem arrangement

The Eurobalise is a data configurable transponder that is mounted in the track. The Eurobalise needs no external power supply as it is energised by the passing train. Once energised, the Eurobalise transmits an electronic telegram back to the train. The Balise Transmission Module (BTM) energises the balise, enabling the balise to transmit its telegram to the train. The Balise Transmission Module then receives the telegram and passes it on to the EVC.

For each BTM equipment manufactured, the operation and requirements need to be tested and verified. That process, currently, shows a major problem: available laboratory certification procedures do not completely address all the needs of the system and require long and expensive field-testing. Even in already tested trains, occasionally problems still arise because the systems have not been tested against the worst case real scenarios that the system may find in the field (e.g. electromagnetic compatibility issues affecting signalling systems).

This research work proposes a Wireless Communication Emulator (WCE) of the Eurobalise/BTM subsystem, in order to be able to emulate the wireless communication in a more realistic way.

2 State of the Art

Due to the noisy railway environment and interferences, air-gap communication can be corrupted and therefore, ETCS service stopped. Some previous experiences have been found as ETCS has been out of service due to the problems found in the air-gap communication. Nowadays, Subset 116 [2] and TREND project [3] have taken steps towards the full definition and modelling of the track noise.

2.1 Subset 116 [2]

Subset 116 is not yet officially published, as some measurement methods are still TBD (mostly for the measuring rolling stock emissions) or open points (real environment vs. test signals). But the test tools, methods and procedures of the first draft applying to the balise immunity setup could be appropriated for a BTM WCE.

The block diagram of the proposal selected for the Subset 116 is depicted in Fig. 3. The balise signal is injected by means of a reference loop and the noise signals are injected through a Wide Loop Antenna.

2.2 TREND Project [3]

TREND (Test of Rolling Stock Electromagnetic Compatibility for cross-Domain Interoperability) project has the objective of addressing this situation by means of the design of a test setup that enables the harmonization of freight and passengers rolling stock approval tests for electromagnetic compatibility (EMC) focusing not only on interferences with broadcasting services but also on railway signaling systems. The thorough analysis comprises measurement, modelization and safety and availability

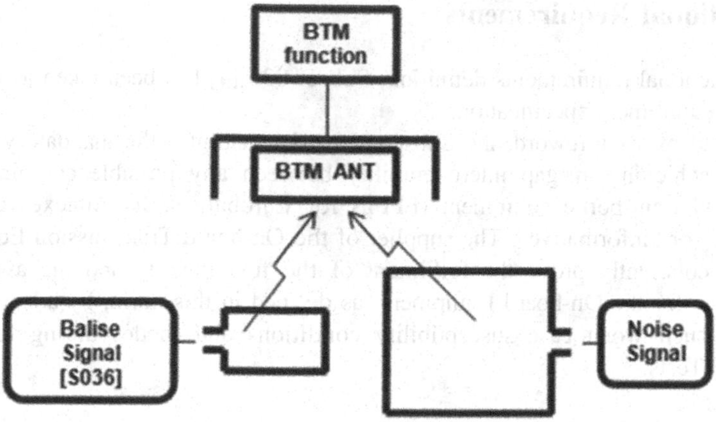

Fig. 3. Architecture proposed in Subset 116

analysis of the effect of rolling stock's EMIs on the neighboring systems. The system potentially affected by these EMIs have been covered.

The wireless channel emulation approach used in the TREND project is presented in Fig. 4. In that case, the balise signal is also injected through the reference loop as in the previous options, but the noise is added to the BTM function directly after the BTM antenna.

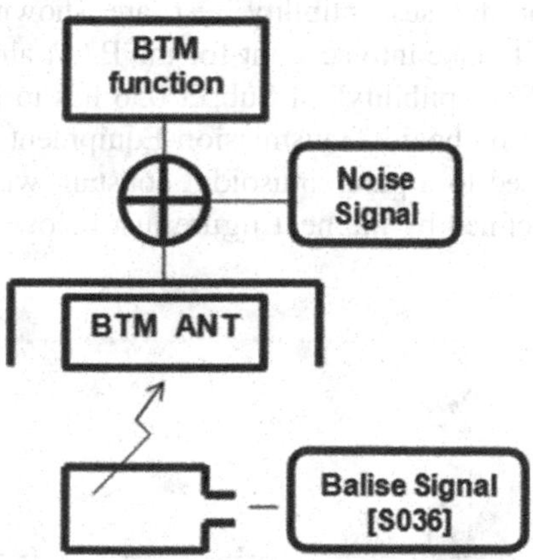

Fig. 4. TREND's approach for BTM WCE

That option would be available for the companies or the manufacturers that could record the noises captured by an antenna at the BTM antenna position, or use someone else recorded files. This way, real noises are taken into account; they could even be obtained with the manufacturer BTM antenna. In order to use the setup of this option, the antenna receiving the balise signal has to be the same used during the measurement campaigns which have recorded the noises. This could be a BTM specific antenna or a MFP, for example.

3 Functional Requirements

For the functional requirements definition, Subset 036 [4] has been taken as the main source of requirement specification.

As stated by its foreword, the Subset 036 [4] constitutes the mandatory requirements for achieving air-gap interoperability between any possible combination of wayside and train-borne equipment (FFFIS for Eurobalise). Its Annexes could be "normative" or "informative". The supplier of the On-board Transmission Equipment shall then coherently prove the fulfilment of the functionality and the availability requirements for the On-board Equipment, as defined in this norm, by adequate simulation of such worst case susceptibility conditions and modes during functional Laboratory Tests.

Table 1. Test specification for BTM

Ambient temperature	25 °C ± 10 °C
Relative humidity	25 % to 75 %
Atmospheric pressure	86 kPa to 106 kPa
Debris in the air-gap	None
Tele-powering mode	CW
EMC noise within the Up-link frequency band	Negligible

The specifications for the susceptibility test are shown in Table 1. Besides, specifically for the threats to take into account for the BTM air-gap, the section "6.7.4 Eurobalise Transmission Susceptibility" of Subset 036 has to be considered. The text defines that the Eurobalise on-board Transmission Equipment (BTM) shall be able to operate when being exposed to a pure sinusoidal constant wave disturbance radiated noise and a transient as defined by the next figure just below (See Fig. 5):

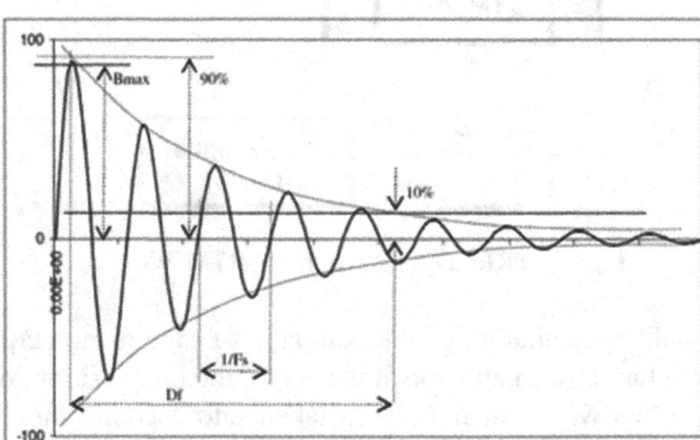

Fig. 5. Shape of the damped interference signal [4]

The parameters and their proposed range are the following:

- Self-Frequency, Fs [1 MHz – 6 MHz]
- Decaying Factor, Df [5 cycles – 30 cycles]
- Repetition Rate [1.5 kHz – 15 kHz]
- Magnetic field strength, Bmax – different depending on the class, see tables just below for transients and CW noises

Requirements regarding the damped oscillation noise and CW noise are defined in Tables 2 and 3.

Table 2. Field Strength Limits for Damped Oscillations [4]

ID	Decaying factor [cycles]	Repetition rate [kHz]	Self-frequency [MHz]	Class H Field strength, Bmax [dBμA/m]	Class M field strength, Bmax [dBμA/m]
DS_01	5	1.5	1.0	95	87
DS_02	5	1.5	2.5	83	80
DS_03	5	1.5	3.9	70	65
DS_04	5	1.5	4.5	70	65
DS_05	5	1.5	6.0	74	74
DS_06	5	5.0	3.9	70	65
DS_07	5	5.0	4.5	70	65
DS_08	5	15	1.0	95	87
DS_09	5	15	2.5	83	80
DS_10	5	15	3.9	70	65
DS_11	5	15	4.5	70	65
DS_12	5	15	6.0	74	74
DS_13	30	1.5	1.0	95	87
DS_14	30	1.5	2.5	83	80
DS_15	30	1.5	3.9	67	60
DS_16	30	1.5	4.5	67	60
DS_17	30	1.5	6.0	74	74
DS_18	30	5.0	3.9	67	60
DS_19	30	5.0	4.5	67	60
DS_20	30	15	1.0	95	87
DS_21	30	15	2.5	83	80
DS_22	30	15	3.9	67	60
DS_23	30	15	4.5	67	60
DS_24	30	15	6.0	74	74

Table 3. Field strength limits for CW noise [4]

ID	Frequency [MHz]	Field strength, RMS [dBμA/m]
CW_01	1.0	100
CW_02	2.5	83
CW_03	3.9	49
CW_04	4.5	49
CW_05	6.0	74

4 System Implementation

Taking into account that the goal of the emulation is to inject the balise signal accompanied by the noise interferers into the BTM function, the sum of the signals could be completed prior to its injection in the air-gap or after it. Moreover, the signals could be summed in the generation or in the reception, in the air or by software.

For the simplicity in the equipment needed for the injection and for the easiest synchronization process of the balise and noise files, the architecture selected in this work is shown in Fig. 6.

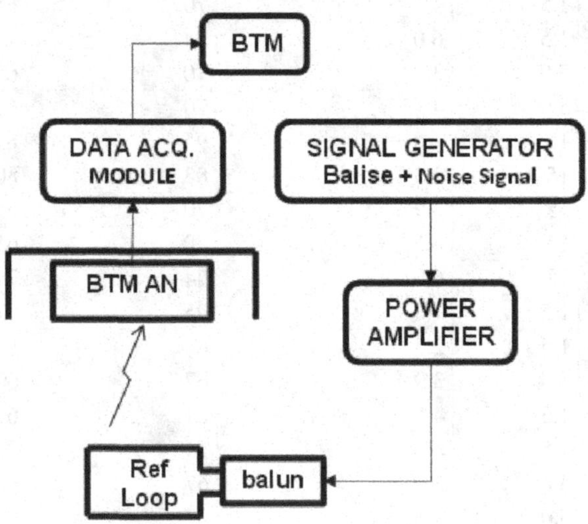

Fig. 6. BTM WCE architecture

The balise and noise signals are generated computationally, following the requirements defined in Subset 036 [4]. Those two signals are amplified in order to obtain the adequate current and field strength values defined in Subset 036 [4]. Afterwards, the added signals are injected to a reference loop and received by the on-board BTM antenna. The physical signal is acquired by a data acquisition module, such as a PXI device, and sent to the BTM function model implement in SW. This model is the one in charge of processing the balise signal and obtaining the information contained in the telegram.

The objective of the calibration process is to obtain the values defined in Subset 036 [4] for the currents in the reference loop for a Standard Size Balise. The calibration parameters to be measured are:

- Signal power in the spectrum analyser (Psa)
- Input power in the Signal Generator (Pin)
- Power amplifier gain (G)
- Waveform scale of the Signal Generator (WS)

Table 4 shows the values obtained for the calibration parameters

Table 4. WCE calibration values

Current	P_{sa}	P_{in}	G	WS
I_{u1} = 37 mA	−15,62 dBm	12,67 dBm	15 %	18 %
75 mA	−9,48 dBm	18,71 dBm	15 %	32 %
I_{u3} = 116 mA	−5,7 dBm	23 dBm	15 %	49 %

Figure 7 shows the physical implementation of the BTM WCE, in which the main components and equipment can be seen:

- Signal generator
- Power Amplifier
- Reference Loop

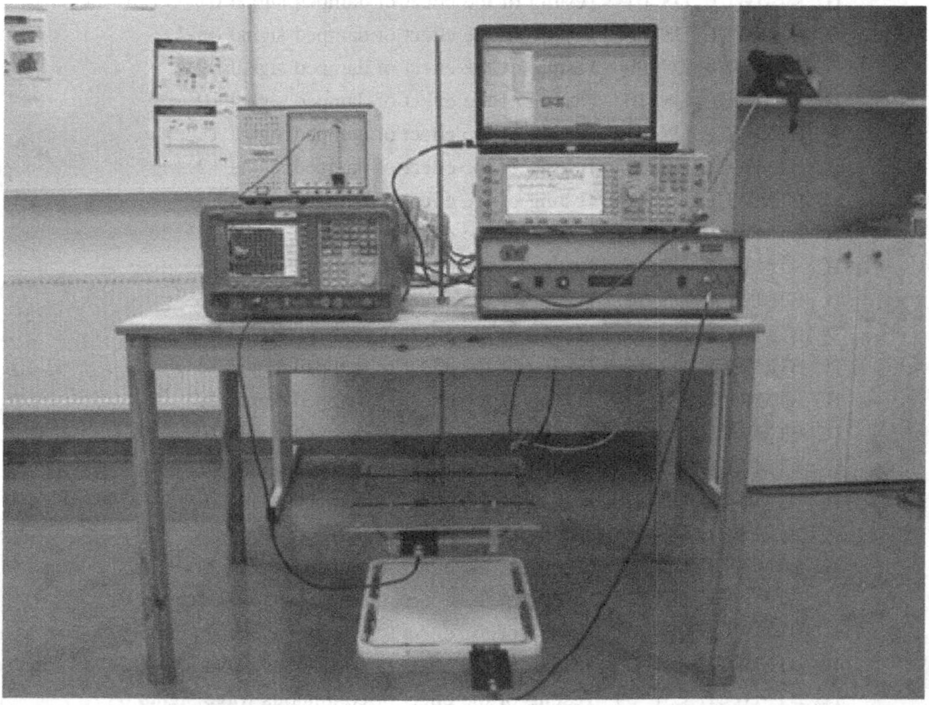

Fig. 7. Laboratory implementation of BTM WCE

- BTM Antenna
- Data Acquisition Equipment
- Auxiliary equipment

5 Results and Validation

The methodology that has been used in order to gather the results and validate the WCE is the following: definition of a test case template, identification of the tests to be performed, results measurement and justify the validation.

In order to identify the list of tests to be performed, the following criterion has been defined: the main objective needs to be the validation of the fulfilment of the functional requirements. Thus, a test per each interferer identified in the requirements has to be carried out.

The test cases that have been identified following this criterion are listed in Table 5:

Table 5. List of test cases

TC_BTMWCE_DS_01	Testing of the effect of damped signal 01
TC_BTMWCE_DS_02	Testing of the effect of damped signal 02
TC_BTMWCE_DS_03	Testing of the effect of damped signal 03
TC_BTMWCE_DS_04	Testing of the effect of damped signal 04
TC_BTMWCE_DS_05	Testing of the effect of damped signal 05
TC_BTMWCE_DS_06	Testing of the effect of damped signal 06
TC_BTMWCE_DS_07	Testing of the effect of damped signal 07
TC_BTMWCE_DS_08	Testing of the effect of damped signal 08
TC_BTMWCE_DS_09	Testing of the effect of damped signal 09
TC_BTMWCE_DS_10	Testing of the effect of damped signal 10
TC_BTMWCE_DS_11	Testing of the effect of damped signal 11
TC_BTMWCE_DS_12	Testing of the effect of damped signal 12
TC_BTMWCE_DS_13	Testing of the effect of damped signal 13
TC_BTMWCE_DS_14	Testing of the effect of damped signal 14
TC_BTMWCE_DS_15	Testing of the effect of damped signal 15
TC_BTMWCE_DS_16	Testing of the effect of damped signal 16
TC_BTMWCE_DS_17	Testing of the effect of damped signal 17
TC_BTMWCE_DS_18	Testing of the effect of damped signal 18
TC_BTMWCE_DS_19	Testing of the effect of damped signal 19
TC_BTMWCE_DS_20	Testing of the effect of damped signal 20
TC_BTMWCE_DS_21	Testing of the effect of damped signal 21
TC_BTMWCE_DS_22	Testing of the effect of damped signal 22
TC_BTMWCE_DS_23	Testing of the effect of damped signal 23
TC_BTMWCE_DS_24	Testing of the effect of damped signal 24
TC_BTMWCE_CW_01	Testing of the effect of continuous wave signal 01
TC_BTMWCE_CW_02	Testing of the effect of continuous wave signal 02
TC_BTMWCE_CW_03	Testing of the effect of continuous wave signal 03
TC_BTMWCE_CW_04	Testing of the effect of continuous wave signal 04
TC_BTMWCE_CW_05	Testing of the effect of continuous wave signal 05

Figure 8 shows an example of a damped noise signal generated by the BTM WCE.

In order to identify more clearly the effect of the injection of the interferers, the interferer is applied to the signal of a balise that transmits a telegram containing the renewal of a Movement Authority. The loss of such a balise telegram should cause the activation of the emergency brake and the train entering in Trip mode.

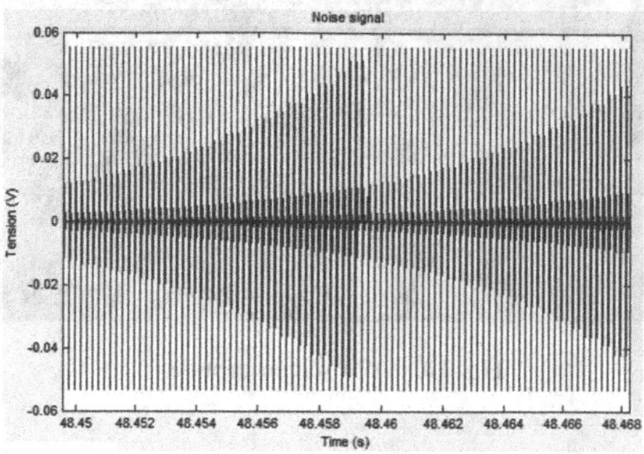

Fig. 8. Damped noise signal generated by BTM WCE

Figures 9 and 10 show the log of an ETCS JRU and the appearance of a DMI in the moment in which the interferer is applied to the balise. The correct activation of the security functions aforementioned can be seen.


```
<StoredJruEvent xsi:type="JruGeneralEvent">
<StoredJruEvent xsi:type="JruGeneralEvent">
<StoredJruEvent xsi:type="JruGeneralEvent">
<StoredJruEvent xsi:type="JruGeneralEvent">
<StoredJruEvent xsi:type="JruEmergencyBrakeEvent">
  <t>92245013.138</t>
  <seq>1</seq>
  <HEADER>
    <NID_MESSAGE>3</NID_MESSAGE>
    <L_MESSAGE>0</L_MESSAGE>
    <DATE>
    <TIME>
    <TRAIN_POSITION>
    <V_TRAIN>11</V_TRAIN>
    <DRIVER_ID>Hector</DRIVER_ID>
    <NID_ENGINE>0</NID_ENGINE>
    <SYSTEM_VERSION>
    Messages.JRU.SYSTEM_VERSION.Class_1__version_1_0__introduced_in_SRS_1_2
    _0_and_re_used_in_SRSs_2_0_0__2_2_2__2_3_0</SYSTEM_VERSION>
    <LEVEL>Messages.JRU.LEVEL.Level_1</LEVEL>
    <MODE>Messages.M_MODE.Trip</MODE>
  </HEADER>
  <M_BRAKE_COMMAND_STATUS>Messages.JRU.M_BRAKE_COMMAND_STATE.Commanded
  </M_BRAKE_COMMAND_STATUS>
</StoredJruEvent>
<StoredJruEvent xsi:type="JruGeneralEvent">
<StoredJruEvent xsi:type="JruGeneralEvent">
<StoredJruEvent xsi:type="JruGeneralEvent">
<StoredJruEvent xsi:type="JruGeneralEvent">
<StoredJruEvent xsi:type="JruGeneralEvent">
<StoredJruEvent xsi:type="JruGeneralEvent">
```

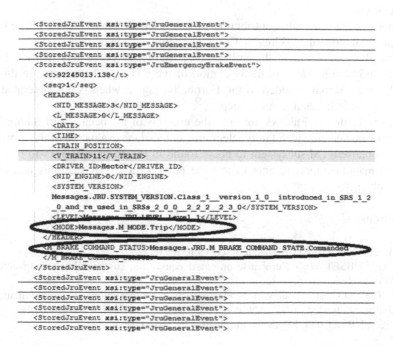

Fig. 9. JRU log capture

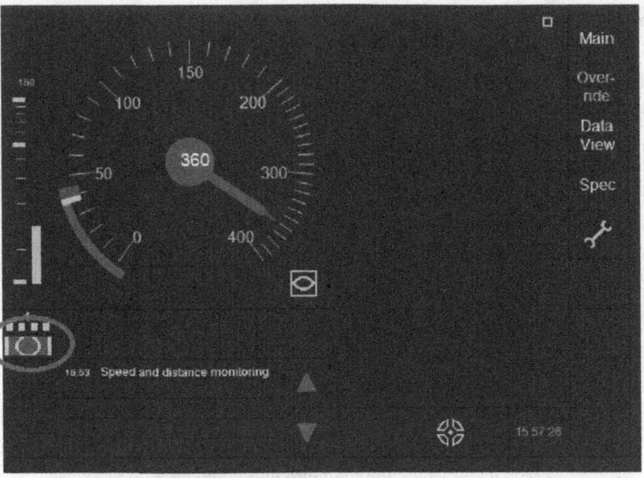

Fig. 10. DMI screen capture

6 Conclusion

The current process of putting ETCS equipment in service is affected by the testing process and laboratory procedures. The laboratory procedures and tools need to be improved in order to reach the objective of "Zero On-Site Testing" searched for long time.

One of the main improvements needed have to do with the capability of reproducing in the laboratory the worst case scenarios that such equipment will encounter when deployed.

In that context, the main contribution of this research work consists of the design and implementation of a Wireless Communication Emulator (WCE) for the BTM subsystem. Its aim is to test the influence of the noises previously defined for the Eurobalise/BTM subsystem, in the operation of the ETCS on-board unit. In this proposal, the noise signal is added to the Eurobalise signal when being generated. The resulting signal is injected to an air-gap.

As a result, this tool allows not only the analysis of the behavior of the on-board equipment when dealing with faulty telegrams, but also the evaluation of the robustness of the Eurobalise/BTM subsystem to noise found in the air-gap. Thanks to this capability, the manufacturers are able to test the equipment's EMC features and correct design problems.

References

1. RSSB: GE/GN8605 - ETCS system description. RSSB (2009)
2. UNISIG: SUBSET 116 - Eurobalise on-board equipment, susceptibility test specification. ERTMS (2011)
3. CEIT: TREND - test of rolling stock electromagnetic compatibility for cross-domain interoperability, EU funded FP7-TRANSPORT contract number 285259 (2011–2014)
4. UNISIG: SUBSET 036: FFFIS for Eurobalise. ERTMS (2010)

Standardisation Roadmap for Next Train Radio Telecommunication Systems

Hervé Bonneville(✉), Loïc Brunel, and David Mottier

Mitsubishi Electric R&D Centre Europe, Rennes, France
h.bonneville@fr.merce.mee.com

Abstract. 3GPP LTE (Third Generation Partnership Project – Long Term Evolution) cellular system first studies started in 2004. The system was designed initially for public voice and data services. Its scope has enlarged later on, to encompass public safety services and Machine-Type Communications (MTC). It targets now vehicular domain (V2X). In parallel, studies for the next generation system, a.k.a 5G, have started recently in 3GPP. This next generation aims at including from its very beginning, requirements for broadband public access services, Internet of Things (IoT) and vertical sectors, the latter ranging from vehicular services to factory automation needs. In Europe, several initiatives are on-going at International Railway Union (UIC), European Railway Agency (ERA) and ETSI (European Telecommunications Standards Institute) to prepare the next train radio telecommunication system that would fit rail community requirements in replacement of GSM-R (Global System for Mobile communications - Railways). Evolutions of 3GPP LTE are candidates, but 5G could jump in the list. This paper aims at providing an overview of current 3GPP status and roadmap toward 5G, and its level of compatibility with next train radio telecommunication system.

1 Introduction

Designing a specific radio communication system for trains makes sure that railway specific requirements are covered but has some cost impact. Besides, interoperability is necessary in Europe to allow trains to seamlessly cross state borders. Hence, it is attractive to benefit from designs and developments made for other deployments, and cellular public access is one of them. However, the evolution pace of systems in railway domain is much slower than the one in public access domain; targets and requirements are different even if 3GPP (Third Generation Partnership) has the intention to care about vertical sectors (e.g., transport, energy, e-health, factory automation) in future releases. Issues are then the choice of the mobile radio component, the timing for switching to a new system and the limitation of migration burden.

This paper is organised as follows: After a short history of GSM-R (Global System for Mobile communications – Railways), Sect. 2 provides some drivers for the next train radio communication system. Section 3 highlights the pros and cons of having specific features embedded in the communication system versus implementing them independently, and makes a tour of railways-related actors' initiatives toward next generation train radio communication system. Section 4 describes the enhancement of

J. Mendizabal et al. (Eds.): Nets4Cars/Nets4Trains/Nets4Aircraft 2016, LNCS 9669, pp. 51–61, 2016.
DOI: 10.1007/978-3-319-38921-9_6

3GPP LTE (Long Term Evolution) for the support of mission-critical communications, while Sect. 5 gives the 5G work status in 3GPP. Finally, Sect. 6 draws a possible time line of 3GPP future releases and their availability for next generation train radio communication system.

2 The GSM-R ERA

In the 90s, the European Union decided to launch a study on a unified train communication system that would facilitate train movement across state borders, in addition to improve signalling and train control required to reduce intervals between trains on dense lines and support high speed trains. Ten years later, ERTMS (European Rail Traffic Management System) was completed. It defines several components, mainly ETCS (European Train Control System), the train control application, and GSM-R, a radio communication part based on GSM and enhanced to support services required for train operation and not provided by the public radio, e.g., group calls, emergency calls, call pre-emption, location-dependent addressing, functional addressing, and direct mode.

GSM-R has been adopted in most of the European countries and worldwide on main lines. However, the deployment is slow due to its heavy cost and the long life cycle of railways equipments. For example in France, SNCF Réseau intends to complete its ERTMS deployment in 2017.

Even if GSM-R fulfils railway needs for train control communications, two points are to be looked at that would drive for an evolution.

Firstly, railway operators' requirements evolve toward a larger use of radio communication system with new applications, e.g., CCTV (Closed-Circuit TeleVision) for look-ahead control and on-board monitoring, train maintenance and configuration, enhanced Public Information System (PIS). Using service-dedicated communication systems is costly in terms of deployment and usage, and having one radio able to support all the services would be beneficial. Such a radio system would need to offer bandwidth capacity out of reach of GSM.

A second driver is related to upcoming GSM obsolescence. The decreasing of industry chain supporting GSM products will negatively impact the availability, costs and maintenance capability of 2G systems. GSM-R industry promises support at least until 2030. However, taking into account the time for technology evaluation, standardisation, product development, trials, certification and migration, it is wise to think about the next generation from now on.

3 Looking at Next Generation Train Radio System

3.1 Off-the-Shelf Versus Native Support

There is a huge difference of product life cycle between the public telecommunication industry and the railway industry. In the public case, we have seen a generation every ten years or so, starting in the 90's with GSM, then UMTS, now LTE and its evolution

(LTE-Advanced), the upcoming 5G tending to confirm this ten-year pace with a deployment target from 2020. In the railway case, the railway industry designs its products with a time horizon which is more about thirty years in mind. However, to keep support and to limit maintenance cost, railways cannot completely ignore what happens in the public telecommunication industry. One solution is to use as much as possible off-the-shelf components for the telecommunication system. But as railways require specific features and requirements, either the service could be designed as an "*over the top*" application over a basic radio system which would be robust enough to support it, or should be – at least partly – embedded in the telecommunication system itself and offered as an integrated service. The first approach enforces the independence between the applications and the telecommunication system, which is not always feasible, and does not take benefit of information the lower communication layers could have or of some optimisation they could offer. The second approach allows a more optimised system at the end, but at the cost of more standardisation effort and less flexibility.

Let us study the example of the push-to-talk service, which is a form of group call feature. Public cellular networks usually do not natively offer this functionality, as they first target point-to-point communications. Conferencing applications could be built up on top of it; several conferencing tools are available today. In 2006, Open Mobile Alliance (OMA) defined specifications of Push to talk over Cellular (PoC) as part of a Core Network (CN) based on IP Multimedia Subsystem (IMS) [1, 2]. 3GPP studied the specifications and confirmed its feasibility [3]. However, the implementation of the feature did not take off, one reason being its poor latency performance. Another drawback of these over-the-top approaches is their poor radio resource usage, each member in a group being served with a separate unicast link even if members are located in the same radio cell. GSM-R, on the other hand, integrates a group call feature and is able to optimise radio resources thanks to multicast whenever it is possible.

Hence, there is a non obvious trade-off between tailoring the communication system to some specific needs and the temptation to have a mass-market, thus hopefully low-cost, solution.

3.2 Preparing the Future

The International Railway Union (UIC) started in 2009 to think about what could and should be the next train radio communication system. A first document defining a set of technology-independent user requirements a new radio telecommunication system must support was released in October 2010 [4]. In 2014, the Future Railway Mobile Communication System (FRMCS) project was officially launched, with the aim to provide all needed information for decisions on the successor of GSM-R. It is composed of three work packages targeting functionality, spectrum, and technology and architecture.

European Union instances are also active on the topic. European Railway Agency (ERA) conducted a survey among all railways stakeholders [5] with the aim to find a common understanding of requirements and possible solutions toward a future radio communication system. Among others, the study mentions 3GPP LTE as a possible basis, but recommends also a monitoring of 3GPP 5G activity and a more active implication of rail sector in 3GPP standardisation in order to ensure that its requirements are taken into consideration.

In ETSI (European Telecommunications Standards Institute), RT-NG2R group (Railways Telecommunications - Next Generation Radio for Rail) was created in July 2015 to address the requirements from the rail transportation domain (including urban, suburban, regional, and long distance rail), to define the related architecture and radio spectrum needs and to identify and fill in standardisation gaps when necessary. RT-NG2R also liaises with relevant 3GPP bodies, e.g., to inform them about current UIC activity on system requirements as relevant input to mission-critical requirements to be considered in 5G [6].

The question of next generation radio system for mission-critical communications is also tackled by the PPDR (Public Protection and Disaster Relief) and the urban rail sectors. Thus, the possibility of sharing a common radio communication system between the PPDR and the rail sectors arises. However, it seems difficult to envisage, due to different requirements in terms of coverage, reliability and management [5], and difficulties to define responsibilities. Regarding urban and long distance rail actors, several initiatives, e.g., in London, tend to indicate a possible merging or at least commonalities between ERTMS and the CBTC (Communications-Based Train Control) systems used currently in urban deployments.

Preparing the next generation means also preparing the migration phase. The timeline shall include end-to-end trials, end-to-end integration, multi-vendor interoperability testing, deployment, co-existence and interoperability between GSM-R and the new system. Considering a possible end of GSM-R from 2030, the new generation should be available in the early 2020s for a safe migration.

4 3GPP LTE Standard

3GPP started first studies of EPS (Evolved Packet System) radio communication system in 2004 as a replacement to UMTS. It is composed of a new Radio Access Network (RAN) called LTE and a new Core Network (CN) named EPC (Evolved Packet Core). Even if EPC can support to some extent radio access technologies other than LTE, for example Wi-Fi, the name LTE is commonly used to address the whole EPS system. We will in the following follow this usage unless there is a necessity to separate the radio access component from the core network part.

LTE was designed initially as a replacement to UMTS, with a focus on public data and voice mobile broadband (MBB) services. It got quick momentum and is today widely deployed worldwide. In a 20 MHz radio channel, it can provide peak data rate of 172.8 Mbit/s for 2 × 2 antennas in the downlink, and 86.4 Mbit/s for 1 × 2 antennas in the uplink, and even if optimised for low user mobility (0–15 km/h), it can support higher speed, up to 350 km/h, despite much lower data rates.

From 2011, 3GPP Release 10, also called LTE-Advanced, is considered as a significant improvement of the LTE system and labelled as a fourth generation mobile cellular system (4G). 3GPP has progressively enlarged the initial LTE scope, by specifying features needed for new services and by enriching the possible deployment architectures. Indeed, broadcast capability was introduced with MBMS (Multimedia Broadcast and Multicast Service), RAN architecture based on large cells and big base stations was completed with the introduction of small cells to cope with dense areas (hot-spots) and home base stations for better indoor coverage as shown in Fig. 1. Enhancements were added to better support Machine-Type Communications (MTC). With the incentive of the US government that has decided that all public safety organisations operating in USA should use a common radio communication system, 3GPP LTE turns to address public safety (mission critical) service requirements. It is an important move since it implies specific features that were not addressed at all when initially considering broadband services. Two important ones are Device-to-Device (D2D) communications and discovery and group communication, called Mission Critical Push To Talk (MCPTT) within 3GPP. Mission critical services were judged important enough to dedicate a working group (SA6) to this topic, in charge of defining application layer functional elements and interfaces to support critical communications. Indeed, with these features, LTE radio access technology could be the next radio of TETRA networks.

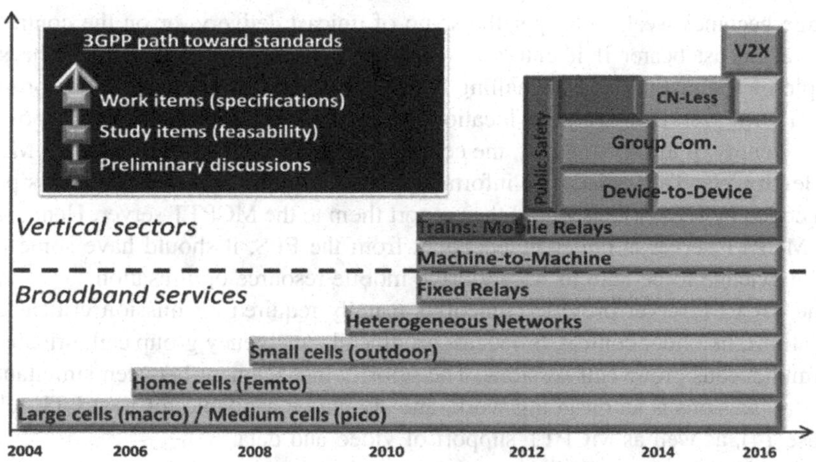

Fig. 1. Expansion of 3GPP scope toward vertical sectors.

4.1 MCPTT Features and Architecture

The approach taken to specify MCPTT is to define interfaces [7] provided by the mobile network to an application server [8]. The interfaces provide enablers allowing the application server to access the mobile network resource so as to support the group communication service. Figure 2 depicts a high level view of the MCPTT architecture. In the downlink, data can be provided to a UE (User Equipment) either through a unicast path, or through a multicast (MBMS) path, although for the uplink only unicast bearers can be established. MBMS can be further optimised if UEs of a group are located in the same cell, with Single-Cell Point to Multipoint (SC-PTM), avoiding radio resource coordination among neighbour cells when it is not necessary.

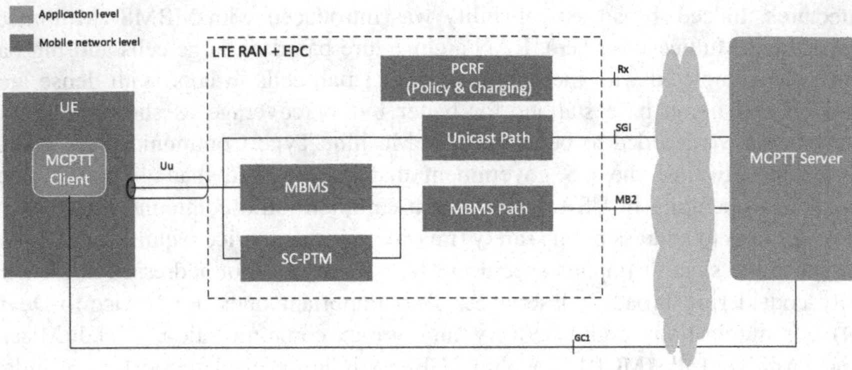

Fig. 2. High level view of 3GPP MCPTT architecture.

The MCPTT server can be guided in its choice of the best data path to use by the UE through application-level signalling between UE MCPTT client and MCPTT server (GC1 interface): For example, the UE warns the application server when its MBMS coverage becomes weak to trigger the setup of unicast delivery, or on the contrary to release a unicast bearer if it enters an area with good MBMS coverage. The same principle of application level signalling could be applied for UE location reporting to the MCPTT server. However, this location information would typically be composed of the cell identity of the serving cell, the cell identities of the neighbour cells, the MBMS area identity, etc. These pieces of information are broadcast by the radio access points and decoded by UEs, which would then report them to the MCPTT server. Hence, even if the MCPTT server is rather independent from the EPS, it should have some radio level knowledge to be able to wisely drive mobile resource optimisation.

The MCPTT server provides functions usually required by mission critical communications, like floor control, broadcast group call, emergency group call, private call, and simultaneous group call sessions. The priority management between simultaneous group call sessions is an on-going work, and should be available for next LTE release (Release 14), as well as MCPTT support of video and data.

4.2 Other Features and On-Going Work

Device-to-device functions [9] include UE discovery, allowing a UE to detect another UE, one-to-many direct communication between UEs, one-to-one direct communication between UEs, and UE to network relaying. Direct communications are supported even when UEs are out of network coverage. Some guidance has been specified for operation in case the link to the core network is lost, for example in disaster situation. It is mentioned as CN-Less in Fig. 1.

Recently, 3GPP started to study the support of vehicular communications (V2X) as understood in ITS (Intelligent Transport System), i.e., vehicle to vehicle, vehicle to pedestrian and vehicle to infrastructure. The study focuses on the automotive domain, but some developments like improved D2D performance could be of interest for railways.

Directly targeting train communications, an on-going work [10] aims to improve performance for mobile broadband public access in high speed trains (up to 350 km/h), with for example proposals for Doppler compensation.

Hence, even if not designed to target train communications, several features offered today by 3GPP LTE-Advanced could fulfil railways requirements. However, some are still missing: for example, location-dependent addressing and functional dependent addressing have not been addressed so far in 3GPP. Furthermore, the data rate offered by LTE in very high speed like 500 km/h strongly decreases in uplink. Depending on the system bandwidth, it may be limiting for services like CCTV. Finally, mixing services with different qualities of service (QoS) on LTE is essential for a railway system where vital services with strong QoS constraints may coexist with best effort traffic. In order to ensure an efficient coexistence, the resource scheduling has to be optimised [11].

5 Toward 5G

Soon after the deployment of a cellular technology, it is time to think about the next generation. Therefore, 5G strategic organisations, e.g., the 5G Infrastructure Public Private Partnership (5G PPP) in Europe and the Fifth Generation Mobile Communications Promotion Forum (5GMF) in Japan, have been put in place in 2014 to coordinate research actions on 5G. At standardisation level, 3GPP started concrete discussions on 5G in 2015 with the organisation of dedicated workshops and the creation of new study items (channel modelling, RAN scenarios and requirements [12, 13], RAN and architectures studies [14, 15]).

Compared to LTE, which first targeted mobile broadband services and then extended its scope to other use cases, there is a will, driven by Europe, to address a wide set of use cases from the beginning of 5G standardisation. Indeed, 5G should not only cover mobile broadband services, but also mission-critical use cases, Internet of Things (IoT) with massive machine-type communications (mMTC), and the so-called vertical sectors, i.e., the automotive, energy, factory automation or e-health industries. Key performance targets are a several-magnitude increase of offered bandwidth, an increased number of supported users, a significantly lower latency (down to the ms or so) and a significantly better terminal battery life. The 5G system is intended to operate on new spectrum bands, from below 6 GHz up to millimetre waves above 24.25 GHz. A new air interface is going to be designed, and eventually a new core network.

3GPP drafted a set of more than 70 use cases and scenarios of interest [16], including high user mobility (up to 500 km/h for high speed trains), ultra-reliable communications, high accuracy positioning, and high availability and service reliability with the help of satellites. Indeed, 5G is not seen as a monolithic system, but as a flexible one able to integrate different radio access technologies.

5.1 Mobile Network Design Evolutions

The 5G core network should be designed to be as much as possible independent from the radio access technology. Hence, the interface between RAN and CN is likely to be completely reviewed.

To support various requirements from services as different as MBB or massive MTC, it is envisaged to rely on network virtualisation that allows defining, on a shared real architecture, so-called network slices that include only the logical network elements needed for a given domain (Fig. 3). Indeed, it is expected to reduce the complexity of each slice, while adding flexibility – new type of slices could be envisaged for new services without impacting the legacy ones – and easier load management – a new instance of a slice could be created or released depending on network load.

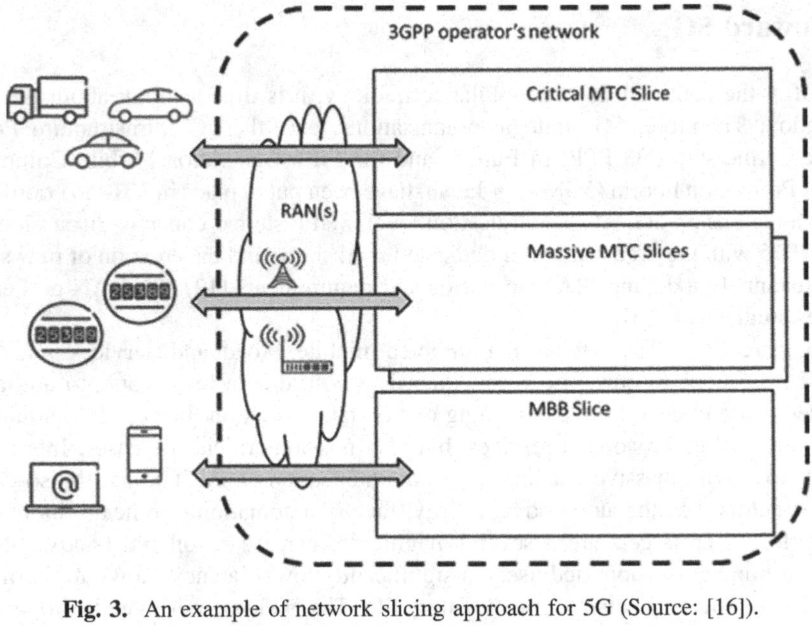

Fig. 3. An example of network slicing approach for 5G (Source: [16]).

The principle of virtualisation could be further extended to network function virtualisation (NFV). With this concept, the network nodes are split into functions that can be dynamically started or released when necessary. For example, MTC being with rather static devices, it could be unnecessary to have the mobility function active for serving them.

Defining new services could be envisaged either over-the-top, without the possibility to benefit from network knowledge, leading to poor optimisation but to a better independence, or embedded into the network, allowing more optimisation but requiring standardisation. Considering the heavy workload in 3GPP, triggering a standardisation effort is challenging for applications or services that do not represent an important market share. However, 5G, by design, is expected to facilitate and speed up the outcome of new services, and NFV approach could be a solution in that direction. For example, if it is possible from an application level to get from the Virtual Network Functions (NVFs) information like the cell serving the UE and the neighbouring cells, this could help implementing a MCPTT service offered at application layer but able to optimise the way–unicast or broadcast – the service is provided to a group of users, without the need to touch UE client and without impacting the network specifications.

However, determining the good NVF granularity level, offering enough flexibility but limiting the complexity coming from the number of elements, is far from obvious. And standardisation work has just started.

6 Possible Roadmap

Figure 4 provides a view of a possible time line of 3GPP releases for the next five years. LTE will continue to evolve, in parallel to 5G development [16]. From the railways' perspective, considering the standardisation progress, the first release to potentially address railway-specific features could be Release 14, which started in early 2016. However, considering the time needed to significantly impact 3GPP community, Release 15 may be a more compatible target. Release 16 could also be a candidate, with a tighter migration time schedule from GSM-R. Indeed, Release 16 5G will surely embed mission-critical features whereas, for Release 15, 3GPP may focus on MBB services in order to be ready for the main salient 5G milestone, agreed worldwide: in 2020, Japan expects to experiment first 5G services for the Tokyo Olympic Games.

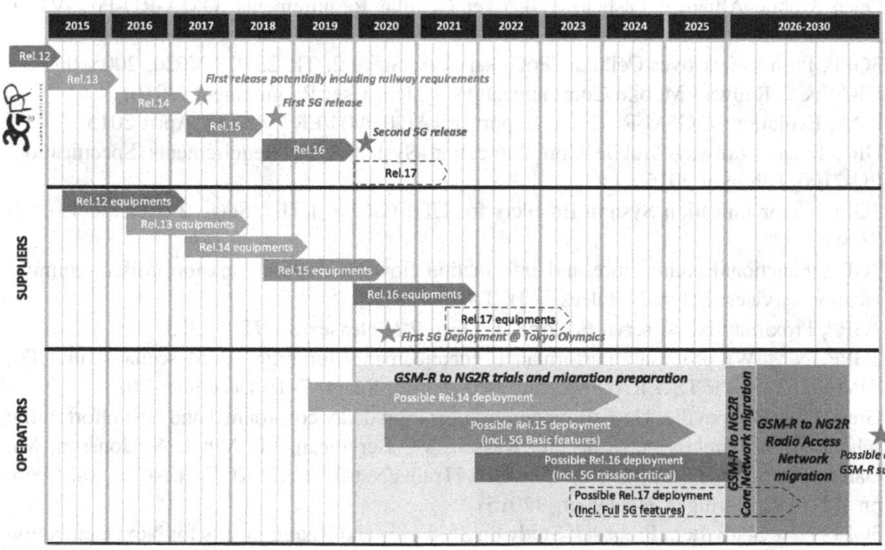

Fig. 4. Possible roadmap of 3GPP releases for the next 5 years.

7 Conclusion

The appearance of new services like CCTV requiring more bandwidth and the expected obsolescence of GSM that should drive the end of GSM-R support from 2030 are drivers for looking at the successor of GSM-R for train communication system.

3GPP LTE was enhanced from its first release and enlarged its scope, embracing in particular public safety services. These enhancements mark it out as a candidate for GSM-R replacement. Hence, LTE could do the job with some further evolutions, but the railway industry should urge to push for these evolutions in 3GPP in order to have a chance to get them in time for migration.

5G could also be a candidate. Time line is tight, but it could be easier for railways stakeholders to be heard in 3GPP on 5G since the specifications are in their infancy and 5G aims at embracing from the beginning use cases more in line with train communication requirements. Moreover, 5G design could eventually allow more flexibility in specific service deployments, which would be a plus. However 5G will not be able to claim the long lasting field-testing LTE has now.

Anyhow, migration will take time and shall foresee a long co-existence between GSM-R and its successor.

References

1. Open Mobile Alliance, Push to talk over Cellular (PoC) – Architecture, OMA-AD-PoC-V1_0, June 2006
2. Open Mobile Alliance, Push to Talk over Cellular Requirements, OMA-RD-PoC-V1_0, June 2006
3. 3GPP, Push-to-talk over Cellular (PoC) services; Stage 2, TR 23.979 V620, 2005–06
4. UIC Spec., Railway Mobile Communication System User Requirement (2010)
5. ERA, Evolution of GSM-R - Final Report, ERA/2014/04/ERTMS/OP, April 2015
6. UIC, Future Railway Mobile Communication System User Requirements Specification, FU-7100, February 2016
7. 3GPP, Communication System Enablers for LTE (GCSE_LTE); Stage 2 (Release 13), TS 23.468
8. 3GPP, Functional architecture and information flows to support mission critical communication services; Stage 2 (Release 13), TS 23.179
9. 3GPP, Proximity-based services (ProSe); Stage 2 (Release 13), TS 23.303
10. 3GPP, New WI proposal: Performance enhancements for high speed scenario in LTE, RP-152263, 3GPP TSG RAN Meeting #70, Sitges, Spain, 7–10 December 2015
11. Gresset, N., Bonneville, H.: Fair preemption for joint delay constrained and best effort traffic scheduling in wireless networks. In: Kassab, M., Berbineau, M., Vinel, A., Jonsson, M., Garcia, F., Soler, J. (eds.) Nets4Cars/Nets4Trains/Nets4Aircraft 2015. LNCS, vol. 9066, pp. 141–152. Springer, Heidelberg (2015)
12. 3GPP, New Study Item Proposal: Study on Scenarios and Requirements for Next Generation Access Technologies, RP-152257, 3GPP TSG RAN Meeting #70, Sitges, Spain, 7–10 December 2015
13. 3GPP, Study on Scenarios and Requirements for Next Generation Access Technologies; (Release 14), TR 38.913

14. 3GPP, New Study on Architecture and Security for Next Generation System, SP-160227, 3GPP TSG SA Meeting #71, Gothenburg, Sweden, 9–11 March 2016
15. 3GPP, Study on NR New Radio Access Technology, RP-160671, 3GPP TSG RAN Meeting #71, Göteborg, Sweden, 7–10 March 2016
16. 3GPP, Study on New Services and Markets Technology Enablers; Stage 1 (Release 14), TR 22.891

Measurement and Analysis of ITS-G5 in Railway Environments

Paul Unterhuber(✉), Andreas Lehner, and Fabian de Ponte Müller

German Aerospace Center (DLR), Cologne, Germany
paul.unterhuber@dlr.de

Abstract. In this paper we present first measurement results of a novel approach in Train-to-Train (T2T) communications. For this measurement campaign an Intelligent Transport System (ITS-G5) communication link was used to investigate the influences of a railway environment on a Car-to-Car (C2C) communication standard based system. The measurements cover a wide range of scenarios from urban to rural environments, forest to open field as well as tunnels and crossings under bridges. The investigated measurement categories are channel characteristics, system performance and environmental aspects. The results should clarify, if a technology transfer from road to railway traffic communications would be expedient.

Keywords: Railway · Train-to-train · Next generation train · Dynamic coupling · Virtual coupling · ITS-G5 · IEEE802.11

1 Introduction

Most of the publications about vehicular communications focus on car communication issues and the related propagation aspects. With good reasons, the individual transport has been increasing tremendously in the last decades. Even though C2C is the biggest market and automotive manufacturer and IT companies are investing billions of dollars, these technologies are also interesting for all other types of vehicles. For railway traffic and management Vehicle-to-Infrastructure (V2I) was the most common communication scenario till now. The last years, a lot of investigations were done on Global System for Mobile Communications-Railway (GSM-R), potential successors like a transfer of Long Term Evolution (LTE) to railway [8] and the availability of those systems for high speed trains in different scenarios [4]. For future applications on railway tracks like dynamic coupling or platooning and with it a more efficient and safe usage, also T2T communications are going to be very important.

T2T communications, like in the Railway Collision Avoidance System (RCAS) are designed for very specific tasks, offering a large coverage but small bandwidth. ITS-G5 would supplement such a system with a higher data rate at short range. Hence, why not using the existing ITS-G5 standard from C2C applications and transfer the technology to railway traffic. To evaluate this possible application and to identify differences on the propagation channel for road and railway environment this measurement campaign was executed.

J. Mendizabal et al. (Eds.): Nets4Cars/Nets4Trains/Nets4Aircraft 2016, LNCS 9669, pp. 62–73, 2016.
DOI: 10.1007/978-3-319-38921-9_7

2 Measurement Campaign

In the same way as it was performed for the RCAS measurement campaign as presented in [2], the purpose of these measurements was to investigate the performance of an existing commercial system in a different environment, as it was designed for. We used Cohda Mobility MK5 On Board Unit (OBU) Enclosure modules [5] as transmitter and receiver. The Cohda MK5 module provides an automotive qualified IEEE 802.11p dual-antenna radio and a Global Navigation Satellite System (GNSS) [6]. With the use of an automotive system in a railway environment several questions were raised: How does a train influence the link in comparison to a car? What are the influences of a railway track environment on the propagation channel? If there are differences between car and train as well as street and track in case of the channel, can the C2C system handle those different circumstances and how is the performance influenced?

To answer these questions a measurement campaign was performed. In Order to investigate different environmental and topological aspects, this campaign was organized similar as the campaign in [2]. Our partner, the "Bayrische Oberlandbahn" (BOB) provided one diesel-hydraulic train-set for the time of the measurements.

2.1 Railway Network

BOB operates with 20 trains on a total network of 120 km with 27 stations and transports around 15,000 people per day within urban, suburban and rural environment. As shown in Fig. 1, the railway network consists of one main line from Munich to Holzkirchen and 3 branches, to Lenggries, Tegernsee and Bayrischzell. The main line is electrified, offers two tracks and is used by the Munich commuter railway system as well. Going on the branches south from Holzkirchen, the network is single track and not electrified. On each run, a combined set of 3 consists departs from Munich central station. In Holzkirchen, one consist splits up to Bayrischzell, two continue to Schaftlach, where they split again and are heading to Lenggries and Tegernsee. On the way back, the consists couple again on the mentioned stations and arrive as one train back at Munich central station. Due to this procedure and the hourly train schedule, only at one place north of Holzkirchen, two trains pass each other. This mentioned single event with two trains and the coupling of the train sets in the stations won't reflect a sufficient distribution of measurement environments. Hence, to cover all kind of different environments and scenarios in T2T communications, the transmitter (Tx) was installed on a BOB train and the receiver (Rx) on the German Aerospace Center (DLR) Safety of Life Communications (SoL) measurement car.

2.2 Environment and Scenarios

The environment along the track varies from urban and suburban in the metropolitan area of Munich to rural areas in the south of Bavaria. The trains passes one tunnel, under several bridges, villages, stations, forests, open field,

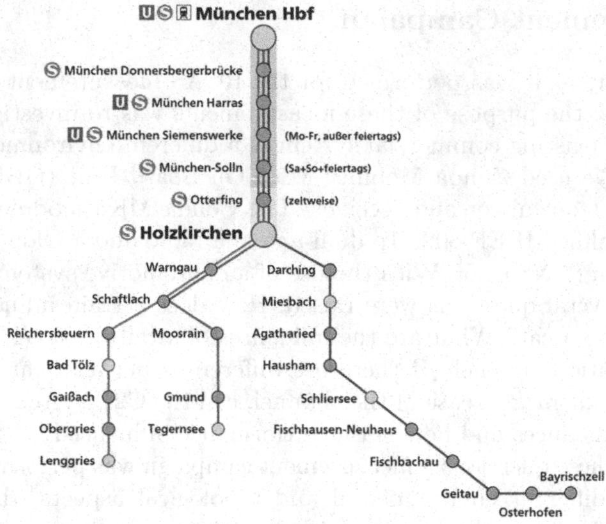

Fig. 1. BOB route network [3]

lakes and mountains. The travel speed of the train goes from 35 km/h near level crossings up to 140 km/h between Holzkirchen and the suburbs of Munich. The variety of scenarios even increases with the possible relative movements of the car to the train. The different measurements can be divided in dynamic and static scenarios as shown in Table 1. Dynamic measurements were done on roads directly next to the railway track; in this way the car emulates a second moving train. Static measurements supplement the scenarios, either the car parks at interesting positions where the train pass by (e.g. on a bridge or next to a level crossing) or both vehicle velocities are zero (e.g. in a railway station).

Table 1. Traffic scenarios in T2T

Traffic scenario		Description
Dynamic	Follow	Train and car driving the same speed in same direction
	Opposing	Train and car driving in opposing direction
	Overtaking	Train overtakes the car or vice versa
	Approach	Train close the gap to the car or vice versa
Static	Pass	Train pass the parked car
	Station	Train and car stop in station

The different scenarios were combined with different environmental aspects as mentioned before. Under consideration of local restrictions and private property along the railway track, 18 different measurement scenarios were investigated in 20 measurement runs.

2.3 Measurement Setup

The measurement setup included two T2T links, ITS-G5 and RCAS and a spectrum analyzer on the receiver side in the car. For all measurements and both T2T links, the train was set as transmitter and the car as receiver as shown in Fig. 2. In detail, we set up one Cohda box as transmitter in the train with a multi-band antenna, including a GNSS antenna and two 5.9 GHz antennas. This antenna was mounted outside of the train on the highest possible point which ensured horizontal transmission. A second Cohda box and antenna were installed in the car as receiver. The Cohda MK5 enclosure offers two independent integrated radios, which were used for different settings as mentioned in Table 2. The transmit power at the Cohda box met the lower bound of the ITS-G5 standard Equivalent Isotropically Radiated Power (EIRP) requirements. Both modules logged the transmitted and received packets. At the train side the Cohda box logged the information of each sent package with a sequential number. The packet information included the GNSS position and time stamp of the train, packet size, modulation and data rate information. At the receiver side in the car, each received packet was analyzed and logged. Next to the received information a time stamp and the GNSS information of the Rx module, the speed of the car, the received power and the sensitivity of both radios were logged.

Fig. 2. T2T measurement setup: Rx on the car in the foreground and Tx on the train in the background

The spectrum analyzer was realized with a software defined radio in the car. The transmitted ITS-G5 signal was received with a separate 5.9 GHz antenna and feed to an Ettus USRP N210 [1]. The spectrum was analyzed at 5.9 GHz with 25 MHz bandwidth for the signal transmitted in channel 180.

The RCAS units and the corresponding antennas and power supply were installed in the train and the car. This system provided detailed information about the train and car position, direction and speed. This was necessary for precise coordination and timing of the measurement campaign. The RCAS system operates with Terrestrial Trunked Radio (TETRA) at 470 MHz with 25 kHz bandwidth and 10 W EIRP.

Table 2. Cohda MK5 radio settings

Radio	A	B
Channel	180	176
Carrier frequency	5.9 GHz	5.88 GHz
Bandwidth	10 MHz	10 MHz
Transmit power	21 dBm, 24 dBm	21 dBm, 24 dBm
Data rate	6 Mbit/s	3 Mbit/s
Modulation	QPSK	BPSK
Coding rate	1/2	1/2
Packet length	150, 400 Byte	150, 400 Byte
Repetition time	100 Hz	100 Hz

3 Data Analysis

The following analysis is based on the data of the Rx Cohda box. As mentioned before, all required information was logged on the box in the car.

3.1 Scenarios

Out of the different measured scenarios as described in Sect. 2.2, three of them are pointed out and the recorded data and evaluated characteristics over time are shown. In Figs. 3a, 4a and 5a the first chart shows the measured received power and the path loss in Line of Sight (LOS) condition calculated with Eq. 1, the second chart shows the distance between Tx and Rx and the last one the speed of the train and the car, as well as the relative speed over the measurement time. Figures 3b, 4b and 5b show a snapshot during each measurement. All three measurements were done with an output power $P_{\text{Tx}} = 21$ dBm.

The first scenario represents a train passing a stopped vehicle with a certain speed. Therefore, the car was parked on a cross bridge as shown in Fig. 3b (on the picture the train is approaching) and the train passed by with 80 km/h (see Fig. 3a bottom chart). The different power level of arrival and departure is cased by the trees marked with a yellow circle. The dense tree marked with a red circle causes the fading between 5 and 6 s. The fading at around $t = 10$ s is cased by the bridge itself when the transmitter is passing under the bridge and car. For the departure ($t > 10$ s) the maximum coverage reaches around 350 m.

The second measurement setup shown in Fig. 4 evaluates a train overtaking another one. The car is driving with approximately 80 km/h and was overtaken by the train with 140 km/h. On Fig. 4b the 470 MHz TETRA antenna, the 5.9 GHz dipole antenna and the white radome including both 5.9 GHz antennas and the GNSS antenna are visible. Left and right of the track was dense forest. The observed fading is caused by the forest environment. The different height of the used vehicles causes variations in antenna gain depending on the position of the vehicles to each other.

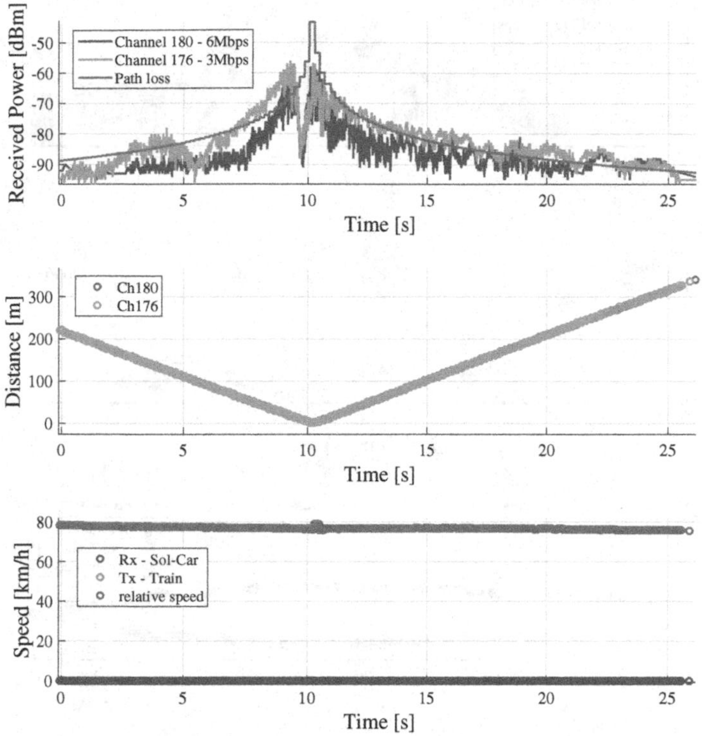

(a) Data

(b) Train passing the car parked on a bridge

Fig. 3. Measurement of a passing train (Color figure online)

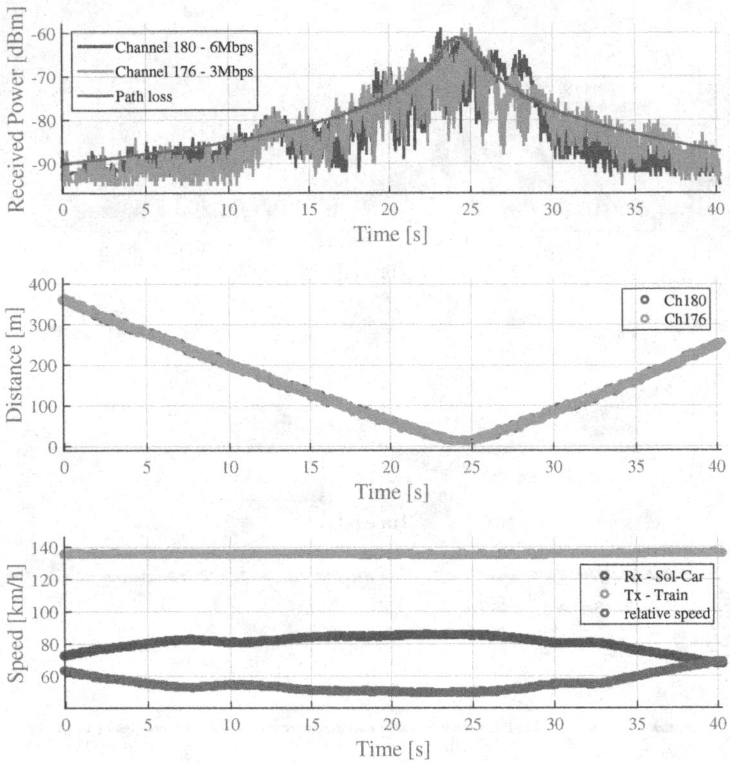

(a) Data

(b) Overtaking maneuver in a forest

Fig. 4. Overtaking measurement (Color figure online)

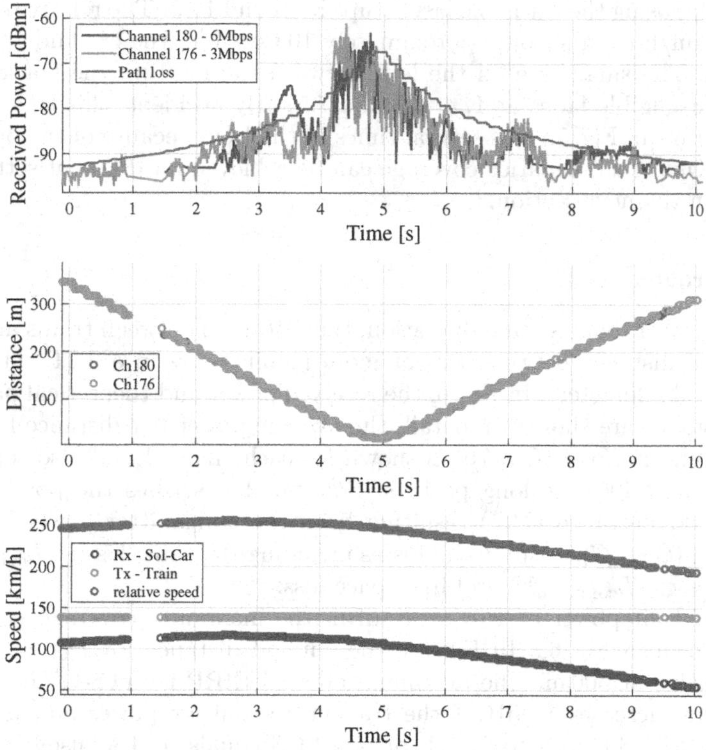

(a) Data

(b) Car and train opposing each other in a village environment

Fig. 5. Opposing measurement (Color figure online)

A train opposing the car is the last setup shown in Fig. 5. The relative speed of around 250 km/h results from approximately 108 km/h of the car and 142 km/h of the train. The small tree on the left, between the road an the track causes several not negligible fades at 1, 4, 6.5 and 7.5 s. By accident, this tree marked with a red circle in Fig. 5b was several times in the LOS because of the opposing movement. Out of all scenarios coverage can be achieved for different settings as mentioned in the next section.

3.2 Coverage

Due to the way of today's train operation, the distances between trains and with it the related distance between two or more mobile users in a T2T network is usually several kilometers. In Fig. 6, the received power and theoretical path loss over the distance are shown. In detail, the average power per distance for radio A (Ch 180) and radio B (Ch 176) is shown for each channel and also separated for 150 byte and 400 byte long packets. Equation 1 describes the power in dB at the receiver entrance (P_{Rx}) resulting from the transmitter power plus the antenna gain (G_{Tx}, G_{Rx}), minus all losses including the cable losses (L_{cable}), the connector losses ($L_{\mathrm{connectors}}$) and free space loss.

For an output power of $P_{\mathrm{Tx}} = 21$ dBm the maximum coverage is around 400 m as shown in Fig. 6a. In Fig. 6b, the cut- off distance for $P_{\mathrm{Tx}} = 24$ dBm is clearly visible at 600 m. The maximum allowed EIRP for ITS-G5 is 33 dBm. Hence, by an increase of 9dB at the transmitter output power and path loss exponents for LOS equals to 2 and for non-LOS equals to 4 as used in [2] the theoretical coverage quadruple for LOS and double for non-LOS. This leads to an estimated coverage up to 2400 m for LOS and 1200 m for non-LOS conditions. Comparing the two different radios, radio B is showing a better performance. This results from the lower data rate and with it a more robust connection. Differences between 400 and 150 byte long packets are negligible for coverage.

$$
\begin{aligned}
P_{\mathrm{Rx}} = P_{\mathrm{Tx}} - L_{\mathrm{cable}} - L_{\mathrm{connectors}} + G_{\mathrm{Tx}} \\
- 20 \cdot log_{10}\left(\frac{4\pi r \cdot f}{c}\right) \\
+ G_{\mathrm{Rx}} - L_{\mathrm{cable}} - L_{\mathrm{connectors}} \qquad (1)
\end{aligned}
$$

3.3 Line of Sight

The design of a railway track is setup for a desired travel speed of the train. Formerly, tracks in rural areas were influenced by the surroundings like rivers, mountains and villages. Nevertheless, the track design and especially the curve radius is setting the maximum speed. In case of propagation aspects, the curve radius and the track width are setting up a minimum given LOS distance. In Table 3, key values of the track are listed. The recorded GNSS data gives the minimum and maximum values for the curve radius R, the track width d_{T} and

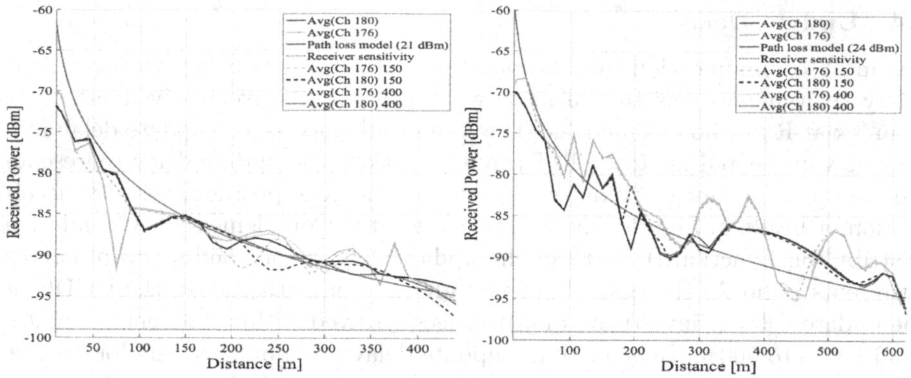

(a) $P_{\text{Tx}} = 21$ dBm (b) $P_{\text{Tx}} = 24$ dBm

Fig. 6. Received power over distance

the train speed v in these sections. Out of the measured data the average values were calculated.

The LOS distance (d_{LOS}) can be calculated with Eq. 2. This calculation describes the worst case scenario: a curved track with obstacles next to the track e.g. buildings or trees. The maximum available coverage could be assumed as a combination of the LOS and the non-LOS component.

The braking distance of a vehicle d_{B} can be calculated from the measured speed, the maximum allowed acceleration for trains ($a_{\text{max}} = 1.5\,\text{ms}^{-2}$). One part counting in the system delay τ_{sys} is added to Eq. 3. One possible application of ITS-G5 in railways could be the communication within a platoon of virtual coupled trains. For a stable drive of the platoon, the coverage of the communication can be less than the braking distance of one consist but large enough to cover the whole platoon including the system delays.

$$d_{\text{LOS}} = 2 \cdot \sqrt{R^2 - \left(R - \frac{d_{\text{T}}}{2}\right)^2} \tag{2}$$

$$d_{\text{B}} = \frac{v^2}{2 \cdot a_{\text{max}}} + \tau_{\text{sys}} \cdot v \tag{3}$$

Table 3. Track analysis

	R [m]	d_T [m]	v [km/h]	d_B [m]	d_{LOS} [m]
min	124	8	35	31	63
avg	400	12	73	137	138
max	2000	20	140	504	400

3.4 Update Delay

For most communication applications the throughput is a key indicator, for safety relevant systems the delay between two consecutive received messages from Tx at Rx is more significant. This value is defined as the update delay of a system as presented in [7]. In T2T communications the update delay represents a quality measure for up to date traffic information e.g. position, velocity, acceleration or heading. Figure 7 shows the investigated Complementary Cumulative Distribution Function (CCDF) of the update delays; the solid series of curves represents radio A, the dashed curves radio B. For both radios, the CCDF of the update delay is investigated for packages received within different coverages from 100 m to 500 m. In general, the update delay probability lowers for shorter communication ranges due to the higher received power. For example take a delay of 0.5 s for radio B, the CCDF for 200 m is $3 \cdot 10^{-3}$ and for 100 m Fig. 7 shows $9 \cdot 10^{-3}$. An increase of the transmit power would have the same effect and would shift the curves down to the left. For this investigation, radio B with a data rate of 3 Mbit/s shows a better performance within all distances. These results reflect power performances of radio A and radio B as shown in Fig. 6.

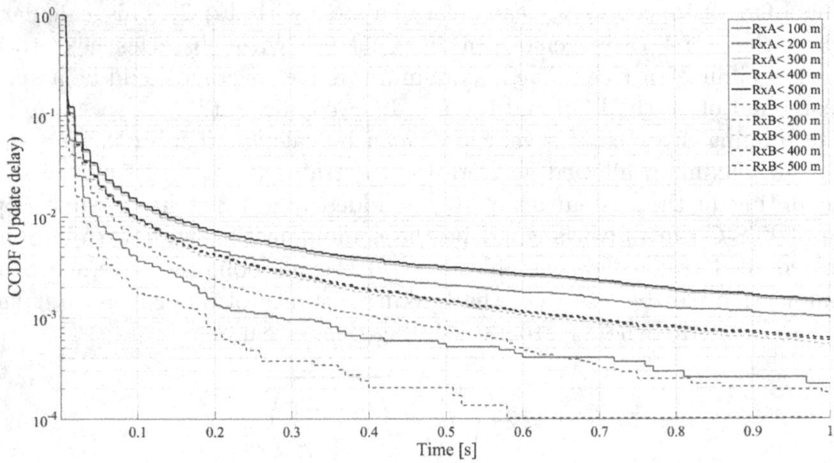

Fig. 7. Update delay for all received packets

4 Conclusion

In this paper the measurement results of a novel approach in T2T communications were presented. The performance of ITS-G5 under railway environment was investigated. One train and one car were equipped with ITS-G5 Cohda units and additional measurement equipment and ran on 20 measurements in 3 days. A wide range of different scenarios from urban, sub-urban and rural were investigated. An extract of these measurements was presented in this paper and the performance of ITS-G5 in railway environments investigated.

With these measurements a proper usage of ITS-G5 in a railway environment is proven. For certain applications within a coverage of up to 1200 m this communication standard is able to handle the diverse environments along a rail track. This measurement data will help to investigate new possibilities in T2T communications for non-high-speed trains. Future channel models out of this data will provide a basement for a development of suitable T2T applications in railway environments.

Acknowledgement. The authors are thankful for the cooperation and support of "Bayerische Oberlandbahn" for these measurements. This cooperation lead to a novel collection of data in T2T communications.

References

1. Ettus USRP N200/N210 Networked Series (2014)
2. Lehner, A., Garca, C.R., Strang, T.: On the performance of TETRA DMO short data service in railway VANETs. Wirel. Pers. Commun. **69**, 1647–1669 (2012)
3. Bayerische-Oberlandbahn GmbH, October 2015
4. Chen, B., Zhong, Z., Ai, B., Guan, D., He, R., Michelson, D.G.: Channel characteristics in high-speed railway. IEEE Veh. Technol. Mag. **10**, 67–78 (2015)
5. de Haaij, D.: Cohda Mobility MK5 OBU Enclosure Design Description (2014)
6. de Haaij, D., Sloman, M.: Cohda Mobility MK5 Module Datasheet (2014)
7. Bernhard Kloiber, C.R., Garcia, J.H., Strang, T.: Update delay: a new information-centric metric for a combined communication and application level reliability evaluation of cam based safety applications. In: ITS World Congress, 1–9 October 2012 (2012)
8. Sniady, A., Soler, J.: LTE for railways - impact on performance of ETCS railway signaling. IEEE Veh. Technol. Mag. **9**, 69–77 (2014)

SDK Definition for Safety Functions for UART, CAN and TCP/IP Communications

Leonardo J. Valdivia(✉), Gonzalo Solas, Javier Añorga, Saioa Arrizabalaga, Iñigo Adin, and Jaizki Mendizabal

CEIT and Tecnun, University of Navarra, Manuel de Lardizabal 15, 20018 San Sebastian, Spain
{lvaldivia,gsolas,jabenito,sarrizabalaga,iadin, jmendizabal}@ceit.es

Abstract. A SDK (Software Development Kit) to test, develop or improve safety-critical systems is presented. The SDK has three main modules: voter, saboteur and sniffer. The voter can be configured as "*m* out of *n*" where m and n can be any number but always $n > m$, each redundant channel uses a microcontroller as a main system. The saboteur examines the information that goes through the information interchange path, altering it and generating faulty data, modification of the evaluation hardware is minimized by using saboteurs in the communication between elements. The sniffer can display the data that passes over a network, it can be configured to handle three different protocols UART, CAN or TCP/IP.

Keywords: SDK · Voter · Saboteur · Sniffer · CAN · UART · TCP/IP

1 Introduction

Critical applications are defined as the ones whose failure have a relevant impact on finances or more important in humans beings. A failure occurs when an application is no longer able to perform its required function. Critical applications can be divided into two sections depending on their impact; when the failure impacts humans being they are called safety-critical or mission-critical if the failure only impacts finances [1].

Any critical system must meet two attributes: safety and availability. A safe system must behave correctly in all operating and environmental conditions. The availability ensures continuous operation of the system and it is also correlated with the capacity to restore after a failure [2, 3]. Regarding system architecture, redundant architecture is commonly adopted in the majority of cases. The redundancy requires a voter, this element is responsible for selecting one of the outputs as correct. In some systems the voter is implemented by hardware (based on relays, digital gates, VHDL, etc.), but depending on the application and the input type this voter cannot be used [4]. Besides the hardware voter are not flexible to test different kind of systems, and in the development stage the flexibility is essential. Therefore, a software voter can be used in most applications, either to test, develop or even improve a system. The problem associated with software voter is to ensure that it does not corrupt data, for this reason, safety elements must be added to prevent this inconvenient [5].

J. Mendizabal et al. (Eds.): Nets4Cars/Nets4Trains/Nets4Aircraft 2016, LNCS 9669, pp. 74–85, 2016.
DOI: 10.1007/978-3-319-38921-9_8

To implement a safety-critical system it is necessary to test that the system is fault tolerant. The saboteurs are a good tool to perform this test, the saboteur is connected to the communication path of the DUT (Device Under Test) this allows to alter the information, this allows to verify how the DUT acts in the presence of faults. Like the voter the flexibility is a feature to consider, because the DUT can receive different kind of messages and configuration settings, and a saboteur that brings the opportunity to the user to select the messages and settings to modify allows to improve the time and effort needed to validate or develop a product.

In the development stage a system that uses any kind of network feature it is always important to have a tool to verify the sent and received messages, it is why a sniffer module that allows to display the data in a network or bus should be used.

This paper proposes a SDK that allows to configure and adapt a voter, saboteur and sniffer, the SDK includes the libraries to implement three of the most used protocols: UART (Universal Asynchronous Receiver/Transmitter), CAN (Controller Area Network), TCP/IP (Transmission Control Protocol/Internet Protocol).

2 SDK

The programming language used to develop the proposed SDK is C, it has three APIs (Application Program Interface) to handle the modules, each API is composed by static libraries with a extension (as shown in Fig. 1).

Because the microcontroller that executes the SDK has to perform multiple tasks, a processor with embedded Linux is proposed to test the SDK. Linux is a good match for commercial grade embedded applications due to its stability and networking ability. It is generally highly stable, it is already in use by a large numbers of programmers, and it allows developers to program hardware [6]. The SDK must be reliable and stable because it can be used in many kind of application including safety-critical. Additionally, the SDK does not use any desktop application and it is completely oriented to technical people. For all these reasons the chosen Operating System (OS) to develop and test the SDK is Debian.

The SDK allows to handle three kind of communication protocols: TCP/IP, CAN, UART. Each protocol can be used in any of the subsystems (voter, saboteur, and sniffer).

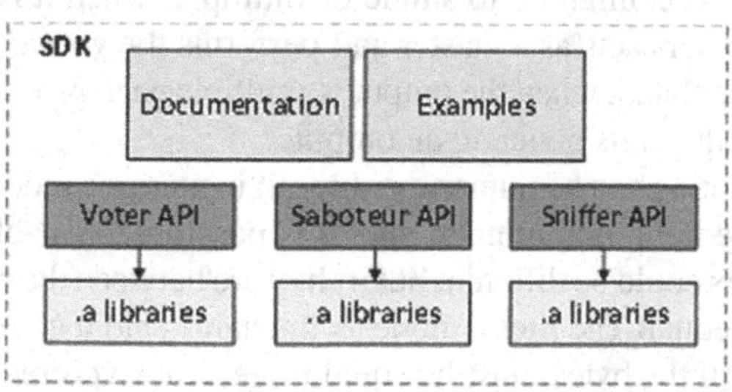

Fig. 1. Modules that compose the SDK

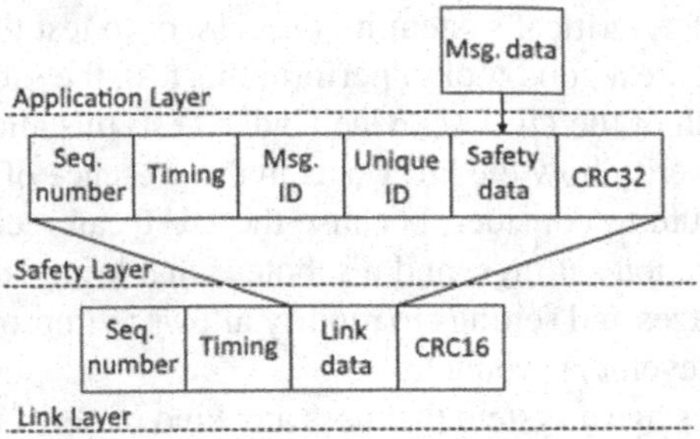

Fig. 2. Layers and fields of the messages

The used protocols must be trusted, hence, they have to support a safety protocol with the requirements of a safety standard like the EN 50159-1 [7]. According to the standard, the trusted transmission system covers the non-trusted transmission and the safety-related transmission functions. Two kind of layers are added to the messages to ensure that all the protocols are trusted and the SDK employs several safety-related artifacts like CRCs, sequence numbers, and timing information to ensure data temporal order and integrity. The Fig. 2 shows the layers and the fields that are added to the messages to meet with the standard.

3 Voter

The voter can be configured as "*m* out of *n*", but for each input is necessary a micro-controller, the Fig. 3 shows the voter's configuration, the microcontrollers are connected together to share their inputs [8]. If the microcontroller *n* sends information to the microcontroller 1 all the other devices acts as a bridges, allowing the communication between *n* and 1.

The voter has some special features that make it more versatile expanding its field of use. These features are listed below:

- Multiple communication protocols: each Processing Unit (PU) has 3 communication protocols (UART, CAN, TCP/IP).
- Voter output: can be configured to single or multiple; when it is simple output one of the microcontrollers acts as a master and performs the voting generating just one output. On the other hand, when the output is multiple each processing unit performs the voting and all the units generate an output.
- Voting type: the voting can be numeric or literal; in numeric mode the voter converts a specific message field to a number, also it is possible to establish ranges of vote, therefore the inputs could be different but if they are between the ranges the messages are considered as equal. The literal mode as the name said it compares the messages byte by byte and all the bytes must be equal to generate a correct output.
- Messages definition: it is possible to configure the input messages to detect specific fields.

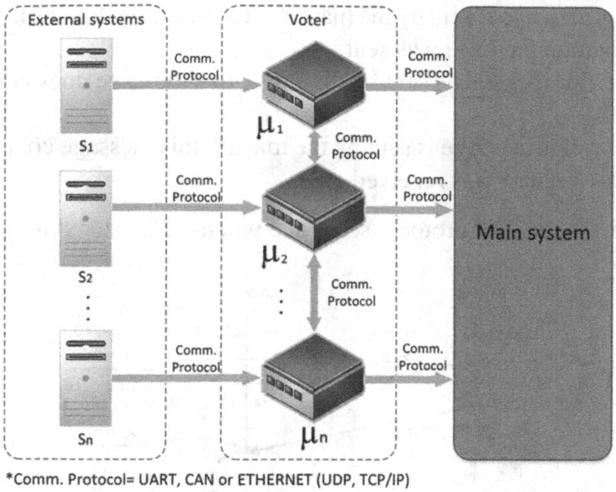

Fig. 3. *m* out of *n* voter schema

- Message layers: a safety layer is used in the all the messages to detect errors, additionally a link layer can be added to improve the safety in the communication protocol with the external systems.
- Result Message: the result message has exactly the same format that the received ones, the voter just replace the voted data in the right place.
- Synchronization: all the microcontrollers that conforms the voter must have the same time reference, to achieve this a synchronization method is performed.

The next subsections describe the synchronization and the voting process.

3.1 Synchronization

All the microcontrollers in the voter have their own system clock and they are not synchronized, hence when a message is sent each microcontroller adds its time in the safety layer causing that all messages have different time reference. Therefore a synchronization method is required. The synchronization has two main objectives in the system:

1. Synchronize all the microcontrollers' system clocks.
2. Send periodical messages to synchronize, so it is possible to detect if a microcontroller is "dead".

To synchronize the voter the Precision Time Protocol (PTP) [9] should be implemented, to use this protocol one of the microcontrollers must act as a master, in other words, the master will start the synchronization and all the other microcontrollers will be synchronized at the master's system clock. This protocol defines four main types of messages:

- Synchronization: this message is sent by the master to start the synchronization, this message does not contain information.

- Follow up: this message is sent by the master, this message contains the time at which the synchronization message was sent.
- Delay request: this message is sent by the slave, this message does not contain information.
- Delay response: this message is sent by the master, this message contains the time at which the delay request was received.

The Fig. 4 shows the PTP protocol sequence when the master synchronizes a slave.

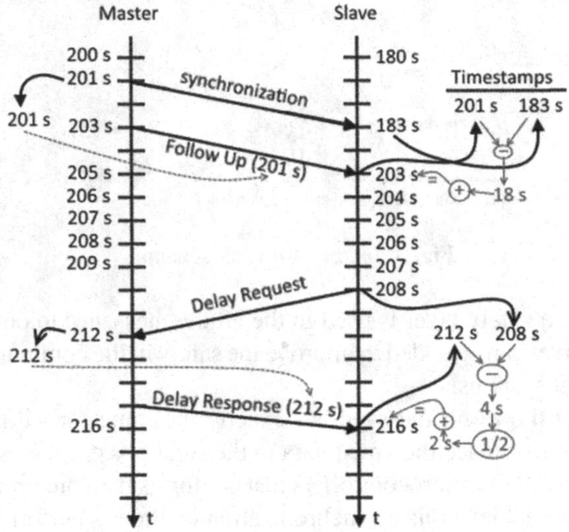

Fig. 4. Synchronization using PTP

3.2 Voting Process

The voting process begins when all the messages have arrived or when a timeout occurs (the timeout is configurable by the user) [10]. The voting can be performed of three different ways: literal, master and numeric. In all the different types of voting the user can set some parameters to customize the process, in the next sections these parameters and each voting type is described.

Literal. This is the most common type of voting, because the information is compared byte by byte and if one byte is different all the message is considered as erroneous. The settings that the user must configure for each input message are:

- Start byte: this is the byte where the data to compare begins.
- End byte: the number of the byte where the data to compare ends.

Master. This type of voting sends an output message equal to the received by the input port (the ports connected to the external system) of the microcontrollers (see Fig. 3), i.e., each PU ignores the others inputs keeping only the message sent by the external system acting as a bridge to the main system.

This type of voting is useful to detect if any of the external systems sends the messages in different time or does not send messages.

Numeric. This is the most complex type of voting, because the data are converted by the voter to a primitive data type and compares it applying ranges. The different parameters that the user must configure are shown below:

- Start byte: this is the byte where the data to be compared begins.
- Data type: this is the data type that is going to be compared, it could be: byte, int16, int32, int64, float (4 bytes), double (8 bytes).
- Range: variation in percentage that can exist between the data (0 to 100 %).
- Output type: the output could be the average or the median value of all the correct values.

The first step is compare all the inputs applying the range previously configured, i.e., a voter 2oo3 performs 3 comparisons using the specified range. The Table 1 shows a 2oo3 voter applying a 10 % range, in this example three comparisons are performed, the process is described next.

Table 1. Numeric 2oo3 voter with all inputs correct

Input	100	105	111	Result
(a)100	OK	OK	NOK	OK
(b)105	OK	OK	OK	OK
(c)111	OK	OK	OK	OK

- The (a) input receives an integer value of 100 when the range is applied it is known that the other inputs must be between 90 and 110, therefore, the input with the 105 value is inside the range and the input with a value of 111 is out. The voter is a 2oo3, so two of the inputs are inside the range son the result is OK.
- In the (b) input the value of 105 is received, when the range is applied (94 to 115) all the inputs all inside the range generating an OK.
- The input (c) receives a value of 111, so as the input (b) all the values are inside the range generating an OK result.

Finally, the voter generates the output or result message but as the inputs are numeric it is probable that they may not be exactly equals. Hence, the voter can provide the result message in different ways, an average or a median value of all the inputs that have the result marked as "OK" could be generated.

4 Saboteur

Interface Saboteurs are placed at wired communication among devices and its aim is to introduce impairments in message communication level. Since it is very common that a fault introduced at any device has its message communication impact, and message modification task does not require many resources consumption, interface saboteurs offer an efficient solution for a fault injection simulation.

Located in wired communication between devices, interface saboteurs modify the communication information between devices. Interface saboteurs are transparent for every device in the test bench and stay as a logical bridge between devices whose communication is intended to be "sabotaged" [11].

Figure 5 shows the saboteur actions between devices. Supposing the case that "Device A" transmits some information to "Device B", interface saboteur acts like a communication bridge as this:

- Interface Saboteur intercepts device A to B communication and responses to device A with a valid response.
- Interface Saboteur modifies the information from A to B.
- Interface Saboteur initiates a connection to device B, if not established, and sends this modified information.

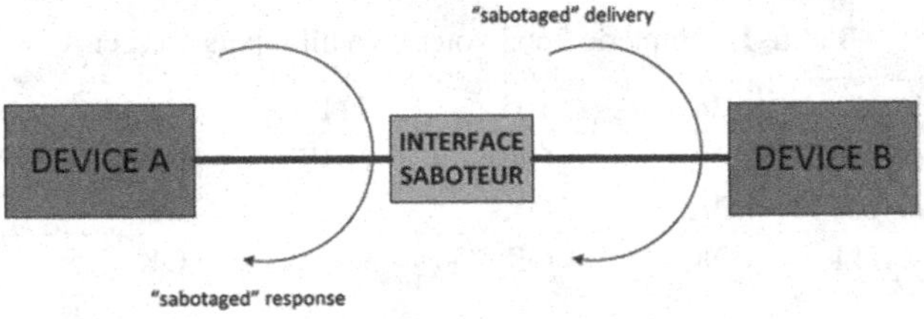

Fig. 5. Saboteur action between devices

The saboteur can alter the information in many manners, therefore, the user must configure the fault to inject and the messages to apply it. The faults that the saboteur can inject are as follows:

- Delete message: the destination device does not receives the message.
- Flip messages: it is possible to interchange the position of two messages.
- Message creation: the saboteur creates and sends a message in certain time, the message must be previously defined by the user.
- Corrupt message: the saboteurs change certain number of bytes to random data.

For all the faults before mentioned the user must indicate the injection time, i.e., when the simulation starts the saboteur has time 0 and increment it each 20 ms, if a message has a time equal or less than the saboteur the fault is injected. The saboteur verifies each 20 ms if there is a fault to inject, hence, it is recommended that the messages have at least 20 ms separation between them.

5 Sniffer

As it is mentioned before the SDK has a sniffer module for each communication protocol. This module gets the information that passes through a network, the sniffer has two ways to display the information:

1. Linux console: the information is printed in the console, therefore, it is necessary to connect a monitor or access to the device remotely.
2. Send by a communication port: in this option the sniffer sends the information via the specified protocol, as the other modules the protocols can be TCP/IP, CAN or UART. The information is sent in text format, i.e., the ASCII code of each byte is sent.

The operation of the sniffer is very similar for TCP/IP and CAN, it is only necessary to connect the device to the network or bus and configure how to display the data. The Fig. 6 shows the sniffer connected to a TCP/IP network and a CAN bus.

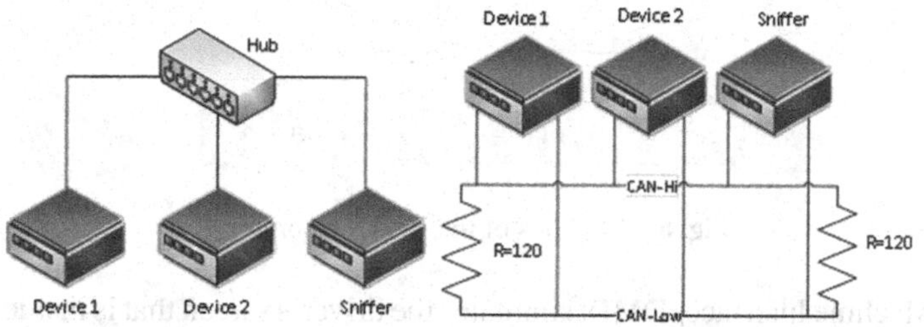

Fig. 6. Sniffer connected to a TCP/IP network and a CAN bus

The UART sniffer has a different configuration because it is very complicated to connect the sniffer to a UART bus, most of the time the devices that use UART as communication protocol are connected directly between them without the possibility to access the bus. Hence, the UART sniffer is connected between two devices, the Fig. 7 shows this configuration, to achieve a bidirectional communication this sniffer uses two UART ports.

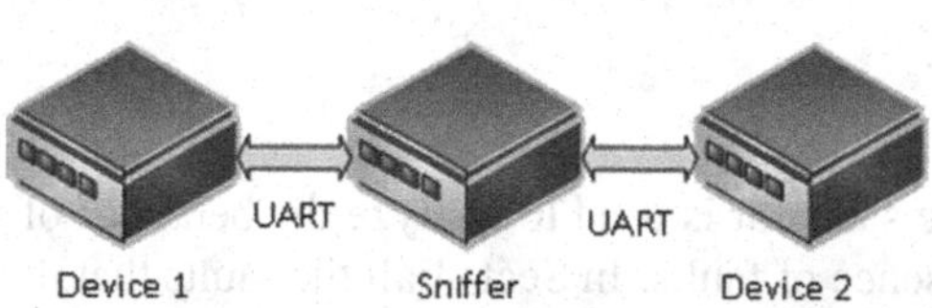

Fig. 7. Configuration of the UART sniffer

6 Using the SDK in a Railway Application

The next example uses the work done in the European project "ETCS Advanced Testing and Smart Train Positioning System" (EATS) [12], in this project a virtual laboratory was developed to simulate a train trip and test the on-board equipment. The trip is a

XML file that contains the information of all the messages sent in a real train. Once the simulation is performed the laboratory generates a JRU file with all the journey information. The EATS project includes to test the behavior of the on-board equipment when faults are injected to the system.

The Fig. 8 shows the modules which forms the EATS laboratory and the place where the faults are injected (interface saboteur). A brief explanation of each module is shown below.

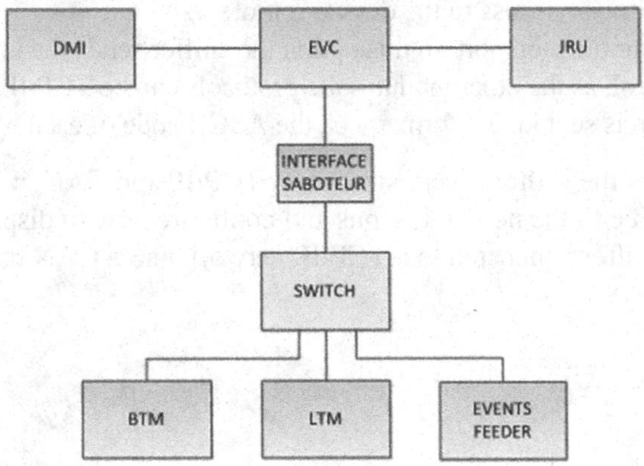

Fig. 8. Modules of the EATS laboratory

- Driver Machine Interface (DMI): simulates the driver's screen that is inside the cabin.
- European Vital Computer (EVC): receives and process all the messages from the other modules, this is the "brain" of the train.
- Juridical Recording Unit (JRU): creates and writes a file with the information processed by the EVC, this is the black box of the train.
- Events feeder: sends the events of the simulated trip.
- Balise Transmission Module (BTM): sends the information of the balises that are present along the track.
- Loop Transmission Module (LTM): sends the information of the loops that are present along the track.

6.1 Saboteur

In this application the saboteur is used to analyze the behavior of the train's on-board equipment in the presence of faults. In Sect. 4 all the faults that the SDK can inject are mentioned, for example, if the delete message is injected to a balise this is equivalent to that the BTM did not detect the balise when train passed over it. Another error could be to change the speed indicated by the odometer.

To achieve the fault injection a commercial board called Beaglebone is used as a saboteur (Fig. 9). The communication protocol between the EVC and the modules is TCP/IP, hence the saboteur must have the same protocol. The Beaglebone only has one Ethernet port and two ports are required (the connection to the EVC and the switch) so a USB to Ethernet converter is used.

Fig. 9. Beaglebone board

The faults that are going to be injected must be saved before the simulation starts, these faults are saved in a database setting the type of fault and the injection time. When the saboteur does not inject faults it acts as a bridge between the EVC and the other modules.

The Table 2 shows the odometer, balise and loop faults that can be injected with the saboteur.

Table 2. Odometer, balise and loop faults

Event id.	Event description
ODO-1	Speed measurement underestimates trains actual speed
ODO-2	Incorrect actual physical speed direction
ODO-3	Distance measurement is incorrect
BTM-H4	Transmission to the on-board kernel of an erroneous telegram, interpretable as correct
BTM-H8	The order of reported balises, with reception of valid telegrams is erroneous
BTM-H9	Erroneous reporting of a balise group in a different track, with reception of valid telegrams
LTM-H4	Transmission of an erroneous telegram/telegrams, interpretable as correct

6.2 Voter

The Fig. 8 shows the modules which form the laboratory of the EATS project, in that configuration the lab only has one EVC, but there is the possibility to have more EVCs, the most common configuration is with three EVCs, as it is shown in the Fig. 10. In this case, the EVCs outputs are send to the voter and the voter compares its inputs to verify that at least two inputs are equal (2oo3 voter), the voter sends the result to the JRU.

For this application the voter only uses one type of voting, the literal (see Sect. 3), i.e., the voter compares that the messages are exactly the same. If all the messages are different the voter can do two things: it does not generate any output (the message is not registered by the JRU) or the voter takes the message form a master EVC and sends it to the JRU (the master EVC must be defined by the user before the simulation starts).

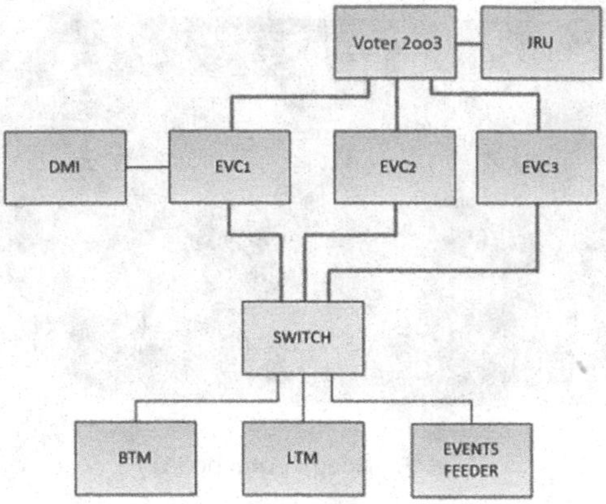

Fig. 10. EATS lab with three EVCs

7 Conclusion

The SDK presented in this paper contains three modules that can be embedded in one device to develop, test or improve safety-critical systems. All the modules can be configured by the user, allowing customize and use the SDK in different kind of applications, this flexibility can be translated into savings of time, effort and money.

The voter has three types of voting, the numerical option provides the opportunity to analyze data that can differ, but this variation does not means that the data is wrong. The voter's capabilities expand the area of use of the device, because it allows to test the ranges that an output can vary or verify is the outputs are exactly the same. On the other hand, the saboteur allows to test a device in a non-intrusive way, thus not changes are necessary in the DUT hardware to check that it is fault tolerant (an essential feature in a safety-critical system).

The voter and saboteur are software based, so it is important to ensure that these devices do not corrupt the data, to achieve this, safety techniques are implemented like CRC, sequence number and timing information.

References

1. Flammini, F.: Dependability Assurance of Real-Time Embedded Control Systems. Nova Science, New York (2010)
2. Knight, J.C.: Safety critical systems: challenges and directions. IEEE Trans. Softw. Eng. **33**, 547–550 (2002)
3. Dunn, W.R.: Practical Design of Safety-Critical Computer Systems. Reliability Press, Solvang (2003)
4. Latif-Shabgahi, G., Bass, J.M., Bennett, S.: A taxonomy for software voting algorithms used in safety-critical systems. IEEE Trans. Reliab. **53**(3), 319–328 (2004)
5. Aizpurua, X., Villaro, A., Legarda, J., Melendez, J.: Implementation details and safety analysis of a microcontroller-based SIL-4 software voter. IEEE Trans. Ind. Electron. **58**(3), 822–829 (2010)

6. Proffitt, B.: What is Linux: an overview of the Linux operating system. https://www.linux.com/learn/new-user-guides/376?showall=1. Accessed 12 Jan 2016
7. Railway Applications. Communication, Signalling and Processing Systems. Safety Related Communication in Closed Transmission Systems. EN 50159 (2010)
8. Yim, K.S., Sidea, V., Kalbarczyk, Z., Chen, D., Iyer, R.: A fault-tolerant programmable voter for software-based N-modular redundancy. In: IEEE Aerospace Conference, pp. 1–20, March 2012
9. Precision clock synchronization protocol for networked measurement and control systems. In: IEEE 1588 (2004)
10. Shye, A., Moseley, T., Reddi, V.J., Blomstedt, J.: Using process-level redundancy to exploit multiple cores for transient fault tolerance. In: Proceedings of the DSN, pp. 297–306, June 2007
11. CEIT: ETCS advanced testing and smart train positioning system, D4.2 v02.00, November 2014
12. CEIT: ETCS advanced testing and smart train positioning system, D2.4 v04.00, March 2015

Inter-cell Interference Coordination for Femto Cells Embedded in a Moving Vehicle

Julien Guillet and Loïc Brunel(✉)

Mitsubishi Electric R&D Centre Europe, Rennes, France
l.brunel@fr.merce.mee.com

Abstract. This paper deals with inter-cell interference coordination (ICIC) techniques based on power control for moving femto cells. Power control is tuned depending on the femto cell position in order to take into account the impact of femto base station transmission onto macro base station terminals in the downlink and take into account the impact of femto base station terminal transmission onto macro base stations in the uplink, while maintaining good spectral efficiency within the femto cell. The proposed techniques are evaluated using system level simulations in a tramway scenario and compared with reference performance results without ICIC or with ICIC using orthogonal resources for femto cells and macro cells. In all cases, the proposed techniques outperform reference techniques.

1 Introduction

In current mobile cellular networks, like 3GPP Long Term Evolution (LTE) networks, heterogeneous deployments mixing macro base stations (MBS) and femto base stations (FBS) are an effective way to ensure both mobility within a large geographical area and high data throughput [1,2]. Furthermore, many vehicles with high density of mobile users, like tramways, subways, buses or trains, circulate in a urban area. These users can be served by FBSs placed in the vehicles, which creates mobile femto cells [3–6], which can also be seen as mobile relays. These femto cells only serve users in the vehicle. We consider co-channel heterogeneous deployments, where femto cells use same carrier frequency as macro cells. Thus, femto cells and macro cells may strongly interfere with each other as depicted in Fig. 1 and we have to control and minimize the impact of femto cells onto macro cells in order to secure the operator MBS data traffic.

In this study, we address both downlink (DL) and uplink (UL), which differ as follows. In downlink, the femto-to-macro impact for a given femto base station (FBS) is geographically limited compared to the macro cell area. Therefore, an interfered macro user equipment (MUE) is mainly highly interfered by a single FBS. Otherwise, a lot of MUE positions within the macro cell coverage are not impacted by FBSs. In uplink, the femto-to-macro interference level for a given

This work was performed within project SYSTUF, which is subsidized by the French ministry of Industry in the framework of the AMI ITS program.

J. Mendizabal et al. (Eds.): Nets4Cars/Nets4Trains/Nets4Aircraft 2016, LNCS 9669, pp. 86–97, 2016.
DOI: 10.1007/978-3-319-38921-9_9

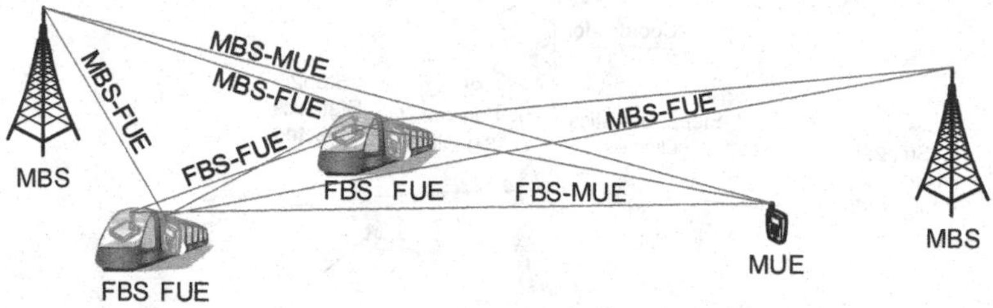

Fig. 1. Heterogeneous networks with macro base stations and femto base stations in tramways (all interferences are depicted by red lines between communication devices).

FBS is identical for all MUEs in the macro cell area. Therefore, each MUE is interfered by all FBSs in the macro cell area and the individual impact of each FBS is small.

In this context, we propose inter-cell interference coordination (ICIC) based on middle-scale power control (PC) at FBS in DL and at the femto cell terminal in UL. Middle-scale PC does not take into account small-scale fading. Due to the potentially high number of femto cells and their mobility, a centralized global optimization is complex. Hence we consider a simpler method based on an individual computation at the femto cell based on a global strategy established in a centralized manner, i.e., in a coordinator for a long term and a large area as shown in Fig. 2. In the proposed method, FBS and user equipments (UE) served by a femto cell (FUE) individually make measurements, e.g., of received power, location or path gain, and their transmit power is computed based on these measurements. The computation of the transmit power according to the measurements aims at optimizing the trade-off between femto and macro performances, the choice of the exact trade-off being an operator choice. The parameters for transmit power computation are quasi-static and can cover a large area of macro cells. As introduced in [7,8] for DL and [9] for UL and depicted in Fig. 2, these parameters can be computed in the coordinator prior to ICIC. A general principle of our approach is equalization as shown in Fig. 3 for the DL case: Each FUE or FBS in a vehicle at each instant must have a similar impact on the macro cell and, for this purpose, the transmit power must be adjusted along time. This is what we call equalization-based ICIC. Here, we adapt and evaluate approaches of [7–9] for the moving context, with a special focus on a tramway case with one FBS per tramway. They have the following characteristics:

- Only femto transmit powers, FBS in DL and FUE in UL, are adjusted for ICIC,
- The transmit powers are adjusted considering the average small-scale fading channel,
- The transmit powers are adjusted independently in each femto cell and there is no coordination between FBSs,

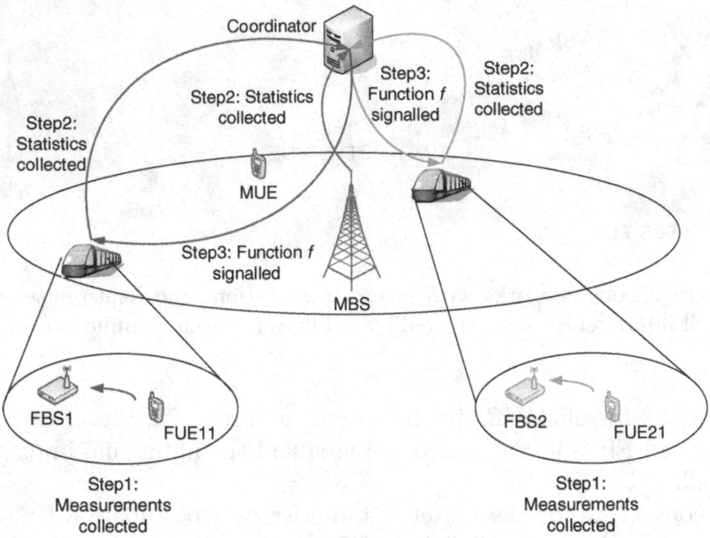

Fig. 2. Interactions in the semi-centralized ICIC.

- The transmit powers in femto cells depend on the MBS deployment but do not depend on the actual MUE locations,
- The transmit powers in femto cells depend on the position of the FBS or more fundamentally on the statistics of MBS-to-MUE link quality around the FBS in DL and of FUE-to-MBS link quality in UL.

This paper is organized as follows: In Sects. 2 and 3, we present the concept of equalization-based ICIC for DL and UL, respectively. We present the performance results of the proposed techniques in Sect. 4 and finally draw some conclusions in Sect. 5.

2 Downlink Equalization-Based ICIC

In order to quantify the impact of a FBS onto a macro cell, we define

- A high interference reference zone (HIRZ) which is a geographical area around the tramway,
- A function g representative of the macro cell performance degradation due to FBS and depending on the useful signal level from the MBS under the coverage of which FBS lies, $P_{U,M-MUE}$, the interference level from neighboring MBSs, $P_{I,M-MUE}$, and the signal level received from the FBS, $PG_{F-MUE} \times P_{t,FBS}$, where PG_{F-MUE} is the path gain between FBS and a MUE and $P_{t,FBS}$ is the FBS transmit power,
- A threshold g_{th} of macro cell performance degradation below which we consider that a MUE is highly interfered by the FBS,

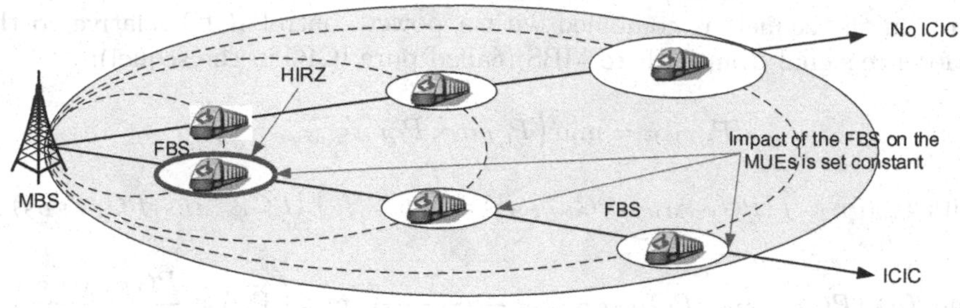

Fig. 3. Equalization-based ICIC for DL.

- An outage probability P_{out} which is the probability that a MUE is highly interfered by a FBS in the HIRZ.

In the DL case, equalizing the impact from FBS onto MUEs means having a same HIRZ, a same function g, a same threshold g_{th} and a similar outage probability P_{out} whatever the FBS location. As macro-cell performance degradation function g, we use the ratio of the MUE Shannon capacity with FBSs and the MUE Shannon capacity without FBSs. The useful and interference powers, $P_{U,M-MUE}$ and $P_{I,M-MUE}$, are obtained at FBS by measuring the received power from surrounding MBSs using a same antenna as a MUE mounted on the tramway. We assume that these powers do not vary within HIRZ. Another option is to use a database and tramway positioning [8]. After some computation [7,8], we obtain $P_{t,FBS}$ as

$$P_{t,FBS} = \min\left(\tilde{P}_{t,FBS}, P_{t,FBS,Max}\right)$$

$$\text{with } \tilde{P}_{t,FBS} = f\left(P_{U,M-MUE}, P_{I,M-MUE}\right) = C_{DL} \times f_{DL}\left(P_{U,M-MUE}, P_{I,M-MUE}\right)$$

$$\text{and } f_{DL}\left(P_{U,M-MUE}, P_{I,M-MUE}\right) = \frac{P_{U,M-MUE}}{\left(1+\frac{P_{U,M-MUE}}{P_{I,M-MUE}}\right)^{g_{th}}-1} - P_{I,M-MUE}$$

where $P_{t,FBS,Max}$ is the maximum FBS transmit power. The constant C_{DL} is related to the mean FBS transmit power and it drives the macro-femto performance trade-off. The constant C_{DL} can be determined from P_{out} and path gain characteristics between FBS and MUE in HIRZ,

$$C_{DL} = 10^{0.1\times\left(-\overline{PG_{F-MUE}|dB}+\sigma_{PG_{F-MUE}|dB}Q_{\mathcal{N}}(P_{out})\right)}$$

where $\overline{PG_{F-MUE}|dB}$ and $\sigma_{PG_{F-MUE}|dB}$ are the mean and standard deviation of $10\log_{10}(PG_{F-MUE})$ in HIRZ. The function $Q_{\mathcal{N}}()$ is the quantile function associated with a standard normal distribution. The value of P_{out} and therefore C_{DL} is an operator choice.

3 UL Equalization-Based ICIC

In order to determine the FUE transmit power $P_{t,FUE}$, a full compensation power control relative to the useful FUE-to-FBS channel (called pure power control in the sequel) is combined with a power control ICIC relative to the interference signal from FUE to MBS (called pure ICIC in the sequel):

$$P_{t,FUE} = \min\left(\tilde{P}_{t,FUE}, P_{t,FUE,Max}\right)$$

$$\text{with } \tilde{P}_{t,FUE} = f\left(PG_{F-MBS}, PG_{F-FBS}\right) = C_{UL} \times f_{UL}\left(PG_{F-MBS}, PG_{F-FBS}\right)$$

$$\text{and } f_{UL}\left(PG_{F-MBS}, PG_{F-FBS}\right) = \frac{1}{PG_{F-MBS}} \min\left(1, \Delta \times \frac{PG_{F-MBS}}{PG_{F-FBS}}\right)$$

where PG_{F-MBS} and PG_{F-FBS} are the path gains between FUE and MBS and between FUE and FBS, respectively, and $P_{t,FUE,Max}$ is the FUE maximum transmit power, i.e., 23 dBm. The constant C_{UL} is related to the mean FUE transmit power and it drives the macro-femto performance trade-off. The parameter Δ allows balancing the combination between a power control through the compensation of the FUE-to-FBS link and a power control ICIC through the compensation of the FUE-to-MBS link. In practice, the constant C_{UL} can also be set to control the ratio IR between the average level of interference from FUEs $P_{I,F-MBS}$ and the Additive White Gaussian Noise (AWGN) level N_0 plus the average level of interference $P_{I,M-MBS}$ from MUEs in neighbouring MBS at the MBS of interest:

$$IR = \mathbb{E}\left[P_{I,F-MBS}\right] / \left(\mathbb{E}\left[P_{I,M-MBS}\right] + N_0\right)$$

We finally obtain

$$C_{UL} = IR \times \frac{\mathbb{E}\left[P_{I,M-MBS}\right] + N_0}{N_f \times \mathbb{E}\left[\min\left(1, \Delta \frac{PG_{F-MBS}}{PG_{F-FBS}}\right)\right]}$$

where N_f is the mean number of FBSs per macro cell and the expectations $E[\ ]$ are taken over all possible tramways positions and on a long term in the area addressed by ICIC. With $\Delta \to 0$ and $\Delta \to \infty$, we obtain pure power control without ICIC and pure ICIC, respectively. We optimize parameter Δ to obtain a specific ICIC that maximizes the femto performance versus macro performance.

4 Performance Evaluation

For evaluation, we consider ideal middle-scale instantaneous power and path gain measurements. We consider at first that the backhaul link between FBS and core network is not handled by MBSs. Thus, we do not consider the effect of the backhaul on UE throughput. All UEs in a tramway with FBS are served by the corresponding FBS and all other UEs are served by MBS. In the evaluation, we consider all interferences depicted in Fig. 1. Users in tramways undergo interference from other femto cells (from FBS in DL and from FUEs in UL) and from all macro cells (from MBSs in DL and from MUEs in UL). Users outside tramways undergo interference from femto cells (from FBS in DL and from FUEs in UL) and neighbouring macro cells (from MBSs in DL and from MUEs in UL). We consider two schemes as references for performance comparison with our ICIC schemes. In the first scheme, all femto cells use constant transmit power. In the second scheme, MBSs and MUEs use resources which are orthogonal to resources used by FBSs and FUEs. The partitioning of resources is the same for all femto cells and maximum transmit power is used for FUEs and FBS.

The results presented in this section are obtained from system level simulations of the physical layer, in which spectral efficiencies are computed taking into account inter-cell interference and small-scale effects as specified by 3GPP [10]. Actual packet transmission is not simulated here. We consider a 3GPP LTE Case 1 deployment [10] with several tramways in a tri-sectorized macro cell deployment in a urban area. There is one FBS in the center of each tramway.

Table 1. Deployment Scenario.

Number of sectors per MBS	3
Macro cell radius	289 m
Number of tramways per square of 578m × 578m	2, 5, 10 (uniform distribution)
Tramway size	2.5 m x 40 m
Number of MUEs per macro cell	10 (uniform distribution)
Number of FUEs per femto cell	10 (uniform distribution in a tramway)
Physical layer	3GPP LTE 10 MHz – MIMO 2x2 – OFDM/SC-FDMA – 50 PRBs – Round Robin scheduling of UEs on 5 adjacent PRBs
Transmit MBS power	46 dBm
Transmit MUE power	3GPP LTE Case 1 full power control
Maximum FBS transmit power	20 dBm
FBS antenna gain	5 dB
FBS directional antenna pattern	Parabolic in dB scale as MBS in [10] Horizontal Beamwidth : 40 degrees Vertical beamwidth : 25 degrees Vertical Tilt : 20 degrees

Table 2. Propagation models for simulated scenarios.

Between MBS and UEs	LTE Macro cell (shadowing standard deviation: 8 dB, non-line-of-sight)
Between FBS and FUEs in same tramway	ITU-InH (shadowing stantard deviation: 4 dB, line-of-sight)
Between FBS and UEs except those in same tramway	ITU-UMi (shadowing standard deviation: 10 dB, non-line-of-sight)

We consider two types of femto cell isolation: *High isolation* with directive FBS antenna and 10 dB penetration loss due to tramway wall and *low isolation* with omnidirectionnal FBS antenna and 5 dB penetration loss. Table 1 presents the details of the deployment scenario. We use 3GPP Case 1 middle-scale and small-scale channel models from [10,11]. In addition, for the FBS-to-UE channel model, we consider two models, one for a FUE in same tramway and another for all other UEs. Table 2 lists the used propagation models. As performance metric, we consider the outage probability capacity, i.e., a spectral efficiency:

$$C_{out} = \arg \max_{R<R_{\max}} \left[R \times (1 - \Pr(C < R))\right]$$

where $\Pr(C < R)$ is the probability that capacity C is smaller than R and $R_{\max}$ is the maximum spectral efficiency offered by the system. $R_{\max}$ is set as 12 bits/symbol in downlink and 6 bits/symbol in uplink.

Figure 4 shows maps representing the MUE capacity in DL at each MUE location, without shadowing, with low femto cell isolation and only one tramway, for two different tramway locations and with and without ICIC. ICIC with g_{th} = 50 %, HIRZ defined as a disc of 30 m radius and P_{out} = 0.981 is used and compared with constant 15-dBm FBS transmit power. We observe that, thanks to ICIC, the impact of FBS onto MUEs is made similar whatever the FBS position.

We now perform global statistical evaluation, which includes results over all possible deployments, i.e., for all realizations of shadowing, FBS positions, UE positions and small-scale channels. These results are representative of the statistical models previously described. We consider full load in FBSs and MBSs. Thus, UEs are always interfered by neighbouring base stations. Figure 5 shows cell-edge 5 %-ile outage capacity results for 5 FBSs in a square of 578 m × 578 m, low isolation and different values of parameter Δ in UL ICIC. As shown in Table 3, a given value of parameter Δ results in a given probability that UL ICIC is actually pure PC. Our optimized ICIC approach performs better than pure ICIC or pure femto PC: It is beneficial to keep a certain balancing between them. Furthermore, pure ICIC performs worse than pure femto PC. In the following, we consider $\Delta = 40$ dB for UL ICIC. Figures 6, 7 and 8 show the macro-femto 5 %-ile capacity trade-off for uplink and low isolation, downlink and low isolation, and downlink and high isolation, respectively. The macro-femto capacity trade-off is explicited by showing the femto capacity versus the macro capacity. Densities of 2, 5 and 10 FBSs in a square of 578m × 578m are shown in these figures. In all cases, the proposed ICIC schemes outperform reference methods with constant transmit power, labelled as *no ICIC*, and orthogonal resources between femto cells and macro cells, labelled as *Orth. resources*. We now consider that the backhaul link between FBS and core network is handled by MBSs. We assume that a maximum

Table 3. Probability of pure PC occurence versus UL ICIC parameter Δ.

Δ [dB]	-10	30	35	40	45	50	110
Probability of pure PC occurence	100 %	88 %	81 %	70 %	60 %	45 %	0 %

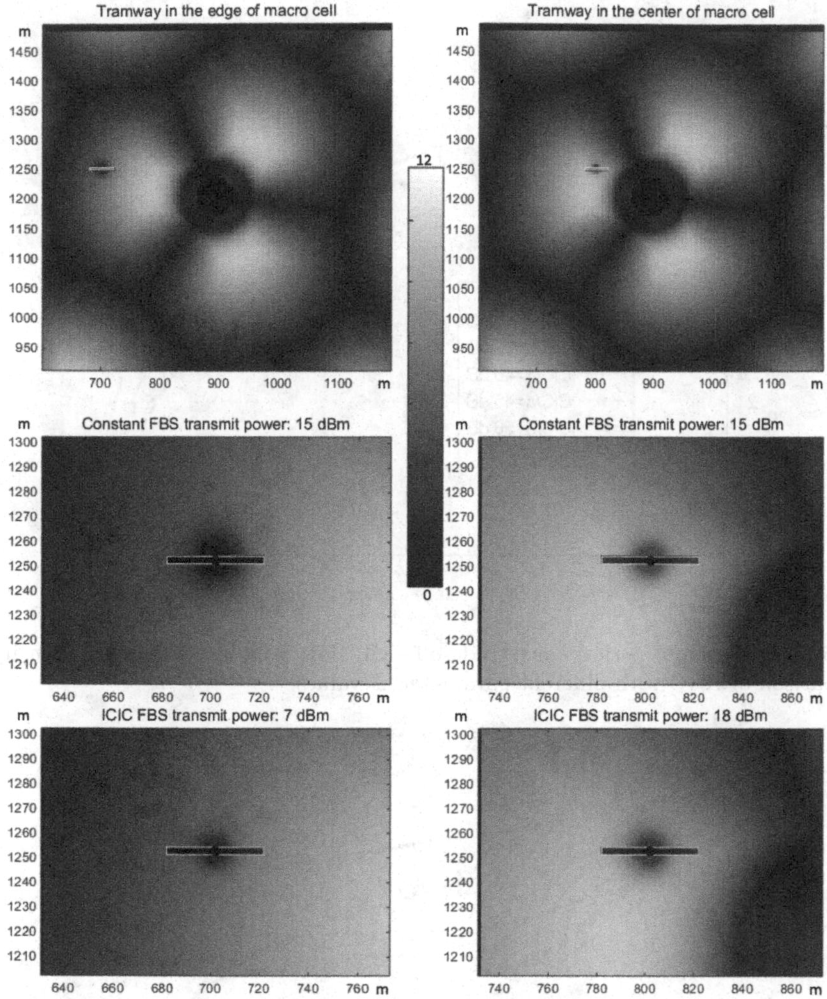

Fig. 4. MUE capacity maps in bits/symbol in DL with a single tramway – Low femto cell isolation, no shadowing – Two tramway positions (tramway in the edge of a macro-cell on the left, in the center of a macro-cell on the right) as shown in the top figures – Zooms around the tramway with constant power FBS transmission in the middle figures and ICIC power setting in the bottom figures.

proportion $\beta = N_{\text{FBS}}/(N_{\text{FBS}}+1)$ of resources, e.g., LTE subframes, is used as backhaul link to the N_{FBS} FBSs under the coverage area of a given MBS. Thus, the FUE aggregated throughput may be limited by backhaul throughput. FUEs are allocated to the remaining resources in order to avoid having FBS simultaneously transmitting and receiving on the same resources. These resources are also used by MUEs. If the FUE aggregated throughput does not require all backhaul resources, MUEs can also use unused resources. The spectral efficiency of

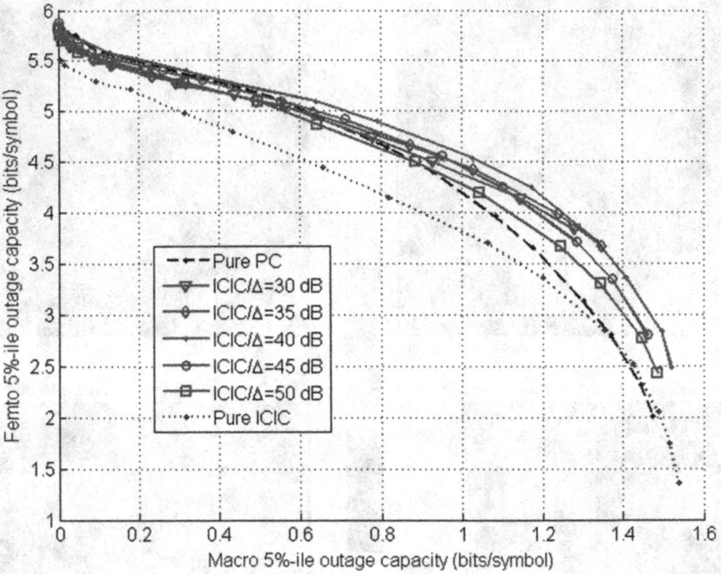

Fig. 5. Macro - femto performance trade-off - UL (low isolation, 5 tramway density) - Comparison of ICIC with different parameter Δ values.

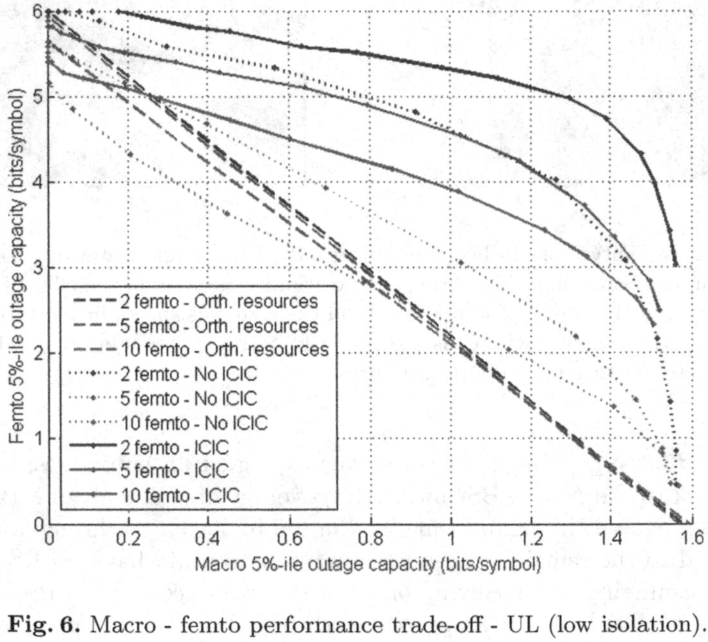

Fig. 6. Macro - femto performance trade-off - UL (low isolation).

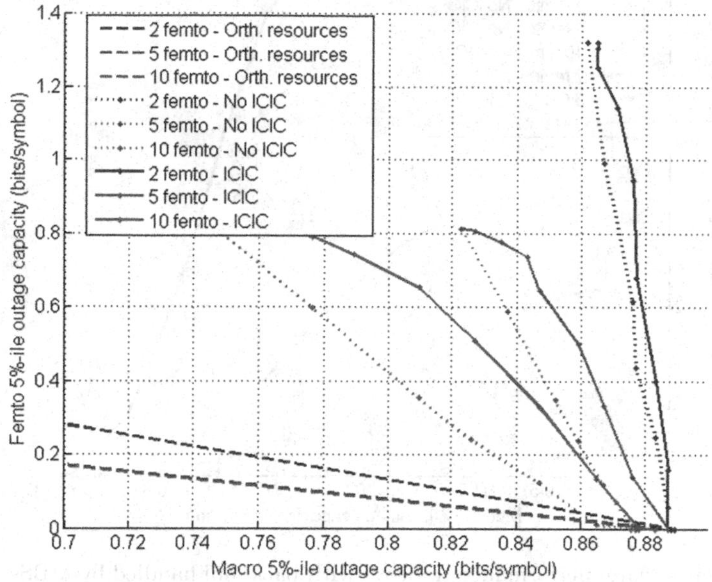

Fig. 7. Macro - femto performance trade-off - DL (low isolation).

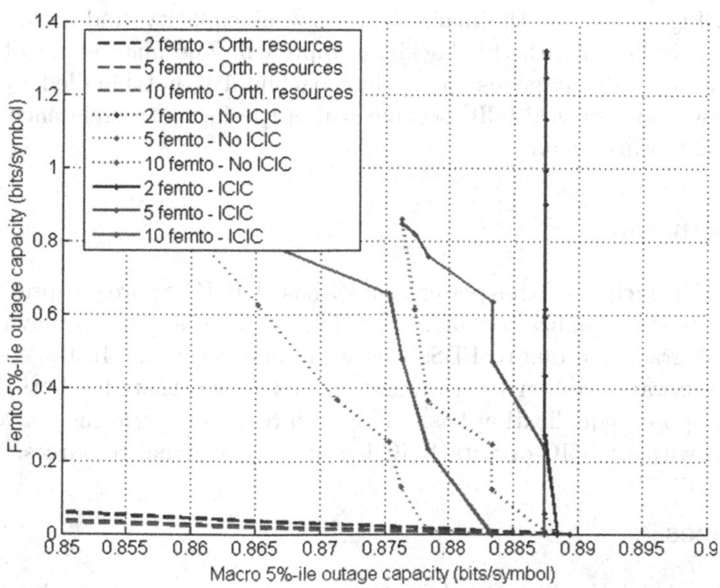

Fig. 8. Macro - femto performance trade-off - DL (high isolation).

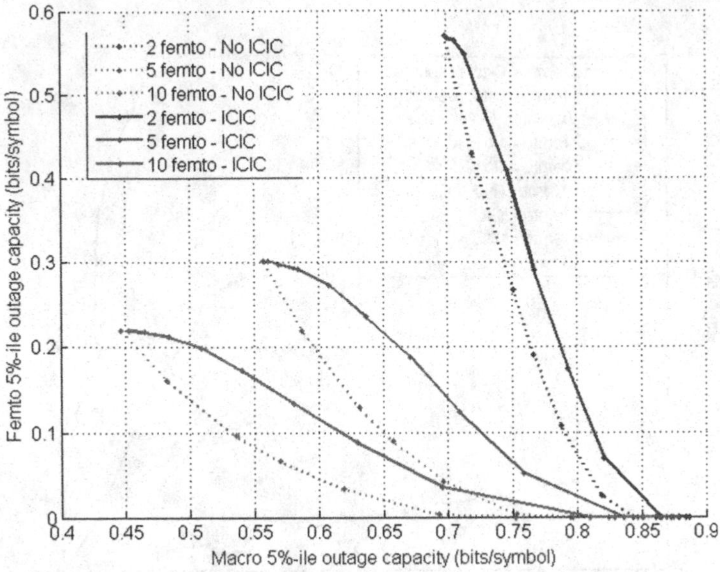

Fig. 9. Macro - femto performance trade-off with backhaul handled by MBSs -DL (low isolation).

backhaul is assumed to be 12 bits/symbol. Indeed, receiving capabilities of FBS for backhaul, e.g., the number of receiving antennas, can be considered as higher than UEs. Figure 9 shows the macro-femto 5 %-ile capacity trade-off for downlink and low isolation with this backhaul approach. The macro-femto trade-off is obviously less advantageous than when backhaul is not handled by MBSs. Nevertheless, the proposed ICIC scheme still outperforms the reference method with constant transmit power.

5 Conclusion

The general principle of the power-control-based ICIC approach presented in this paper is the equalization of macro degradations aiming at having similar macro degradation due to FBSs whatever their positions. In the context of FBSs in tramways, system level evaluation has shown that, for both UL and DL, the proposed equalization-based ICIC approach outperforms conventional approaches without ICIC or with ICIC based on orthogonal resources.

References

1. Chandrasekhar, V., Andrews, J.G., Gatherer, A.: Femtocell networks: a survey. IEEE Commun. Mag. **46**(9), 59–67 (2008)
2. López-Pérez, D., Valcarce, A., De La Roche, G., Zhang, J.: OFDMA femtocells: a roadmap on interference avoidance. IEEE Commun. Mag. **47**(9), 41–48 (2009)

3. Haider, F., Wang, H., Haas, H., Yuan, D., Wang, H., Gao, X., You, X.-H., Hepsaydir, E.: Spectral efficiency analysis of mobile femtocell based cellular systems. In IEEE 13th International Conference on Communication Technology (ICCT), pp. 347–351. IEEE (2011)
4. Noriega-Vivas, P., Campo, C., Garcia-Rubio, C., Rodriguez-Carrion, A.: MOFETA: a network architecture based on MObile FEmtocells to enhance cellular connectivity on TrAins. In: Vinel, A., Mehmood, R., Berbineau, M., Garcia, C.R., Huang, C.-M., Chilamkurti, N. (eds.) Nets4Trains 2012 and Nets4Cars 2012. LNCS, vol. 7266, pp. 174–185. Springer, Heidelberg (2012)
5. Chen, Y., Lagrange, X.: Downlink capacity gain analysis of mobilerelay in lte-advanced network. In: 11th Annual IEEE Consumer Communications & Networking Conference, CCNC 2014 (2014)
6. Sui, Y., Guvenc, I., Svensson, T.: Interference management for moving networks in ultra-dense urban scenarios. EURASIP J. Wireless Commun. Networking **1**, 1–32 (2015)
7. Guillet, J., Brunel, L., Gresset, N.: Downlink femto-macro ICIC with blind long-term power setting. In: IEEE 22nd International Symposium on Personal Indoor and Mobile Radio Communications (PIMRC 2011), pp. 212–216. IEEE (2011)
8. Guillet, J., Brunel, L., Gresset, N.: Downlink femto-macro ICIC with location-based long-term power setting. In: IEEE 17th International Workshop on Computer Aided Modeling and Design of Communication Links and Networks (CAMAD 2012), pp. 1–5. IEEE (2012)
9. Guillet, J., Brunel, L., Gresset, N.: Uplink femto-macro ICIC with semi-centralized power control. In: IEEE 22nd International Symposium on Personal Indoor and Mobile Radio Communications (PIMRC 2011), pp. 142–146. IEEE (2011)
10. 3GPP: Further advancements for E-UTRA physical layer aspects. In: 3rd Generation Partnership Project (3GPP), TR 36.814, March 2010
11. 3GPP: Spatial channel model for multiple input multiple output (MIMO) simulations. In: 3rd Generation Partnership Project (3GPP), TR 25.996, September 2014

A Multi Bearer Adaptable Communication Demonstrator for Train-to-Ground IP Communication to Increase Resilience

Christian Pinedo(✉), Marina Aguado, Igor Lopez, Marivi Higuero, and Eduardo Jacob

Faculty of Engineering, University of the Basque Country UPV/EHU,
Alameda Urquijo s/n, 48013 Bilbao, Spain
{christian.pinedo,marina.aguado,igor.lopez,
marivi.higuero,eduardo.jacob}@ehu.eus

Abstract. This paper presents the setup of a demonstrator based on Multipath TCP protocol to provide a multi bearer—WiFi and WiMAX—and resilient agnostic layer to support train-to-ground IP communication. The adaptable communication and resilient architecture consists of three main blocks: an Acquisition System, a Detection System and a Multipath Communication System. Several tests carried out with jamming devices disturbing the data transfer established between the end devices demonstrate the resilient capability and performance of the proposed architecture to overcome electromagnetic attacks.

Keywords: Adaptable communication · Resilience · MPTCP · FRMCS

1 Introduction

Nowadays, the European train control industry is facing the challenge of searching a successor of GSM-R—the underlying communication technology in ERTMS. There are multiple alternatives such as the natural evolution from GSM-R towards GPRS, the possibility to migrate directly to LTE or the identified as the Future Railway Mobile Communication System (FRMCS) architecture—a multi bearer technology agnostic reference network.

Under this migration scenario, the European Commission—and in a next step the on-going Joint Undertaking Shift2Rail—provides its support to numerous research projects and initiatives. The EU FP7-SEC- 2011-1 Collaborative Research Project entitled SECurity of Railways against Electromagnetic aTtacks (SECRET)[1] is also outlined in this context. SECRET project main goal, carried out from 2012 to 2015, was to identify, assure and cope with intentional electromagnetic interferences that might affect current and future communication technologies in railways.

[1] http://www.secret-project.eu.

J. Mendizabal et al. (Eds.): Nets4Cars/Nets4Trains/Nets4Aircraft 2016, LNCS 9669, pp. 98–100, 2016.
DOI: 10.1007/978-3-319-38921-9_10

Our contribution in the SECRET project was focused on the design and implementation of a resilient communication architecture—in accordance to ongoing design of an all-IP multi bearer and agnostic FRCMS—whose aim was the ability to face electromagnetic attacks [3,4]. The architecture is based in three main building blocks: the Acquisition System (AS) which is responsible of collecting and processing electromagnetic data in the train and track-side; the Detection System (DS) which is the entity governing the overall resilient communication system; and, finally, the Multipath Communication System (MCS) which provides to the DS multiple communication interfaces and paths in order to dynamically overcome the electromagnetic attacks.

The basis of the behaviour of the MCS is the Multipath TCP (MPTCP) protocol [1]. MPTCP is an extension to the TCP protocol in order to support multi-homed devices, in other words, to support devices with multiple communication interfaces and multiple IP addresses. Thanks to this protocol it is possible to simultaneously use all the IP interfaces of the host for one MPTCP connection, when due to original constrains of the TCP/IP protocol the normal and current behaviour is to use only one interface and IP address.

In the SECRET project we developed a redundant scheduler for MPTCP, which sends the same information replicated through all the available interfaces with the aim of increasing the resilience of the communication whereas the delay and jitter are reduced because MPTCP/TCP retransmissions are minimized [5]. The code of this new scheduler for MPTCP was made publicly available[2] once the SECRET project finished and then we also collaborated to achieve the inclusion of a redundant scheduler in the official implementation of MPTCP for the Linux kernel[3]. The patch[4] that was finally included in the official MPTCP implementation was not only based on the proposal of the SECRET project but also on a second proposal of a redundant scheduler published afterwards [2].

2 Description of the Demonstrator

The demonstrator focuses on showing the increase on the resilience of the wireless communications thanks to the use of MPTCP and, more precisely, thanks to the use of the new redundant scheduler.

The setup, see Fig. 1, consists basically on two devices that needs to transfer real-time MPTCP/TCP information through wireless links. In order to proceed with data transmission, these wireless devices have two different wireless transceivers: one WiFi transceiver at 2,4 GHz and one WiMAX transceiver at 5 GHz. Under normal conditions, devices are configured to use the WiFi transceiver instead of the WiMAX one.

This baseline setup will be disturbed with the help of a jammer that will interfere and finally raise down the WiFi connection. Thus, it will disturb the data transfer established between the end devices.

[2] http://github.com/i2t/rmptcp.
[3] http://github.com/multipath-tcp/mptcp.
[4] http://github.com/multipath-tcp/mptcp/pull/109.

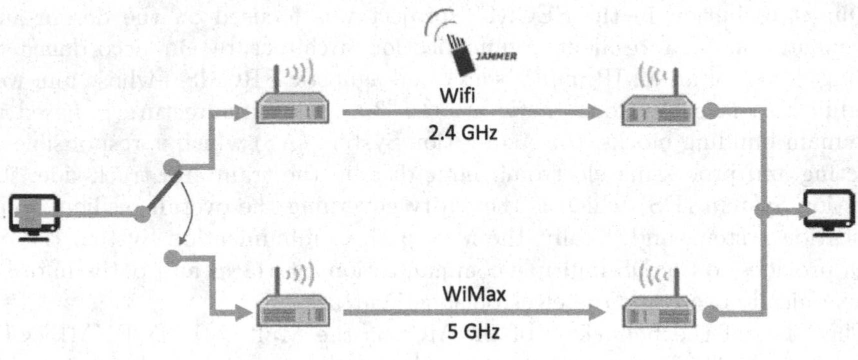

Fig. 1. Setup of the demonstrator.

The demonstrator will allow to appreciate how established connections can switch from one interface to another without losing connectivity and consequently without requiring to re-establish the connection again.

Acknowledgements. The work described in this paper is partially supported by the EU FP7-SEC-2011-1 Collaborative Research Project entitled SECRET and by the Spanish Ministry of Economy and Competitiveness through the SAREMSIG TEC2013-47012-C2 project (Contribution to a Safe Railway Operation: Evaluating the effect of Electromagnetic Disturbances on Railway Control Signalling Systems). This work is produced within the Training and Research Unit UFI11/16 funded by the UPV/EHU.

References

1. Ford, A., Raiciu, C., Handley, M., Bonaventure, O., Paasch, C.: TCP extensions for multipath operation with multiple addresses. Internet-Draft draft-ietf-mptcp-rfc6824bis-05, IETF Secretariat. http://www.ietf.org/internet-drafts/draft-ietf-mptcp-rfc6824bis-05.txt
2. Frömmgen, A., Erbshäußer, T., Zimmermann, T., Wehle, K., Buchmann, A.: Remp TCP: Low latency multipath TCP. In: Proceedings of the 2015 CoNEXT on Student Workshop, CoNEXT Student Workshop 2015. ACM (2015)
3. Gransart, C., Pinedo, C., Aguado, M., Heddebaut, M., Jacob, E., Lopez, I., Higuero, M.: Cyber attacks in the guided transport domain. In: Proceedings of the Computer & Electronics Security Applications Rendez-vous (C&ESAR 2014), Rennes, France, November 2014
4. Heddebaut, M., Mili, S., Sodoyer, D., Jacob, E., Aguado, M., Pinedo, C., Lopez, I., Deniau, V.: Towards a resilient railway communication network against electromagnetic attacks. In: Proceedings of the Transport Research Arena 2014 Conference (TRA 2014), Paris, France, April 2014
5. Lopez, I., Aguado, M., Pinedo, C., Jacob, E.: SCADA systems in the railway domain: enhancing reliability through Redundant MultipathTCP. In: Proceedings of the 2015 IEEE 18th International Conference on Intelligent Transportation Systems (ITSC), pp. 2305–2310, October 2015

Nets4cars

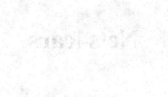

Communication Technologies for Vehicles: eCall

Olatz Iparraguirre(✉) and Alfonso Brazalez

CEIT and TECNUN, University of Navarra, Pamplona, Spain
oiparraguirre@ceit.es

Abstract. Traffic accidents are one of the major causes of deaths and injuries in Europe. A timely and efficient intervention of emergency services is crucial to save lives and reduce human suffering. In order to reduce the fatality rate in the EU the European Commission is working since 2009 to develop the eCall system. eCall is a project design for the improvement of road safety by providing rapid assistance to motorist involved in a collision anywhere is the European Union. In case of an accident the intended solution establishes automatically a communication with emergency services and sends a set of data such as location, vehicle type and other relevant information timely and reliably from the in-vehicle system (IVS) over the cellular network. This paper provides a general vision of how it works and different kinds of eCall. In addition, it describes the studies that have taken place to validate the deployment of eCall based on 112 across Europe and introduces some future targets.

Keywords: ecall · European commission · Emergency · 112

1 Introduction

Road fatalities in the EU have fallen 18 % since 2010 [1], when the Road Safety Strategy (2010–2020) started. While achievements to date are good – cutting the number of annual deaths by almost one fifth in this period– they are not quite in line with the ambitious target. Even with these improvements, traffic incidents are still one of the major causes of deaths and injuries in Europe [2]. According to the European Commission (EC), there were 26,000 deaths and more than 1.4 million people injured on road network during 2014 [3]. The Intelligent Car Initiative had a significant positive impact, but in order to halve the number of road deaths by 2020, the road fatality numbers must go down at a higher speed from today and onwards.

In 2010 the EU Commission launched the European Intelligent Transport Systems (ITS) Action Plan, which covered a section for Road safety and security. This section promotes support for a harmonized introduction of the Pan European eCall, including awareness campaigns, upgrading Public Service Access Points (PSAP) infrastructures and an assessment of the need for regulation. Feasibility studies by the European Commission have indicated that eCall can make a significant reduction to the number of people died on the road and reduce the severity of injuries, by enabling an early intervention by the emergency services, providing more rapid access to medical services in that vital “golden hour” following an incident.

J. Mendizabal et al. (Eds.): Nets4Cars/Nets4Trains/Nets4Aircraft 2016, LNCS 9669, pp. 103–110, 2016.
DOI: 10.1007/978-3-319-38921-9_11

Emergency calls made from vehicles or mobile telephones using wireless technology can assist in significantly reducing road deaths and injuries. However, in many situations, the passengers of a vehicle involved in an incident may not be in a position to call using a mobile phone, because either they have been injured or trapped or do not know the local emergency number to be called. Additionally, they have inaccurate location details, especially if travelling on rural roads or whilst travelling abroad. Furthermore, travellers driving abroad may have language problems trying to communicate with emergency services.

The objective of implementing the Pan European in-vehicle emergency call system (eCall) is to automate the notification of a traffic accident from anywhere in the European Union and associated countries, using the same technical standards.

2 How eCall Works

eCall is a 112 emergency call triggered either manually by vehicle occupants or automatically as soon as an in-vehicle sensor detects a serious accident.

When activated, the in-vehicle system (IVS) will establish a voice connection directly with the relevant Public Safety Answering Point (PSAP). After the triggering of the eCall, other communications that are in progress are suspended, if needed. Microphone and loudspeakers are fully dedicated to the emergency call. At the same time an emergency message, the minimum set of data (MSD) including key information about the accident, such as time, location, driving direction and vehicle description, is sent with the voice call.

The mobile network operator (MNO) handles the eCall like any other 112 call and routes the call to the most appropriate emergency response centre. The PSAP operator will receive both the voice call and the MSD.

The information provided by the MSD will be decoded and displayed in the PSAP operator screen. The PSAP operator may at any time request for a new MSD (e.g. data appears corrupted or inconsistent, or the PSAP operator believes that the data may have changed). In the meantime, audio link is established and the operator will be able to hear what is happening in the vehicle and talk with the occupants of the vehicle if possible. This will help the operator ascertain which emergency services are needed at the accident scene (ambulance, fire brigade, police) and to rapidly dispatch the alert and all relevant information to the right service. Once the communication with the vehicle is finished, only the PSAP is allowed to clear down the call. Even so, in-vehicle equipment remains registered to the network in order to allow the call back.

Furthermore, the PSAP operator will be able to immediately inform the road/traffic management centres that an incident has occurred in a specific location, facilitating rapid information to other road users and thus preventing secondary accidents, helping to clear the carriageway, and therefore reducing congestion (Fig. 1).

2.1 eCall Flag

Some emergency services have required a system to separate eCalls from 112 calls in order to route the calls differently. This is the main reason of the eCall flag implementation. The eCall flag is also able to differentiate automatically and manually initiated eCalls.

The flag is included in the MSD information. That way, the flag enables the telecommunication mobile network operator to route to a different long number (E.164 number) depending of the nature of the call (eCall or 112 call).

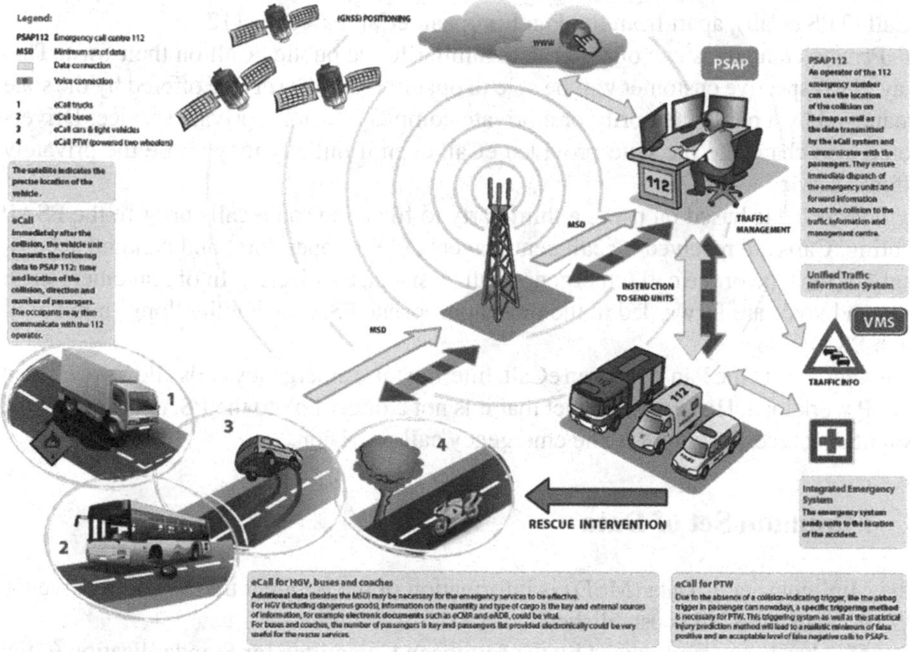

Fig. 1. Graphic of eCall operating summary (extracted form: Infrastructure Harmonised eCall European Pilot (IHeERO) http://iheero.eu/about_ecall/)

2.2 In-Band Modem eCall

Communication between the passengers of the crashed vehicle and emergency services is based on a quasi-simultaneous data and voice link over the same channel. In-band modem eCall uses Circuit Switched (Cs) technology. This system forces to mute the voice path while the MSD is being transmitted.

3 Pan European and Third Party Services eCall

The Pan-European eCall concept benefits from its direct prioritised emergency link to the appropriate PSAP through the existing 112 mechanisms. The 112 call over the mobile network is required to work in all European countries for free, even if no roaming agreement between the vehicle's home network and the guest network is in place. For the pan-European eCall, the priority given to normal 112 calls in the mobile network also applies to the eCall data transmission. Therefore, the coverage and availability of the eCall service is maximized. [4].

Otherwise, European legislation leaves room for the existence of Third Party Service eCall (TPS eCall), apart from the Pan European eCall based on 112.

Private companies can offer services similar to the public eCall on their own. That way, the respective customer will be able to opt either for the service offered by the state (managed by a public authority or a private company) or for a private service. Drivers could also change to the state-provided eCall even if initially they chose the privately offered service.

TPS eCall is based on using a third party to filter and route calls prior to the PSAP routing. Calls are received by call centre agents (TPSP operators) and handled accordingly of the type of the call (emergency call, assistance call, etc.). In of real emergency, data and voice are forwarded to the most appropriate PSAP using the 'long' number of each PSAP.

Compared to the Pan European eCall, filtering false emergency calls allows to lighten PSAP work load. However, the fact that it is not a direct link to the PSAP increases the potential sources of failure in the emergency call provision.

4 Minimum Set of Data

The Minimum set of Data (MSD) is information of the accident that would receive the PSAP when the eCall is established.

MSD has been standardised by the European Committee for Standardisation (CEN TS 15722: 2015) [5]. The information from the MSD can be divided in two categories: mandatory and optional. The mandatory information includes: message ID, vehicle identification, vehicle propulsion storage type, time stamp, vehicle location and direction and format field.

- *Message identifier:* MSD format version as well as a message identifier. The message identifier will initially have a value of 1, which will be incremented with every MSD retransmission after the incident event.
- *Activation type:* whether the eCall has been manually or automatically generated (0 for automatic and 1 for manual).
- *Call type:* whether the eCall is a real emergency or a test call (1 for test call and 0 for an emergency call).
- *Vehicle type:* passenger vehicle, buses and coaches, light commercial vehicles, heavy duty vehicles or motorcycles.
- *Vehicle identification number* (VIN) according to ISO 3779.

- *Vehicle propulsion storage type:* This is important particularly relating to fire risk and electrical power source issues (e.g. Gasoline tank, Diesel tank, compressed natural gas (CNG), etc.)
- *Time stamp:* the time of the accident, expressed in seconds elapsed since midnight January 1st 1970 UTC.
- *Vehicle location:* determined by the on-board system at the time of message generation. It is the last known vehicle's position (latitude and longitude).
- *Position Confidence:* this bit is to be set to "Low confidence in position" if the position is not within the limits of ± 150 m with 95 % confidence (1 for low confidence in position or 0 if the position can be trusted)
- *Direction:* helpful to determine the carriageway vehicle was using at the moment of the incident
- *Format field:* It contains information regarding the optional additional data. 0– No optional additional data, 1– Binary data, 2– BCD, 3– XML encoded data, 4– ASN. 1 BER defined data, 5– ASN.1 PER defined data, 6– ASCII encoded data.
- *Recent vehicle location n (Optional):* vehicle's position in (n-1) and (n-2).
- *Number of passengers (Optional):* number of fastened seatbelts

5 Important Standards

The most efficient way to address interoperability issues in the eCall implementation is to use the agreed common standards. The European Standardisation Bodies CEN and ETSI are working on eCall standards since 2004 and, as a result, the following technical and operational standards have been developed so far:

- CEN EN 15722: Intelligent transport systems - eSafety - eCall minimum set of data
- CEN EN 16062: eCall- High Level Applications Protocols
- CEN EN 16072: Pan European eCall Operating Requirements
- EN/ISO 24978: ITS Safety and emergency messages using any available wireless media - Data registry procedures
- ETSI TS 126 267: In-band modem solution, general description
- ETSI TS 124 008: Pan-European eCall discriminator

6 Privacy and Data Protection

Although the added value of a service such as eCall cannot be easily questioned, concerns about the data privacy should be well addressed. It is worth separating Public eCall service from TPS eCall service for this issue.

The public Pan European 112 eCall in-vehicle system is not connected to mobile network and therefore there is no tracking or data transmission unless a serious accident takes place. Only in this case or after a manual activation, the information contained in the Minimum Set of Data is transmitted to the PSAP. On top of that the data included in the MSDS are those strictly needed by the emergency services to handle the emergency situation.

On contrast there is the TPS eCall system. If a car is equipped with TPS devices, it usually offers additional services such as GPS navigation, integrated hands-free cell phones, road assistance, and so on. In consequence, since it might need to transmit data depending on the other services provided, a dormant eCall device cannot be guaranteed.

7 About HeERO

The pre-deployment evaluation of eCall as a part of ITS action plan started with the EU co-founded R&D projects "HeERO" and "HeERO 2" (Harmonised eCall European Pilot).

HeERO addresses the Pan European in-vehicle emergency call service "eCall" based on 112, the common European Emergency number. For three years (January 2011 to December 2013), the nine European countries forming the HeERO 1 consortium (Croatia, Czech Republic, Finland, Germany, Greece, Italy, The Netherlands, Romania and Sweden) carried out the start-up of an interoperable and harmonised in-vehicle emergency call system.

The second phase of the HeERO project - HeERO 2 - started on 1st January 2013 and lasts 2 years. 6 new countries (namely Belgium, Bulgaria, Denmark, Luxembourg, Spain and Turkey) have joined the other 9 pilot sites of HeERO 1. Furthermore, other countries who wished to become HeERO partners, but have not succeeded for several reasons, (Hungary, Cyrus, Iceland and Israel) became associate partners, a status allowing them to benefit from the expertise of HeERO 1 and 2 but not granting them access to EC funding [6] (Fig. 2).

Those projects have paved the way for the deployment of eCall based on 112. The architectures to be used are defined and the published standards have also been validated. Now, the I_HeERO project (January 2015 to December 2017) proposal draws directly from these results and as such adds real value to the work already undertaken to achieve the mandated deployment of eCall based on 112 for member state PSAP by 1st October 2017 and for vehicles 6 months after that date (31st March 2018).

This project proposal, I_HeERO, ("I" for "Infrastructure") also addresses the mandated pan European in-vehicle emergency call service based on 112.

I_HeERO will

- Upgrade the necessary PSAP infrastructure to support eCall as a Pan European concept.
- Boost Member States investment in the PSAP infrastructure and interoperability of the service within the roadmap including the cross-border communications.
- Prepare for deployment for eCall for HGV and Dangerous Goods and Long Distance Coaches.
- Prepare for deployment for eCall for Powered two wheeled vehicles.
- Define and then perform PSAP Conformity Assessments, which is a legal obligation for all PSAP handling eCall based on 112.
- Look at advancements in the management of data and next generation 112 for eCall.
- Provide Associate Partnership for I_HeERO open to both Member States and Commercial Organisations who are involved in eCall deployment [7].

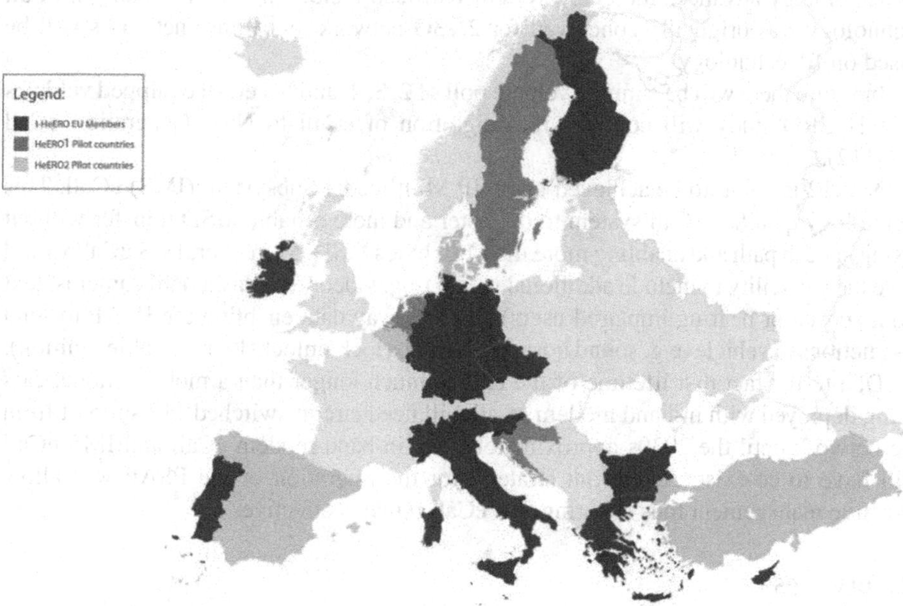

Fig. 2. HeERO project Member States. (extracted form: Infrastructure Harmonised eCall European Pilot (IHeERO) http://iheero.eu/about-iheero/)

8 eCall Benefits

Getting an immediate alert in the event of an accident and knowing the exact location of the crash site reduce the reaction time for the emergency services by 50 % in rural and 40 % in urban areas [8]. Thanks to this gain in time, eCall system is expected to save several hundred lives, and to mitigate the severity of tens of thousands of injuries in the EU annually when fully implemented. eCall will also result in faster treatment of injured people, thereby giving accident victims better recovery prospects.

The early arrival to the accident scene will also allow faster clearance of crash sites, thus reducing the risk of secondary accidents, decreasing congestion times, cutting fuel waste and lowering CO2 emissions.

In addition, the value of life saved and severe injury prevented must be also translated into monetary benefits. Road collisions cost the EU around 160 billion €/year, but if all cars were equipped with the eCall system, up to 20 billion € could be saved annually. [9].

9 Next Generation eCall

As technology advances the eCall system will also include necessary changes. eCall technology was originally conceived for 2&3G network, but future networks will be based on IP technology.

In future there will be a mixed vehicle poll of 2, 3, 4, and 5G eCall equipped vehicles so I_HeERO study will consider the migration of eCall to Next Generation eCall (NG112).

NG112 is going to be achieved using IP Multimedia Subsystem (IMS) eCall. This technology qualifies eCall system to do faster and more reliable MSD transfer without losing speech path and enabling more than 140 bytes MSD. Moreover, IMS eCall would have the capability to include additional media (e.g. video from dashboard cameras, text from speech or hearing impaired users) and two-way data enabling the PSAP to send instructions to vehicle (e.g. sound horn, flash lights, lock/unlock doors, disable ignition).

Due to the fact that lifetime of the cars is much longer than a mobile phone, cars being deployed with in-band modem eCall will need circuit switched 112 support from the network until the 2030s approximately. So, in-band modem eCall and IMS eCall will have to co-exist. A relevant strategy for the migration of the PSAP will allow effective management thus ensuring that eCall remains effective.

References

1. Road safety in the European Union. Trends, statistics and main challenges. European Commission, Mobility and Transport DG, BE-1049 Brussels. March 2015. http://ec.europa.eu/transport/road_safety/pdf/vademecum_2015.pdf. Last query 23rd March 2016
2. EENA Operations Document – eCall, April 2012
3. Road safety evolution in EU from CARE (EU road accidents database) or national publications. European Commission, Mobility and Transport DG, February 2016
4. EENA Operations Document – eCall, p. 10, April 2012
5. EN15722: eCall minimum set of data (MSD)
6. Harmonised eCall European pilot (HeERO) – About HeERO. Last query March 2016. http://www.heero-pilot.eu/view/en/heero.html
7. Infrastructure Harmonised eCall European Pilot (IHeERO) – About I_HeERO. Last query March 2016. http://iheero.eu/about-iheero/
8. Infrastructure Harmonised eCall European Pilot (IHeERO) – About eCall. Last query March 2016. http://iheero.eu/about-ecall/
9. Harmonised eCall European Pilot – About eCall. Last query March 2016. http://www.heero-pilot.eu/view/en/ecall.html

Machine Learning for Autonomic Network Management in a Connected Cars Scenario

Gorka Velez[1(✉)], Marco Quartulli[1], Angel Martin[1], Oihana Otaegui[1], and Haytham Assem[2]

[1] Vicomtech-IK4, Paseo Mikeletegi 57, 20009 San Sebastian, Spain
{gvelez,mquartulli,amartin,ootaegui}@vicomtech.org
[2] Cognitive Computing Group, Innovation Exchange, IBM Ireland, Shelbourne Road, Ballsbridge, Ireland
haythama@ie.ibm.com

Abstract. Current 4G networks are approaching the limits of what is possible with this generation of radio technology. Future 5G networks will be highly based on software, with the ultimate goal of being self-managed. Machine Learning is a key technology to reach the vision of a 5G self-managing network. This new paradigm will significantly impact on connected vehicles, fostering a new wave of possibilities. This paper presents a preliminary approach towards Autonomic Network Management on a connected cars scenario. The focus is on the machine learning part, which will allow forecasting resource demand requirements, detecting errors, attacks and outlier events, and responding and taking corrective actions.

Keywords: 5G · Connected cars · Machine learning · Network management

1 Introduction

The Internet of Things (IoT) vision promotes the interconnection of objects that have traditionally worked offline, creating new opportunities for more direct integration between the physical world and computer-based systems. However, current 4G technology is approaching its limits, and will not be capable of covering the necessities of the huge amount of devices that are expected to utilize this network [1]. Due to these vast and huge increase in the number of devices, network management challenges are becoming more and more complicated [2]. Hence, the 5G which is the new generation of radio systems and network architecture will need to specially take into account IoT challenges in relation to network management [3]. Apart from being able to make maximum use of available spectrum and data transmission rates, it will need to largely manage itself. Virtualisation will play a key role here. Instead of building a network to meet an estimated maximum demand, the network will need to provision itself dynamically to meet changing demands.

J. Mendizabal et al. (Eds.): Nets4Cars/Nets4Trains/Nets4Aircraft 2016, LNCS 9669, pp. 111–120, 2016.
DOI: 10.1007/978-3-319-38921-9_12

Machine Learning is expected to be one of the main key technologies that will enable this vision of self managing network. Machine Learning technologies can learn from historical data, and make predictions or decisions. Instead of following static programming instructions, it can dynamically adapt to new situations learning from new data [4]. This technology has been successfully used in image analysis, language recognition and many other applications. It has also a great potential in the network management area. For example, it can be used to forecast resource demand requirements, detect security threats and error conditions, and react correctly to them.

The transportation sector is one of the key sectors that will be benefited from 5G. Autonomous and semi-autonomous cars, which are expected to decrease significantly the chance of accidents, will depend heavily on connectivity. Cars will become complex electronic devices that have to cope with multiple, high-bandwidth, heterogeneous and asynchronous data sources such as cameras, radars, GPS, etc. So the network must ensure high data rates of big volumes of data at potentially high travelling speeds, what supposes a great challenge.

The aim of this paper is to show the potential of machine learning for its application on the softwarisation and virtualisation of common network functions, in the specific case of a connected cars scenario. This article focuses on the concept and architecture of our approach and also proposes an evaluation criterion.

The rest of the paper is structured as follows. Section 2 describes the state of the art on the main technologies involved in Autonomic Network Management. Section 3 defines a connected cars scenario highlighting the main challenges. Section 4 proposes a generic solution based on machine learning for the problem presented in Sect. 3. Finally, Sect. 5 concludes the paper.

2 Background

5G breakthroughs will not only lay on the radio access network, by means of additional spectrum bands and higher spectral efficiency, in order to achieve higher capacity for dense deployments but will also bring solutions to empower the core network. These new approaches at the network design will aim to provide connectivity to a increasing number of users and devices [5]. Rising demand for mobile traffic will enforce new ways of enhancing capacity, such as dense deployment, as well as intelligent traffic steering and offload schemes while reducing operational expenditure [6].

The strategy from industrial partners, network operators, equipment vendors and standardization bodies, like European Telecommunications Standards Institute (ETSI), is to decouple hardware from software and move network functions towards software. For example, virtual network functions (VNFs) could virtualize a router a base station, core mobile nodes GGSN, SGSN, RNC, EPC (all-IP mobile core network for the LTE networks), firewalls, intrusion prevention IPS, etc.

Introducing a new software-based solution is much faster than installing an additional specialized device with a particular functionality. It boosts network adaptability and provide elasticity to make network easily scalable. So, with simpler operation, new network features are likely to be deployed or teared-down more quickly.

However, there is a need for mechanisms to manage the network due to the increase of the network complexity. To organize all the VNF instances under common goals and policies, a policy manager and orchestrator is needed for the life cycle. MANO stands for Management and Orchestration setting up, maintaining and tearing-down VNFs. Moreover MANO entity communicates with OSS/BSS (Operation Support System/Business Support System) system of the telco operator. OSS deals with network management, fault management, configuration management and service management. BSS deals with customer management, product management and order management etc.

Open Source projects such as OpenStack[1], OpenMano[2], OpenBaton[3] or OpNFV[4] implement network functions virtualization (NFV) and MANO stacks. While solutions, like OpenFlow[5] open standard, deploy innovative protocols in production networks by means of communications interface defined between the control and forwarding layers of an SDN architecture.

Going beyond, the transformation of operative switching and forwarding into programmable and configurable functions enable autonomous network management. The key challenge is to enable direct access and manipulation of the forwarding plane of network devices (e.g. router, switch) by moving the network control out of the networking switches to logically centralized control software. A logically centralized network intelligence can tune the network control directly without taking care about the underlying infrastructure that is completely abstract for applications and network services. Thus, networks turn into flexible, programmable platforms with intelligence to meet dynamically performance and react to degradation symptoms.

Today, this vision is not yet realized. The is not a reliable solution that addresses the problems for flexible creation by scaling up/down or in/out an elastic network in an automated way [7]. We propose to overcome autonomous network management by means of the application of Machine Learning to data streams originating from the forwarding plane of network devices.

3 Scenario Definition

The connected cars scenario is a complete and challenging scenario to test future 5G capabilities. Vehicles can exchange information with other vehicles (V2V), with the roadside infrastructure (V2I), with a backend server (e.g., from a vehicle manufacturer or other mobility service providers) or with the Internet (V2N), with a pedestrian (V2P), etc. The term Vehicle-to-Everything (V2X) is used to

[1] http://www.openstack.org/.
[2] https://github.com/nfvlabs/openmano.
[3] http://openbaton.github.io/.
[4] https://www.sdxcentral.com/listings/opnfv/.
[5] https://www.opennetworking.org/sdn-resources/openflow.

refer to all these types of vehicular communication. Typical automotive use cases for V2X include [8]:

- Advanced Driver Assistance Systems: In this application, connected cars periodically provide either status information (e.g., position, speed, acceleration, etc.) or event information (e.g., traffic jam, icy road, fog, etc.). This information is usually packed into stateless, individual messages or probes which are either locally disseminated to neighboring vehicles, or sent to a central point (base station, backend) where it can be aggregated and then disseminated to other vehicles to make use of it.
- Enhanced navigation: An efficient connectivity is needed to enable a collaborative navigation, where each car can receive information in real-time from other cars or from roadside infrastructure about noticeable events such as road works or traffic congestions.
- Information society on the road: people are demanding high data rate and low latency connectivity when travelling inside vehicles. The introduction of the autonomous vehicle will increase the consumption of data traffic on the move, as drivers no longer need to be focused on driving tasks.

One critical factor in the connected cars scenario is performance. Network performance degradations could potentially impact people lives by affecting the vehicle safety for instance by causing delays in the network. The cause of such issues must be detected in advance, and avoided such that no performance degradations occur in the network.

Moreover, in the current deployments and in order to encompass the connected cars scenario, the system will need to be highly over provisioned (i.e., more resources are available in the network) based on the peak time connectivity requirements. This requires that a large amount of resources can be made available very fast by the system at any time. This continuous time availability is very expensive to maintain. Therefore, an efficient and accurate service demand prediction in the connected cars scenarios is necessary to accordingly provision the network. This should lead to optimizing performance and the use of available network and VM resources, maintaining the Quality of Service (QoS).

4 Proposed Solution

4.1 Architecture

The high-level architecture proposed to solve the problems stated in the connected cars scenario is depicted in Fig. 1. In a nutshell, we propose defining a Machine Learning cluster, the Data Analyser, and two data flows: an input data flow for measurements and monitoring, and an output data flow for policies. Therefore, we need two APIs to interact with our solution. Using these APIs, the deployment and integration of an existing virtualized infrastructure with the proposed solution is limited to the data ingest and the policy recommendation embodied in two APIs that decouple our solution from the analysed and optimized system. The APIs would be based on HTTP, and would use JSON/Openstack like structured data.

The Data Analyser, which is the core Machine Learning module, is fed by metrics data that aim to describe the state of the network. Some of this data comes from the telecommunications operator, while the rest of the data is conventional data gathered from individual VMs or from the VM management software. The Data Analyser contains different Machine Learning algorithms, that are used to detect different kind of events. The main aim of the Data Analyser is to generate rules and to inform the Policy Manager for resource provisioning.

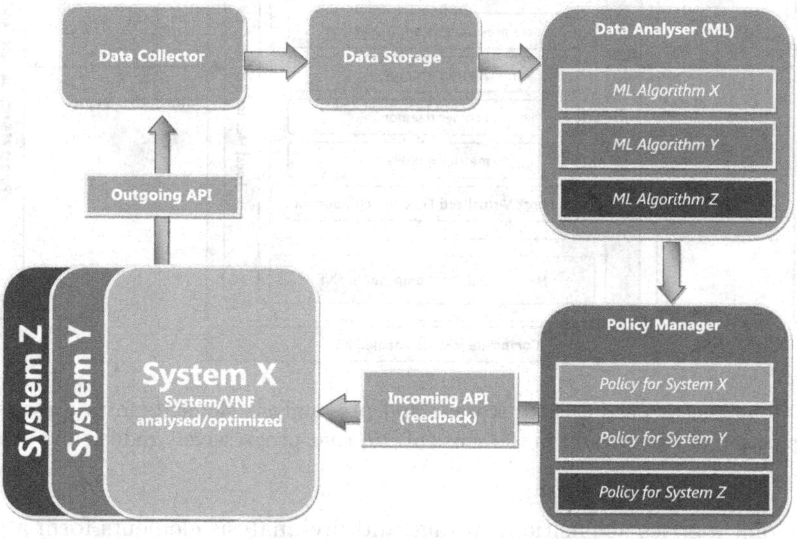

Fig. 1. High-level architecture for machine learning based network management.

As it is evident, the autonomic management of virtualized telecommunication network infrastructures inherently represents a Big Data problem, as it naturally encompasses issues of data Velocity, Variety and Volume: decisions need in principle to be taken in real-time, based on incomplete information represented in large collections of high-dimensional measurements jointly acquired by different layers of the networking stack and therefore residing in largely separated descriptor sub-spaces. This characteristic of the problem needs to be taken into account when devising a working solution to the problem.

If the Machine Learning subsystem needs to execute network load classification and forecasting functions in order to support operational and cost-effective management decisions, then we consider that this effectivity requires both that:

- The metrics acquisition, storage and the initial data reduction and analysis components are physically co-located as close as possible in order to minimize the cost of transferring large volumes of data from one component to another.

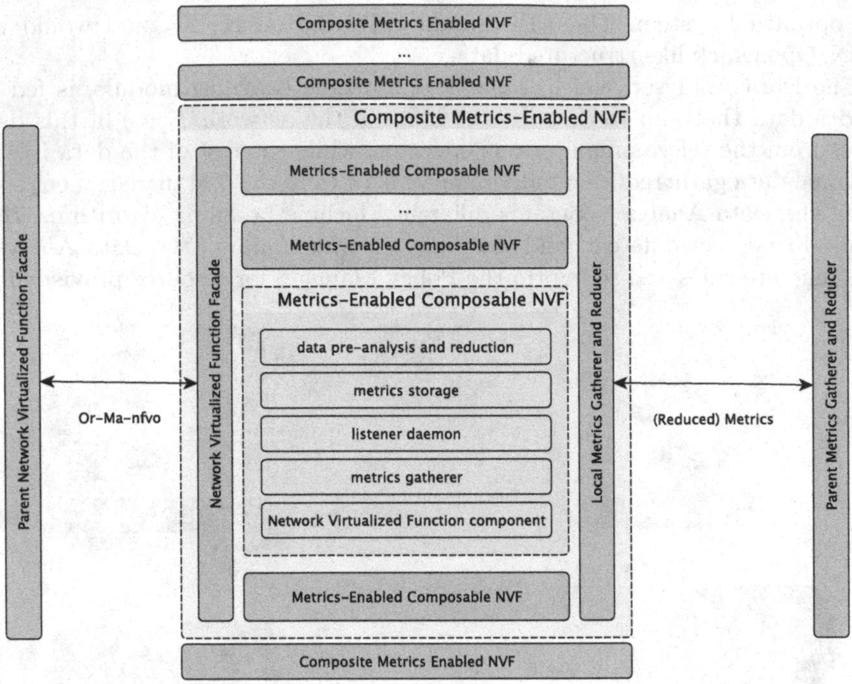

Fig. 2. Joint metrics acquisition, storage and pre-analysis elements form a pyramidal decomposition of Composites in the sense of [10] that progressively reduce and abstract metrics.

- The joint metrics acquisition, storage and pre-analysis elements form a pyramidal decomposition of Composites in the sense of [10] (cfr. Fig. 2) that progressively reduce and abstract metrics to higher and higher levels, proposing (e.g. horizontal and vertical scaling) remediation measures at a local level while delegating higher-level contextual ones to parent levels in a Map/Reduce pyramid [11].

Distributed real-time analytics architectures beyond the Lambda need to be considered for the effectual processing of this kind of streaming data.

While large scale near real-time data processing is a crucial component, standard architectures typically only permit batch processing strategies on large scale metrics collections.

As per [12], we propose instead to consider the streaming approach as the standard one for cognitive NVF self-management, adapting large and historical batch data processing to a near-real time scenario by task queueing and smart scheduling. To this end, we propose to consider how the organization of the data on N-dimensional lattices and the locality of access patterns in the spatio-temporal and in the resolution dimensions can allow us to define and exploit a methodology that is based on streaming cluster computing frameworks [13], Hilbert curve scheduling [14] and multi-scale pyramid decompositions for optimizing access to distributed storage and computing resources and maximize perceived processing speed in real-time operations.

In doing so, we propose adapting an architectural approach from the field of Earth Observation data mining to improve on the 'Lambda architecture' [15], the prevalent approach in managing the contradiction between the large sizes of metrics data and the significant data rates their processing involves.

4.2 Required Components and Proposed Methods

Network Sensorization. The collection, management and analysis of metrics describing the state of a virtualized telecommunications network requires that components are set up and assembled in a proper architecture (see again Fig. 2) to that end.

Requirements for this set of components include:

- The availability of a well-defined querying API allowing standardized access to the collected metrics.
- Fully automatic setup and deployment for the components and the resulting composed architecture.
- Open metric protocol defining the ways in which metrics data is formatted and transmitted through the network.
- Scalability of the resulting component set, especially with respect to scenarios in which the generation, transmission, storage and processing of a large volume of small I/O operations represents the normal mode of operation of the subsystem.

Required components include:

- A metrics gathering component capable of receiving the relevant measures generated by the monitored system, such as StatsD[6]
- Listener daemons capable of aggregating metrics from multiple gathering components. It is in this case fundamental to anticipate and address performance issues at scale, for instance by exploiting highly concurrent implementations
- A metrics database capable of locally storing the aggregated measures so that at least short term historical analysis is possible. Again, availability issues at scale need to be addressed.
- A trend analysis component that implements and makes available the Machine Learning core functionality.

Distributed Optimization and Machine Learning. It is important to note that all problems that are solved through data analysis, particularly through the use of Big Data statistical and machine learning algorithms, share a few key characteristics. First, the datasets are often extremely large, consisting of hundreds of millions or billions of training examples; second, the data is often very

[6] https://github.com/etsy/statsd.

high-dimensional, because it is possible to measure and store very detailed information about each example; and third the data can be stored or even collected in a distributed manner. As a result, it is essential to develop algorithms that are both rich enough to capture the complexity of modern data, and scalable enough to process huge datasets in a parallelized or fully decentralized fashion.

For our particular problem, mathematical optimization can be used as an aid to a human decision maker, system designer, or system operator, who supervises the dimensioning of an NFV architecture, checks the results, and modifies the problem (or the solution approach) when necessary. In a number of scenarios excluding on-line applications, this human decision maker also carries out any actions suggested by the optimization problem. As an alternative, for on-line scenarios embedded optimization procedures can be used to automatically make real-time choices, and even carry out the associated actions, with no (or little) human intervention.

4.3 Scenario Evaluation

In scenarios dedicated to the management of important telecommunication infrastructures such as the one considered here, is crucial to define and execute appropriate validation activities proving that an operational solution is feasible, applicable to different operational contexts, and that it will bring the expected performance benefits.

Here, performance capturing through probes that enable quantitative assessment becomes a key side of the solution. The KPIs and Quality of Service (QoS) are widely used. KPIs depend in a highly intricate manner on the structure and dynamics present in the network. While QoS score is determined by the transport network design and provisioning of network access, terminations and connections.

The connected cars scenario can be developed in two different configurations, depending on whether the application is based on low-level data (e.g., raw data from camera sensors) or based on high-level data (objects or events detected) [8]:

- High-level data transmission requires a medium data rate (up to 1 Mbit/s) with a very low tolerance on errors (10^{-5}).
- Low-level data (mainly video streaming) requires a high data rate (up to 10–20 Mbit/s) with a medium tolerance on errors (10^{-2}).

The connected cars scenario also requires:

- End-to-end latency of less than 5 ms for message sizes of about 1600 bytes.
- Data is sent either event-driven or periodically with a rate of about 10 Hz.
- Minimum throughput: 3 Mbit/s. The system under consideration requires high reliability rather than high throughput [9].

In order to measure these parameters and apply policies there is a set of frameworks and plugins that can be used on top of an OpenStack infrastructure. Neutron[7] is the interface of OpenStack to configure the network that helped

[7] https://blueprints.launchpad.net/neutron/+spec/quantum-qos-api, https://blueprints.launchpad.net/neutron/+spec/ml2-qos.

by ML2 driver provides network attributes. While other solutions like Ryu[8] or OpenDaylight[9] allows setting QoS policies over Open vSwitches using an Open vSwitch database (OVSDB).

5 Conclusions and Future Work

Current network management devices are generally proprietary and closed, and have very low improvement potential. The state-of-the-art methods force network operators to implement complex policies and tasks with a limited set of low-level device configuration commands. The softwarisation and virtualisation of common network functions can raise the level of abstraction, simplifying and making more flexible the network configuration process.

This new network management paradigm can also impact on the automotive sector, specially with the future adoption of 5G technology, which is expected to be aligned wit this paradigm. V2X communications will need to deal with a big amount of data in an efficient and reliable way. A software-based self-managing 5G network could more easily fulfill the requirements needed for this purpose. Furthermore, there can be a great number of new applications due to the introduction of technologies that allow improved performances.

In this article, we focus on machine learning as a key enabling technology for autonomic network management. We first identify the features and challenges of a connected cars scenario, and then we propose a preliminary approach towards autonomic network management. However, it does not exist a generic machine learning mechanism suitable for all use cases. Developers need to design a specific learning path for each use case, which may combine multiple approaches or algorithms together. So instead of proposing a specific approach, we propose a generic architecture that can accommodate different machine learning strategies.

The deployment and validation of our solution require further and intensive research and development work, which is planned to be done inside the framework of an ongoing H2020 European Project.

Acknowledgments. This work was fully supported by the EC project CogNet, 671625 (H2020-ICT-2014-2, Research and Innovation action).

References

1. Wang, C.-X., et al.: Cellular architecture and key technologies for 5G wireless communication networks. IEEE Commun. Mag. **52**(2), 122–130 (2014)
2. Kim, H., Feamster, N.: Improving network management with software defined networking. IEEE Commun. Mag. **51**(2), 114–119 (2013)
3. Shariatmadari, H., et al.: Machine-type communications: current status and future perspectives toward 5G systems. IEEE Commun. Mag. **53**(9), 10–17 (2015)

[8] http://osrg.github.io/ryu/.
[9] https://wiki.opendaylight.org/.

4. Mohri, M., Rostamizadeh, A., Talwalkar, A.: Foundations of Machine Learning. MIT Press, Cambridge (2012)
5. Sun, S., Kadoch, M., Gong, L., Rong, B.: Integrating network function virtualization with SDR and SDN for 4G/5G networks. IEEE Network **29**(3), 54–59 (2015)
6. Hernandez-Valencia, E., Izzo, S., Polonsky, B.: How will NFV/SDN transform service provider opex? IEEE Network **29**(3), 60–67 (2015)
7. Szabo, R., Kind, M., Westphal, F.-J., Woesner, H., Jocha, D., Csaszar, A.: Elastic network functions: opportunities and challenges. IEEE Network **29**(3), 15–21 (2015)
8. 5G-PPP: 5G automotive vision. White paper (2015). https://5g-ppp.eu/wp-content/uploads/2014/02/5G-PPP-White-Paper-on-Automotive-Vertical-Sectors.pdf
9. Yao, Y., Rao, L., Liu, X.: Performance and reliability analysis of IEEE 802.11p safety communication in a highway environment. IEEE Trans. Veh. Technol. **62**(9), 4198–4212 (2013)
10. Gamma, E., Helm, R., Johnson, R., Vlissides, J.: Design Patterns: Elements of Reusable Object-Oriented Software. Pearson Education, Upper Saddle River (1994)
11. Dean, J., Ghemawat, S.: MapReduce: simplified data processing on large clusters. Commun. ACM **51**(1), 107–113 (2008)
12. Quartulli, M., Lozano, J., Olaizola, I.G.: Beyond the lambda architecture: effective scheduling for large scale EO information mining and interactive thematic mapping. In: IEEE International Geoscience and Remote Sensing Symposium (IGARSS), pp. 1492–1495. IEEE Press (2015)
13. Zaharia, M., Das, T., Li, H., Shenker, S., Stoica, I.: Discretized streams: an efficient and fault-tolerant model for stream processing on large clusters. In: Proceedings of the 4th USENIX Conference on Hot Topics in Cloud Computing 2012, p. 10. USENIX Association (2012)
14. Drozdowski, M.: Scheduling for Parallel Processing. Springer, London (2009)
15. Marz, N., Warren, J.: Big Data: Principles and Best Practices of Scalable Realtime Data Systems. Manning Publications, Westampton (2015)

Vehicular Ad-hoc Network's Privacy Assessment Based on Attack Tree

Sara Bahamou[1,2](✉), Jean-Marie Bonnin[1], and Moulay Idriss El Ouadghiri[2]

[1] Télécom Bretagne, Rennes, France
{sara.bahamou, jm.bonnin}@telecom-bretagne.eu
[2] IT Labs, TAR Team, Faculty of Sciences, Meknes, Morocco
dmelouad@gmail.com

Abstract. In the recent years, Vehicular Ad hoc NETworks (VANETs) have known a significant interest in terms of security and dependability. Moreover, we cannot ignore that this kind of networks request further work to provide different privacy related issues. Meaning that, the private data of users of this kind of network have to be prevented from different threats that may abuse their privacy. In this paper we propose an overall sight on the privacy threats in vehicular networks and we give our approach that addressing this issues. The goal here is providing the VANET dependability, by preventing the system assets from the potential threats that targets a vehicular system in order to more understand all ways in which the system can be attacked, that could help us to conceive countermeasures to counteract different possible attacks. Which could be done by applying the attack tree model on the vehicular system use case, in order to retrieve from it different informations in order to evaluate the system. Countermeasures could be added to the attack trees, that leads to the attack-defense tree model.

Keywords: Vehicular system · VANET · Security · Privacy · Countermeasures · Attack tree · Attack-defense tree

1 Introduction

Serval research aims to develop wireless ad-hoc networks and their applications, in order to offer an efficient communication between different entities in Vehicular Ad-hoc Networks (VANETs). VANETs entities could be mobile or fixe with a deterministic properties or random such as: Roads infrastructure, bus, cars or trains, etc.

Our work focus on vehicular networks (VANET) security, where the main objective is to provide road safety measures or information about vehicles speed and its location coordinates, which are transmitted between the vehicles with or without the deployment of the infrastructure. The communication between vehicles or Vehicle to Vehicle Communications (V2V) is made by a medium of inter-vehicle communication. The communication also enlist various road infrastructure equipments, with the intermediary of the vehicle communication to infrastructure (V2I). Also there are hybrid models obtained by the combination of V2V and V2I. Our main objective is to

J. Mendizabal et al. (Eds.): Nets4Cars/Nets4Trains/Nets4Aircraft 2016, LNCS 9669, pp. 121–130, 2016.
DOI: 10.1007/978-3-319-38921-9_13

improve the security level of exchanged data in these kind of networks. Our aims is to develop a general security architecture for vehicular communications in the ITS field, this kind of communication forms a network called Vehicular Ad-hoc Network (VANET), wherein our research works aims particularly this kind of networks. We can see VANET networks as a new form of Mobile Ad-hoc NETwork (MANET), which defines the communications between vehicles or with infrastructure located at roadsides zones. Compared to a conventional ad hoc network, VANET networks are characterized by high mobility of nodes makes the network topology highly dynamic. The following figure explain more the hierarchical relationship between different wireless/fixed networks. We can extract the mobile ad hoc networks (MANETs) which composed by different nodes linked via a wireless communication. These topics are the most groundbreaking in wireless networks fields.

However, by proceeding further, we can say that, VANET could be not considered as a particular case of MANET. Due to the communication type, which does not really requires a global communication, covering all the network nodes (just a local one). Also the defined mobility in VANET which is defined and fixed by the environment properties. Based on these specifications, several difficulties in securing the communication in VANET can be foreseen. However, VANETs presents many security challenges due to their high mobility and changing infrastructure. As an example, an attacher can eavesdrop the wireless medium and access to several informations about communicating nodes that allows tracking them, such as, vehicles identifiers, and locations. Also, an attacker can impersonate a legitimate user identity in order to broadcast false informations, which could compromise and change the normal functionality of the vehicular networks, that may lead to a serious problems. Therefore, the need to solidify the privacy aspect in this type of networks. Ensuring VANET security can touch its privacy, means to allow a secure vehicular system, we need to have the access to vehicle's identity, location and more important informations, which are broadcasted without being encrypted through the network. Thus our work here is to provide a simplified process for location privacy preservation in VANETs. Where we try to introduce different privacy threats and the defense techniques. In this paper we focus on the privacy analysis of VANET communicating systems, by using simplified and close to real world modeling of different possible attacks in order to predicts the most possible attacks which help us to secure the vehicular system and determine the appropriate defense strategy.

As a reminder for the paper, in section II we presents the privacy issues in VANETs, section III we introduce our system model and our building of attack tree for the system model privacy. Also the attack defense tree is presented to show some of possible countermeasures against each attack. Section IV conclude the paper.

2 Privacy Issues for VANETs

2.1 The Importance of Privacy in VANETs

Providing a network privacy it might be defined as ensuring that an exchanged information is observable, readable and decipherable only by who are supposed to do it. Less researches focus on the privacy issue in this kind of networks. And this related to the fact that most researchers consider privacy as a part of security. It means, that by providing such a network security assume that the privacy is also provided. In the one hand, this can be true, if we consider that the role of authorities (car manufacturers and system operators) is to ensure user's data privacy and that their identities will stay safe during the communication between different nodes. But they requires the access to these kind of informations in order to operate in case an issue arises. Most of proposed security protocols and solutions need to know the communicating nodes identification and state in order to provide their security. Which lead us to recognize the fact that there is an important *trade-off* between privacy and security [14]. It is also hard to ensure the real time constraints when we apply such a security or privacy protocol.

In our case, we see that this tow aspects as a tow overlaid layers, which must be guaranteed in a parallel manner. First question that we can ask is: Why interesting to Privacy in a VANET network? What are the threats that can influence this aspect?

Starting with the first question, it is obvious to see that in a vehicular system, many personal behavior of drivers can be derived just from their ways of driving. Moreover, in the near future vehicles will be fully equipped with advanced navigations systems with a high level of communication capabilities. Thus all connected cars or drivers will have a huge number of informations about the movement patterns in the network. Unfortunately, most people are not aware of this problem. Hence the importance to raise their sensitivity to the fact that once the privacy is lost, it is very complicated to re-established it again.

2.2 Privacy Threats in VANETs

Before talking about different privacy requirements in a VANET system, we should underline that privacy requirements may contradicts with security requirements. To more understand that and to response to the asked previous questions, we consider a specific vehicular system model. And we identify the different requirement to achieve adequate privacy 17, 18.

First of all, a taxonomy of privacy issues in VANETs is presented in the Fig. 1. As we can conclude that privacy concerns tow main interests. Content-oriented and context-oriented concerns. Content-oriented regards the privacy protection of collected or requested data. Contextual privacy concerns the contextual informations, which includes the locations privacy of nodes and timing and pattern of the traffic flows.

After sitting the different aspect of the privacy in vehicular ad hoc networks, it becomes less complicated now to define different ways that an attacker may follow in order to reach the network privacy. We can clearly realize that the first step to do for each vehicular network is to ensure its context-oriented privacy. For our system model we focus on the node's location privacy and the temporal of exchanged messages. It consist in preventing the spatio-temporal information from being leaked. Most of existed research work on VANET location privacy based on preventive techniques, such as: Group signature based technique [1], mix-zone based approach [2, 3] or pseudonym based approaches [4]. The main goal of this kind of techniques is preventing the compromising of user location privacy, but the issues here, that these

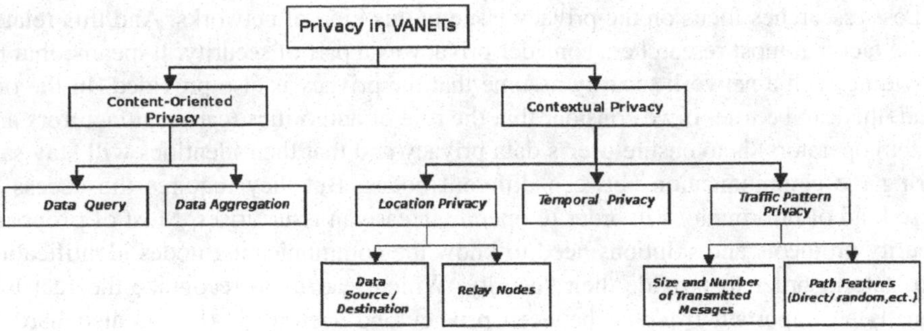

Fig. 1. Privacy in vehicular ad hoc networks

techniques cannot address the unexpected privacy issues. Thus the important to identify before system's deployment, the critical security threats and attacks strategies. In [5, 6], authors proposed a general method for risk evaluating for location privacy based on cost and technical difficulties of the vehicular system. However many limitations could be introduced in their presented model. If we ensure that and adversary can't change nor modify the exchanged informations, but he can tries to infer the creation time of informations from the time when they are received. *Temporal privacy* [15] can be defined here, as, the mutual information between creation and reception of such information packets. So providing privacy issues can be defined as a minimization problem of this mutual information. Buffering information packets in different intermediates nodes (exp. vehicles) between the source, which is in our case a sensor nodes and the receiver. Next section details more clearly these aspects illustrated by a vehicular system model. Where show how additional techniques can enhance privacy.

3 Building Attack Tree for Vehicular Networks Privacy

3.1 The System Model

Our research work is considered as a part of an emerging topic which is the Internet of Things (IoT) in smart cities. So we spotlight one of the major issues of this kind of sustainable cities is the data collection by using of low cost wireless sensors, that can be interconnected via different type of medias such as 3G, Wi-Fi, etc, which suffer also from many obstacles related to their deployment and are broadly expensive. Hence the idea of integration a smart system, based on the vehicular communication techniques. Where the vehicular network in all its forms is dedicated to the service of smart cities, with regard to data collection from low energy devices, we named this mechanism by DC4LED (Data Collection for Low Energy Device), that may be destined for their central servers, and emphasizing the security-related aspects. So by given importance to the data exchanged on these networks, an attacker can as an example, in the absence of the security measures, change the behavior of vehicles by adding false data into traffic, or extract information related to the identity of a vehicle broadcast messages. So our goal is to ensure anonymity, in order to prevent an adversary part locates or retrieve information about vehicles that communicates in the network, by taking into account specific security properties and requirements, also the quality of service in VANET. As well, DC4LED studies are based on a simple portrayal, where VANET systems link between the smart city via different wireless sensors and the central servers. As presented in the following scheme (Fig. 2). As we can conclude that, our purpose here that the system model is related to the data collection processing. Here we can divide this scheme into different main parts where we try to cover and see different research work, handling the security between WSN and VANET, then between VANET network and the access gateways, without forgetting the direct or the end-to-end communication, from WSN to the servers.

Moreover, in our system model, the communication is divided into three parts: vehicle to vehicle, Vehicle to the on board unit (OBU), and vehicle to internet (internet access of vehicles). We make also the assumption of the existence of a third party CA (certificate authority), where vehicles are registered to it. The CA is the responsible of identity dissemination to each vehicle, also a set of pseudonyms are assigned to these vehicles by the CA. The broadcasting of vehicle's position/ location is done periodically. And the most important hypothesis that we consider that the communicating parties (vehicles, OBU) are trusted, which means that attacks could not be done by an internal entity. Now we can move to the construction of our attack-tree for that system.

3.2 Attack Tree Construction

3.2.1 Attack Tree Basis

Attack tree is a way to analyze the security of a network agains its threats. However we can utilize it to construe threats that can be produced in the communicating system by an outsider or insider attacker. Attack trees help us for quantifying security in term of losses caused by attacks [3] or defender's gain from applying such security mechanisms. Quantitative security lead to calculate a probabilistic risk analysis of a system, which enforce development of a communicating systems. In a first stage, defense mechanisms are not included in the basic attack tree. Thus the first interest on basic attack tree building and in next sections will present our attack-tree model where we place different defense mechanisms. Like most mathematical tree models, attack trees are a diagrams where the root node is the goal of the attack and leaf nodes are the attacks. Each leaf nodes are considered as subgoals, and their children are ways to achieve that subgoal. The attack goal (root) bust be chosen carefully. Moreover, for complex systems, we can have many root nodes representing different goals. Nodes can be linked via connective operators (logical operators) in particular AND and OR gates [1, 2], as presented in the following figure.

As shown in Fig. 3. In an attack tree construction, "OR" gates are used to represent the different ways to achieving the same attack goal. Attack goal can be attained by achieving *leaf Node_1* OR the *sub-Goal*. While "AND" operator is used to depict different steps in achieving the attack goal. Based on what have been mentioned above, we built our attack tree model for the vehicular network system, selecting some important Privacy issues as attacker's goals. A stage by stage analysis for the construction of the attack tree is proceed in the next section. Represented attacks can be

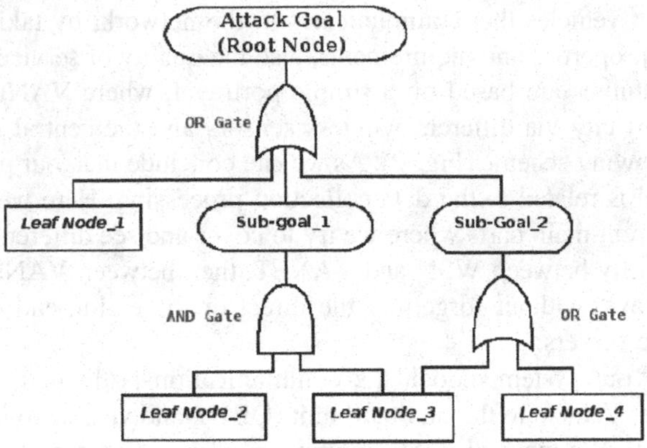

Fig. 2. Basic attack tree.

partly decomposed in several detailed steps, they are represented graphically in the figure. Similarly, we should note that in the previous figure, we consider that the interaction between adversaries and the communicating system takes place at the leaf node. For this reason, some people call attacks of leaf nodes as *stabs*. Each minimum combination of events at the level of the leaf node is known as an attack scenario. The purpose of establishing the attack tree is to define the most probable scenario that may occur in the system. The full set of attack scenarios for an attack tree shows the different possibilities that are available to an attacker that has infinite resources, capabilities and motivations.

3.2.2 Attack Tree Construction for Location Privacy

First step in the building of the attack tree, besides to the modeling of the vehicular system (as presented in the previous section, is the definition of the system leakage, which is here the node's position privacy, so the attack goal here, denoted by G is the D*isclosure of Node's Position (*As shown in Fig. 3). Node here can be a vehicle, sensor deployed over the network or the vehicle's constructers (other authorities). So to achieve this goal we can imagine many possibilities, for example an attacker can get the location of the nodes via the listening to the communications between nodes, because in VANETs most nodes broadcast clearly their locations with no encryption mechanisms. Or by inquiring directly the location from the target node. Or via the physical stealing of the vehicle. So its becomes easy now to define the intermediate causes of the attack goal. The attacker goal is then reached if any of the three intermediate causes is achieved. The following figure represents our tree building based in the illustration presented in [8]. Taking as an example the first attack sub-goal event "eavesdropping", an attacker can achieve the node's privacy via two possibilities: By attacking the Application Layer or Eavesdropping the MAC Layer (See Fig. 4). These to attacks could be produced due to four-attacks (we note them by A1, A2, A3, A4, A5 and A6). And similarly to the others subgoals [8].

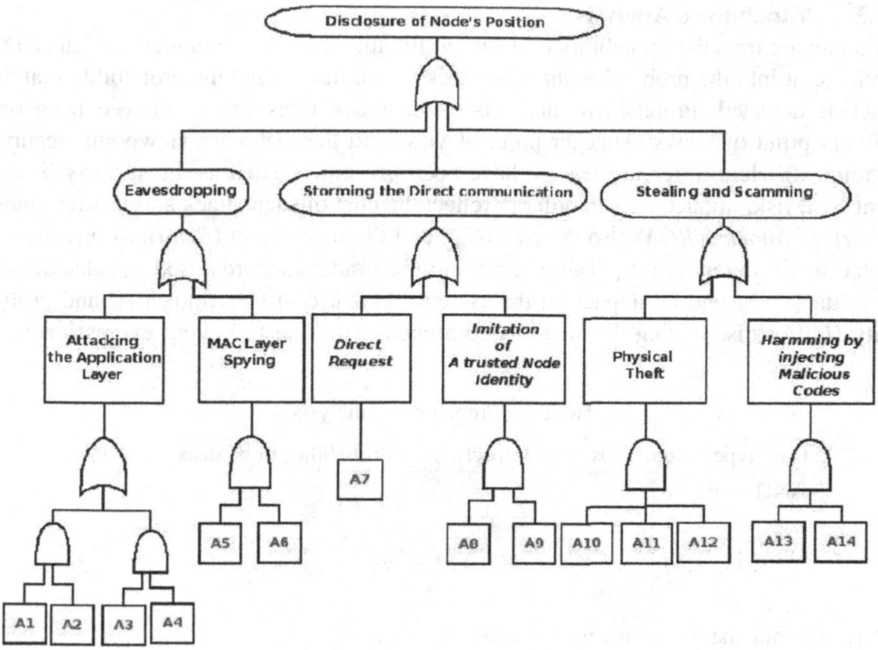

Fig. 3. Attacks on location privacy

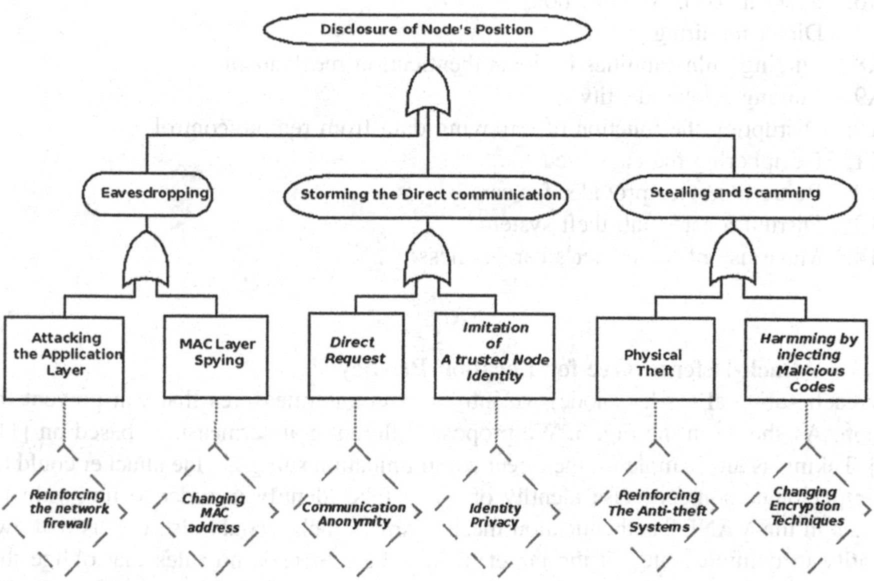

Fig. 4. Attack-defense tree for location privacy

3.2.3 Probabilistic Analysis

For an attack tree, the probability of a successful attack can be computed, which can be further split into the probability that the attack is undetected and the probability that the attack is detected. Probabilistic analysis using attack trees can be viewed from two different point of views: Attacker point of view and the Defender viewpoint (security techniques). Here different measure have been presented (such as the security investment cost, risk, impact, etc.) in order to reflect the cost of such attack and its investment (*Return to Attacker ROA*) also the cost (C_{Ai}) and the investment (*Return to Investment*) related to the defender [16]. Table 1, present the grade standards used to calculate the total attack cost and its impact on the system. Attack cost (C), impact (I) and probability (P_d) of discovering the attack is computed using the following expressions:

Table 1. Probabilistic analysis

Gate type	Attack cost (C)	Impact (I)	Probability to be discovered P_d
AND gate	$\sum_{i=1}^{n} C_{A_i}$	$\sum_{i=1}^{n} i_{A_i}$	$\sum_{i=1}^{n} P_{A_i}$
OR gate	$min^{i=1\ldots n} C_{A_i}$	$max^{i=1\ldots n} C_{A_i}$	$max^{i=1\ldots n} P_{A_i}$

A1: Obtain the signal receiver
A2: Analyze the adopted pseudonym mechanism's weakness
A3: Climbing over the network's firewall
A4: Be familiar with the wireless network's weak security feature
A5: Protocol Vulnerability Analysis
A6: Reset its own configuration
A7: Direct inquiring
A8: Finding vulnerabilities in the authentication mechanism
A9: Making a fake identity
A10: Disrupting the function of removing data from remote control
A11: Deciphering the encrypted file
A12: Being a service provider for cars
A13: Disrupt a car's anti-theft system
A14: Make use of the owner's carelessness.

3.2.4 Attack-Defense Tree for Location Privacy

For each sub-goal (or leaf node) we introduce countermeasures that can prevent the action. As shown in the Fig. 3. We propose different countermeasures based on [11–13]. Taking as an example for the direct communication sub-goal, the attacker could try to impersonate someone else identity or make fake identity in order to find vulnerabilities in the VANET authentication mechanism. Attacker could also use its real own identity to communicate wit the target node, where there is no rules that oblige that node to verify it.

As we can see from the figure, the lake of the sensitivity about privacy is the main cause of this kind of attacks. Anonymity of the VANET should be ensured in the first time also enforcing the public key infrastructure (PKI) makes the network more robust against this kind of attacks.

4 Conclusion

Attack trees depends on the complete attackers knowledge, their possible resources and access level. But it dose not provide us a manner to incorporate these kind of informations in the attack-defense tree model. Means that attack trees dose not provide informations about skills that should be presents to achieve a defense task or an attack goal. Many processes can be realized on the attack tree, this analysis requires values and attributes to be given to each leaf nodes. But thats depends on many things which will be presented in our future work, also an assessment of the attack- defense tree is under investigation for our system model. Where we will try to answer to the following question [1]: *how attack trees can derive security requirements, or influences the architecture design.*

Acknowledgment. We take this opportunities to thank all the conference's committee and we would like to thanks for the anonymous reviewers for their remarks and opinions.

References

1. Schneier, B.: Attack trees: modeling security threats. Dr. Dobb's J. (1999)
2. Schneier, B.: Secrets & Lies: Digital Security in a Networked World. Wiley, New York (2000)
3. Cremonini, M., Martini, P.: Evaluating information security investments from attackers perspective: the return-on-attack (ROA). In: Proceedings of 4th Workshop on the Economics of Information Security (2005)
4. Lin, X., Sun, X., Ho, P.-H., Shen, X.: GSIS: a secure and privacy- preserving protocol for vehicular communications. IEEE Trans. Veh. Technol. **56**(6), 3442–3456 (2007)
5. Freudiger, J., Raya, M., Felegyhazi, M.: Mix-zones for location privacy in vehicular networks. In: Proceedings of ACM WiN-ITS 2007 (2007)
6. Freudiger, J., Shokri, R., Hubaux, J.-P.: On the optimal placement of mix zones. In: Goldberg, I., Atallah, M.J. (eds.) PETS 2009. LNCS, vol. 5672, pp. 216–234. Springer, Heidelberg (2009)
7. Leinmuller, T., Schoch, E., Maihofer, C.: Security requirements and solution concepts in vehicular ad hoc networks. In: Proceedings of the 4th Annual Conference on Wireless Demand Network Systems and Services (2007)
8. Ren, D., Du, S., Zhu, H.: A novel attack tree based risk assessment approach for location privacy preservation in the VANETs. In: 2011 IEEE International Conference on Communications (ICC), pp. 1–5, 5–9 June 2011
9. Du, S., Li, X., Du, J., Zhu, H.: An attack and defense game for security and privacy in vehicular ad hoc networks, Peer-to-peer networking and application. Special Issue on Machine to Machine Communication (2012)
10. Dotzer, F.: Privacy in vehicular ad hoc networks. In: 5th International Workshop, PET 2005, Cavtat, Croatia, 30 May–1 June 2005

11. Freudiger, J., Manshaei, M., Hubaux, J.-P.: Non-cooperative location privacy: a game theoretic analysis. In: CCS 2009, DC (2009)
12. Bistarelli, S., Dall'Aglio, M., Peretti, P.: Strategic games on defense trees. In: Dimitrakos, T., Martinelli, F., Ryan, P.Y., Schneider, S. (eds.) FAST 2006. LNCS, vol. 4691, pp. 1–15. Springer, Heidelberg (2007)
13. Beresford, A.R., Stajano, F.: Location privacy in pervasive computing. IEEE Pervasive Comput. **2**(1), 46–55 (2003)
14. Kapadia, A., Triandopoulos, N., Cornelius, C., Peebles, D., Kotz, D.: AnonySense: opportunistic and privacy-preserving context collection. In: Indulska, J., Patterson, D.J., Rodden, T., Ott, M. (eds.) PERVASIVE 2008. LNCS, vol. 5013, pp. 280–297. Springer, Heidelberg (2008)
15. Pandurang, K., Xu, W., Tr. Zhang, W.: Temporal privacy in wireless sensor networks. In: 27th International Conference on Distributed Computing Systems, 2007, ICDCS 2007, p. 23, 25–27 June 2007
16. Du, S., Zhu, H.: Security Assessment in Vehicular Networks. SpringerBriefs in Computer Science. Springer, New York (2013). doi:10.1007/978-1-4614-9357-0_1
17. Mardacany, E.: Smart cities characteristics: importance of built environments components. In: IET Conference on Future Intelligent Cities, London, pp. 1–6 (2014)
18. Guizani, M., He, D., Ren, K., Rodrigues, J.J.P., Chan, S., Zhang, Y.: Security and privacy in emerging networks: Part II [Guest Editorial]. IEEE Commun. Mag. **53**(8), 40–41 (2015)

Overview of an ITS Project: SCOOP@F

Hasnaâ Aniss(✉)

Institut Français des Sciences et Technologies des Transports, de l'aménagement et des Réseaux (IFSTTAR), Bouguenais, France
Hasnaa.aniss@ifsttar.fr

Abstract. The SCOOP@F project aims at deploying cooperative ITS in a nation-wide scale. 2,000 km of road are to be equipped with Road Side Units and 3,000 vehicles with On-Board Units to enable communication between the infrastructure (the road operator) and the user (the driver). Ile de France, Bordeaux and its ring, Paris-Strasbourg highway, Brittany and Isère counties, will be the field of the first deployments.

Keywords: C-ITS deployment · SCOOP project · Technical architecture · Cross-test

1 Introduction

Among all the deployment strategies of Cooperative Intelligent Transport Systems (C-ITS) across the world [1, 2], in France, the choice has been made to consider for C-ITS pre-deployment hybridizing of ITSG5 and G4 technologies with a strong commitment of road operators and cars' manufacturers.

The main objectives are to increase travel and operation safety, while improving travel quality. The Ministry of Environment, Energy and Sea is in charge of the SCOOP@F project, which aims at deploying Cooperative ITS from 2014 onwards. It is a nation-wide project, which will equip 3000 vehicles and 2000 km of streets, intercity roads and highways in 2016.

The ministry manages this project which involves partners such as local authorities, State services in charge of national road management, automotive industries, automotive suppliers, study centers, universities and research centers, from which Cerema and IFSTTAR.

Five test sites are considered (Fig. 1):

- intercity roads in Ile-de-France,
- Brittany,
- highway between Paris and Strasbourg: A4,
- Bordeaux City and its ring road,
- county roads in the Isère County.

J. Mendizabal et al. (Eds.): Nets4Cars/Nets4Trains/Nets4Aircraft 2016, LNCS 9669, pp. 131–135, 2016.
DOI: 10.1007/978-3-319-38921-9_14

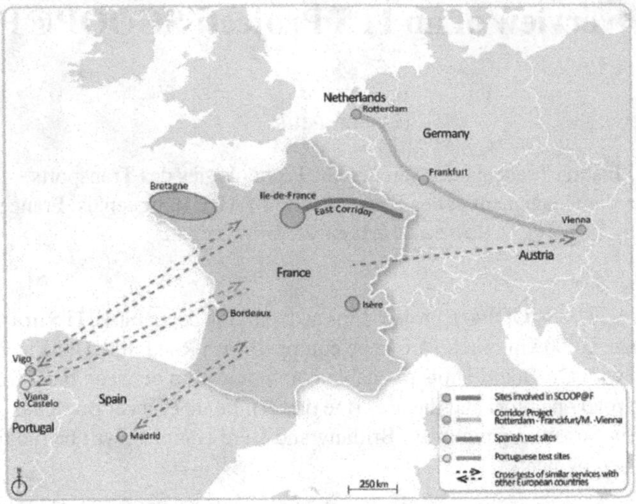

Fig. 1. SCOOP@F test sites

In addition of the French test sites, 3 countries are participating to the project: Spain, Portugal and Austria. Considering their own deployment strategies, interoperability across borders must be evaluated and hopefully be guaranteed.

After a general presentation of the technical architecture and services chosen in the SCOOP Project, the paper will focus on impact studies and interoperability issues.

2 Technical Architecture and Services

C-ITS networks are based on the V2X communications [3]: Vehicle to vehicle and vehicle to infrastructure communications. The infrastructure is based on Roadside units connected to the traffic management center through a central ITS station (Fig. 2).

All the ITS stations are based on the reference architecture of the European Telecommunications Standards Institute (Fig. 3).

Roads infrastructure and vehicles will communicate through wireless networks (access layer) using

- ITSG5 (based on IEEE 802.11p)
- public cellular networks (3G-4G LTE) [4].

Neworking and transport layer are defined by different protocols:

- Geonetworking: The GeoNetworking protocol is a network layer protocol that provides packet routing in an ad hoc network. It makes use of geographical positions for packet transport. GeoNetworking supports the communication among individual ITS stations as well as the distribution of packets in geographical areas [5].
- BTP: The Basic Transport Protocol (BTP) provides an end-to-end, connection-less transport service in the ITS ad hoc network It allows protocol entities at the ITS

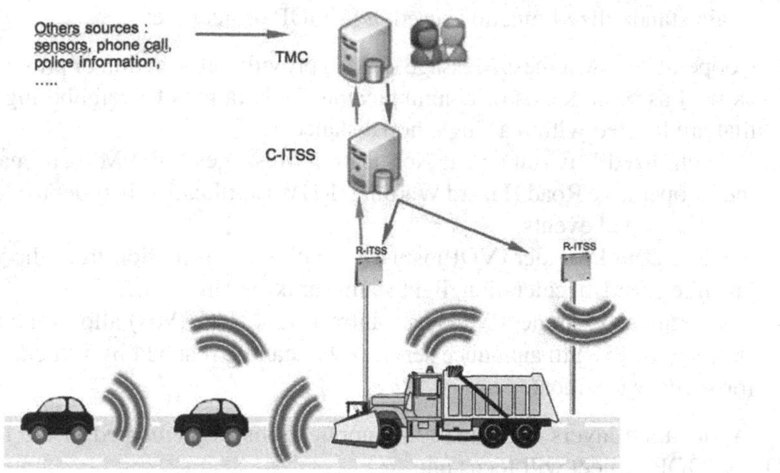

Fig. 2. Functional architecture

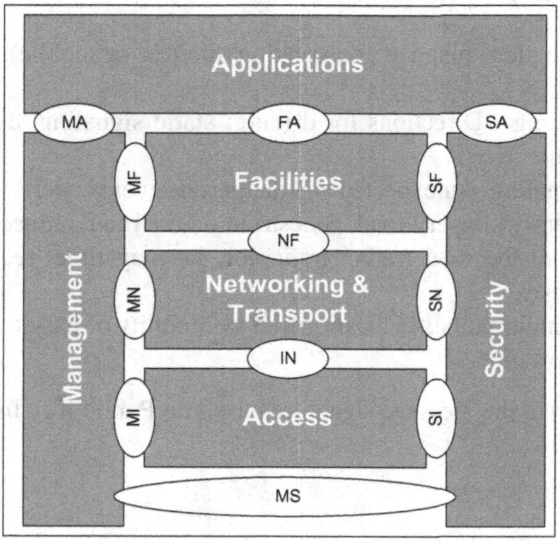

Fig. 3. Reference architecture of C-ITS

facilities layer to directly access the services provided by the GeoNetworking protocol.

- IPV6/IPV4

The facilities layer is a middleware composed of multiple facilities. A facility is a component that provides functions, information or services to ITS applications. It exchanges data with lower layers and with management and security entities of the ITS-S.

Main standardized functions used in SCOOP project are:

- Cooperative Awareness Message (CAM) provide information of presence, positions as well as basic status of communicating ITS stations to neighboring ITS stations that are located within a single hop distance.
- Decentralized Environmental Notification Messages (DENMs) are mainly used by the Cooperative Road Hazard Warning (RHW) application in order to alert road users of the detected events.
- Vehicle Data Provider (VDP) is used to collect information from the vehicle CAN bus like speed, acceleration, light status, braking strength…
- Cooperative Awareness Message –Infrastructure (CAM-I) allows the roadside ITS station (R-ITSS) to announce services that can be reached by vehicles (like request for security certificate).

Application layers is related to all applications implemented in the ITS Network. The SCOOP Project will focus on:

- Data collection: vehicle data (position, speed, direction, cape), road event data inputted manually by driver (animal on the road, etc.), automatic data (impact, emergency brake,…)
- Construction site alert: planned construction site (fix or mobile), vehicle of winter maintenance.
- In-vehicle signaling - Directions for driving: static signaling, dynamics of speed, VMS embedded.
- Road hazard signaling – unexpected and dangerous events: alerts from the European directive (temporary slippery road, pedestrian on the road, reduced visibility,…)
- Information about the road traffic: traficolor, journey time, recommended route, access to services…
- Parks relay and multimodality: location and availability of parking relays, schedules of public transportation.

Security layer is about the message signature based on Public Key Infrastructure (PKI) architecture.

3 Studies

Experimentation, conducted on open road during 1 year in a naturalistic way, will allow researchers to study impact of these technologies at different level:

- Legal and Regulatory impact
- Organizational Impact
- Technical evaluation
- Evaluation of benefit and economic impact
- Evaluation of social acceptability
- Evaluation of impact on driver behaviour
- Evaluation of acceptability of ITS system
- Evaluation of accidentologic gains

- Evaluation of limitations related to driver distraction
- Evaluation of traffic impact

In parallel, activities on cross-borders interoperability will take place in test sites (Bordeaux, Vigo, Vienna, Lisbon, Madrid) after a first series of experimentation in laboratories and closed test tracks. Some issues are already been identified like implementation of the geonetworking protocol, parameters of the DEN messages (like event cause code) and of course the implementation of the security layer and the PKI process.

4 Conclusion

During the keynote, details on architecture and studies will be discussed. The focus is to carry out research aspects on C-ITS system which will be raised by all the studies conducted in the SCOOP project. They can be identified although all the layer of the reference architecture (especially on access and networking layer) and evaluations.

References

1. Yogarayan, S., Azman, A., Rama, K.J.: A framework on cloud based connected car services. In: Kim, K.J., Joukov, N. (eds.) Information Science and Applications. Lecture Notes in Electrical Engineering, vol. 376, pp. 11–20. Springer, Singapore (2016)
2. Xiong, G., Zhu, F., Dong, X., Fan, H., Hu, B.: A kind of novel ITS based on space-air-ground big-data. IEEE Intell. Transp. Syst. Mag. **8**(1), 10–22 (2016)
3. Alam, M., Ferreira, J., Fonseca, J.: Introduction to intelligent transportation systems. In: Alam, M., Ferreira, J., Fonseca, J. (eds.) Intelligent Transportation Systems: Dependable Vehicular Communications for Improved Road Safety. SSDC, vol. 52, pp. 1–17. Springer, Heidelberg (2010)
4. Gholibeigi, M., Heijenk, G., Moltchanov, D., Koucheryavy, Y.: Analysis of a receiver-based reliable broadcast approach for vehicular networks. Ad hoc Netw. **37**, 63–75 (2016). Elsevier
5. García-Costa, C., Egea-López, E., García-Haro, J.: Evaluation of MAC contention techniques for efficient geo-routing in vehicular networks. Ad hoc Netw. **37**, 44–62 (2016). Elsevier

Towards Solutions for Current Security Related Issues in ETSI ITS

Sebastian Bittl(✉)

Independent, 80997 Munich, Germany
sebastian.bittl@mytum.de

Abstract. Vehicular ad hoc networks are a promising approach for increased safety of driving. Hence, there is a high interest to enable their mass roll out in upcoming years. Thereby, intended safety critical use cases require a rigid security system. The provided analysis of standardized security mechanisms identifies three main weaknesses. Firstly, end-to-end encrypted multi-hop communication is not supported. This affects the whole communication system, as it limits the capability for required distribution of pseudonym certificates indirectly hindering single-hop communication, too. Secondly, pseudonym certificate management requires a dedicated start up strategy after node start up. Thirdly, basic data sets of time and position are acquired from sources lacking security mechanisms and are used in a partly inconsistent way. Enhancements to overcome the identified issues are proposed and discussed.

Keywords: ETSI ITS · VANET · Security

1 Introduction

Vehicular ad hoc networks (VANETs) are in the wake of mass roll out in upcoming years. They are regarded as enablers of cooperative advanced driver assistance systems (ADAS) for enhanced safety of driving. Thereby, security of data exchange is a core point of concern, due to safety critical use cases.

Similar approaches for secure message exchange are standardized within ETSI Intelligent Transport Systems (ITS) and Wireless Access in Vehicular Environments (WAVE) [3,16,18]. Thereby, message authenticity and integrity are provided by digital signatures. Most messages within VANETs yield pure information dissemination. Thus, they do not require data confidentiality [18,31].

An extra security challenge in VANETs is given by the need to ensure privacy of participants. To realize it, so called pseudonyms are used as temporary identities of all nodes. The used pseudonym is changed frequently to avoid tracking. Thereby, a pseudonym change requires a new pseudonym certificate (PSC) holding the dedicated cryptographic parameters for validation of a nodes messages' signatures. Retrieval of such a new certificate over the air (i.e., a pseudonym certificate update) requires encryption to keep this future identifier private.

J. Mendizabal et al. (Eds.): Nets4Cars/Nets4Trains/Nets4Aircraft 2016, LNCS 9669, pp. 136–148, 2016.
DOI: 10.1007/978-3-319-38921-9_15

In contrast to WAVE, ETSI ITS supports multi-hop communication. However, our analysis shows that currently end-to-end encrypted messages cannot be delivered over multiple hops, due to malformed protocol design.

PSCs updates within nodes are also affected by the found issue, as single hop communication from node to a backbone server is infeasible in practice. Moreover, this requirement of multi-hop communication for PSC updates also causes the extra need for a valid PSC within a node to request a new PSC. We propose a solution for this problem which does neither need long lifetimes of general PSCs, nor does it require PSC revocation.

Furthermore, we address the security related handling of time and position in VANETs. This includes the recently found security problem of time synchronization in VANETs [13]. It strengthens the requirement for frequent PSC distribution to nodes, which highlights the importance of the mechanisms mentioned before. Time synchronization in a VANET is usually achieved by using Global Position System (GPS) time as a reference [13,32]. However, this leads to vulnerability of the VANET security scheme against GPS spoofing attacks. The threat analysis from [13] is extended to the location component of GPS signals and an extended review of alternative reference time sources is given. Thereby, terrestrial time broadcast is found to be an appealing candidate for a source of more robust time synchronization in VANETs. Moreover, the requirement of mutual consistency of time and position as well as a data format issue within the security envelope of ETSI ITS and WAVE are discussed.

Most outlined issues do not arise from the definition of security mechanisms on its own. Instead, interaction with other layers, especially with the network layer, causes serious cross layer issues.

The further outline is as follows. Related work is looked at in Sect. 2. Section 3 treats the outlined issues of encrypted multi-hop communication in general and specifically secured PSC update requests. Security related handling of time and position data sets is looked at in Sect. 4. Finally, Sect. 5 provides a conclusion about achieved results and gives topics of future work.

2 Related Work

Much work has been done to enable usage of VANET technologies over the last years. However, none of the conducted field tests used the protocol stack or security system from current standards [12,30,31]. Basic operation and interoperability checks have been done during so called ITS Cooperative Mobility Services Events. However, the amount of conducted tests is still relatively small. The issues addressed in this work have not been identified by them so far.

2.1 Encrypted Multi-hop Communication

Prior work on multi-hop communication in VANETs has so far concentrated on routing [11,16]. To the best of the knowledge of the authors no prior work dedicated to security of multi-hop communication in VANETs has been published.

Security for multi-hop communication in ad hoc networks is studied in [19], but privacy requirements of VANETs have not been considered. An extensive survey on privacy and security within VANETs is available in [26].

In general security within VANETs is based on a public key infrastructure (PKI) scheme. Thereby, participants (i.e., nodes) use so called pseudonym certificates (PSCs, or authorization tickets) or mutual authorization. Thereby, the used PSC is changed frequently to avoid tracking. However, this requires new PSCs to be distributed to nodes quite often, as pre-distribution of many PSC to each node is discouraged. PSCs may contain three kinds of validity restrictions. These relate to PSCs' lifetime, a geographical validity region and applications whose messages may be secured by it. The latter ones are identified via so called ITS-AIDs (Application Identifiers) [12].

The general approach for PSC distribution to nodes is described in [4]. It includes to generate a new public/private key pair at the node and send the public key to a CA. The CA generates a valid PSC by providing at digital signature for the public key and its accompanying meta data, e.g., a PSC's validity time. To achieve privacy of a node requesting a new PSC, such requests are encrypted. Typically, fixed road side units (RSUs) are used to propagate messages between a node and a corresponding certificate authority (CA) [16,26]. Within ETSI ITS such CAs are often called authorization authorities (AAs) [12]. PSC updates benefit from multi-hop communication, as it reduces the amount of required RSUs to cover the road network in comparison to single-hop communication.

2.2 Secure Time and Location Information

The need for accurate time synchronization and localization of VANET participants has been identified in numerous works [16]. However, findings about security weaknesses of the proposed GPS based approach have been published quite recently [13]. While the work in [13] concentrates on time synchronization, a first extension to localization is given in this work. Feasibility of the attacks from [13] is supported by recent findings in [33], strengthening the need for secure ways to obtain time and position information, especially in VANETs.

Approaches from similar domains for secure time synchronization (and partly also localization) cannot be easily ported to VANETs, due to specific characteristics of VANET systems. For example, work in [28] assumes that the attacker cannot shield the node from the real signal of the location and time providing system. However, this is not the case in VANETs [13]. The approach from [35] requires a static node setup, while nodes in VANETs are highly mobile.

Prior work on secure positioning in VANETs has concentrated on relative positioning [34]. However, VANET security mechanisms, like certificate validity restrictions [12], require absolute positioning. Moreover, position and time of a node do not only need secure and accurate obtaining on their own, but mutual consistency of both values has to be ensured, too. We show, that the currently standardized mechanisms require enhancement in regard to this issue.

The time synchronization weakness is an extra reason for short lived PSCs with onetime usage, in addition to an increase in privacy in comparison to a longer lived PSC pool with reused members [26]. However, short lived PSCs require frequent encrypted PSC updates over the air. For details about the PSC update process see Sect. 2.1.

3 Core Security Mechanisms

The overall security mechanisms of ETSI ITS and WAVE are quite similar [4,5,12]. However, as the WAVE system does not support multi-hop communication [2], its corresponding security system does not need to support this feature, too.

3.1 Encrypted Communication

The ETSI ITS security entity provides basic mechanisms for encrypted communication. However, analysis of the interface between network layer and security entity shows that end-to-end encrypted communication can only be performed over a single hop connection. The network layer can only use the interfaces called encapsulate (for a to be sent message) and decapsulate (for a received message) [11]. Additionally, the payload inside a security envelope can only have a single element with one of the properties encrypted, signed, signed and encrypted or unsecured [12]. The encapsulate and decapsulate methods perform the required cryptographic operations on the provided payload and add or remove the meta data of the security envelope.

An illustration of dedicated message parts at the ETSI ITS network layer (often called GeoNetworking layer) is given in Fig. 1.

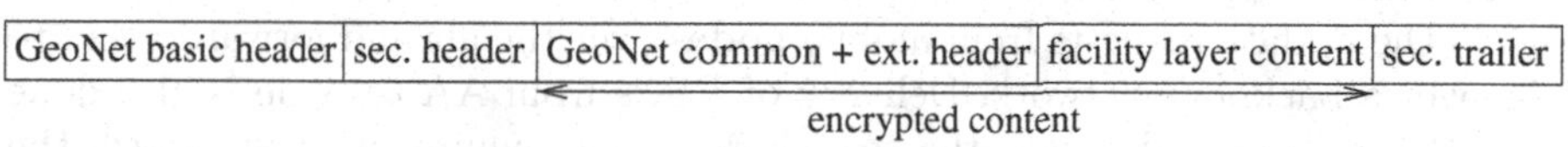

Fig. 1. Encrypted message at the network layer.

Routing information of the network layer, as required for multi-hop communication, is contained in the so called extended GeoNetworking header. It is part of the payload given to the security entity [11]. Hence, it will be encrypted together with all the remaining payload. Thus, any receiver not being identical to the intended end point of communication will not be able to access the routing information. It is encrypted with a secret key only known to the final target, but not to the packet forwarders. Thus, the packet will be discarded and not delivered to the target, except single hop communication is possible. Hence, at the current stage of standardization, the ETSI ITS framework does not provide the possibility to have multi-hop communication with end-to-end encrypted content.

Preceding versions of the security envelope standard provided support for multiple payloads with different security properties [7]. One could use that mechanism to encrypt (and sign) only the confidential part of higher level payload, but only sign the network layer header fields holding routing information. However, the support for multiple payloads received criticism, e.g., in [24]. This lead to the support being dropped. However, the support for encrypted multi-hop communication was (unintentionally) dropped by this move, too.

Moving the routing information to the unsecured part of the network layer header fields outside the security envelope would circumvent the above described problem. However, this would open a possible security flaw. An attacker could capture multi-hop packets to inject them with modified routing information into the VANET causing bogus traffic by valid nodes forwarding the injected packets. Thus, one should stay back from such kind of approaches.

A solution for the issue could partly reintroduce multiple payloads within the security envelope. To address the increase in complexity mentioned in [24], one could limit the number of payload fields to a well defined maximum. This was not the case in [12]. A maximum of two differently secured payloads would be sufficient for the important use case of pseudonym updates. The data exchanged between originator node and AA would be signed and encrypted, while the routing information should only be signed.

3.2 Pseudonym Update Procedure

In order to perform privacy conserving pseudonym changes, a vehicle has to retrieve new pseudonym certificates from an AA from time to time. Pre-caching of many PSC within a node is disregarded and a short lifetime of PSCs in the area of minutes is recommended, e.g., in [13,18]. Thus, a node has to obtain new PSCs over the air. We show that the combination of resulting requirements can only be fulfilled by adding a special on-demand used PSC for PSC updates.

A common approach to realize PSC updates is to use RSUs. Thereby, RSUs receive the update requests from mobile nodes over the air and forward them to AAs over a backbone network. Delivery of PSCs from AA to node is also done using RSUs, but in this case the sender does not require privacy. Hence, the AA can just encrypt its answer using the public encryption key of the node and sign it with its public verification key. Thus, the following mechanisms are only required for the request messages, but not for the answering delivery messages.

The general data content of a PSC request has been defined in [4]. Thereby, the to be signed PSC is contained together with the long term certificate (LTC) of the node, which is used to sign the whole request on the facility layer level, and some extra meta data. To send a PSC request, the facility layer part of the cross layer security entity generates a packet with the aforementioned content. Then, it is handed over to the network layer, which adds its own header fields. Moreover, the network layer passes the package to the network layer part of the security entity. This is done to embed the package into a so called security envelope consisting of a header and trailer. Moreover, the packet is encrypted using the public encryption key of the AA. This process is illustrated in Fig. 2.

The dedicated header and trailer fields within the security envelope are added in dependence of a so called security profile. Currently only profiles for CAM and DENM as well as a generic profile for other messages have been specified [12].

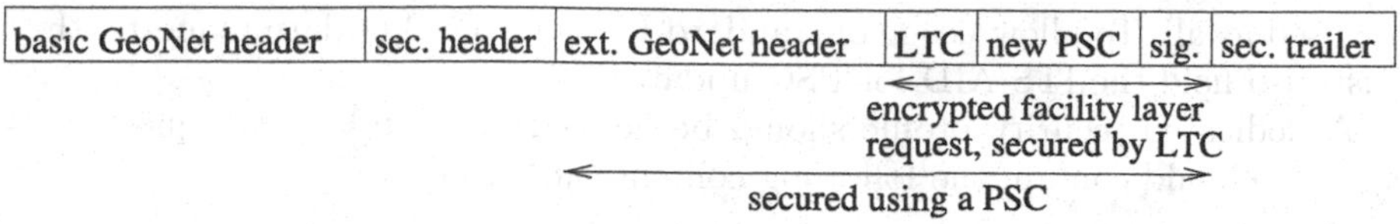

Fig. 2. A PSC update request within a security envelope at the network layer level.

The signer cannot identify itself in the security envelope by its LTC, as this unique identity has to be kept private. Only the AA may obtain the long term identity by decrypting the LTC in the encrypted payload. Hence, only a PSC can be used to authenticate the request message against other nodes. Otherwise other nodes do not forward the packet disabling multi-hop delivery, as unauthenticated packets are dropped. Thus, a node requires a PSC to be able to obtain another PSC via a multi-hop connection.

Like mentioned above, RSUs are used to forward PSC request to AAs. Thus, such requests always require multi-hop communication. Even in case the request can reach an RSU in one hop, the RSU should still be able to authenticate the request message. Otherwise, RSUs would have to forward arbitrary messages to AAs. This should clearly be avoided, as this would allow an attacker to flood AAs via one or even many RSUs with bogus requests to perform a (distributed) denial of service ((D)DOS) attack.

As outlined above, ordinary PSCs should have a short lifetime to prevent misuse and protect privacy of nodes. However, this poses the problem of how to obtain a PSC for message generation after node start up, when all stored PSCs are outdated. We propose to overcome this issue by using a dedicated PSC, denoted by PSC_U, with a lifetime long enough to be still valid after a node's restart. To protect against misuse of this PSC_U for generation of malformed messages like CAMs, the PSC_U has to be only valid for PSC update requests. This limitation can be applied by only assigning the ITS-AID for PSC updates to the PSC_U. Thus, the PSC_U is not valid for securing other kinds of messages.

An attacker can generate future PSC update requests using the attack from [13]. However, he cannot access the issued PSC from the CA's answers, as these are encrypted with the long term encryption key only known to the node. Moreover, the extra load caused in the VANET from sporadic bogus PSC update messages should be minor.

If a node has no standard PSC available, e.g., after start up, it uses the PSC_U to setup the protocol stack. Pseudonym identifiers on the different protocol layers (StationID, network layer address, MAC address) can be derived from it. As no valid PSC for standard messages like CAMs is available, such messages are not sent by the affected node until a corresponding PSC is obtained. The node only generates PSC update requests, which are signed by the PSC_U. After a PSC has been obtained, sending of standard messages is started. Moreover, the obtained PSC is used to request a new PSC_U from the AA to avoid reusing it, which may endanger privacy of the node. In case a PSC is available at a node the PSC_U is not used at all. To allow usage of standard PSCs for PSC update requests, they must also hold the ITS-AID for PSC updates.

A dedicated security profile should be defined for pseudonym request messages. It should contain the following content (at least).

- Header fields holding
  - signer identifier (either a standard PSC or a PSC_U),
  - generation time which allows dropping of outdated requests,
  - ITS-AID for pseudonym update, together with
- a payload field of type 'signed and encrypted', and
- a trailer field holding an ECDSA signature (same as for CAM or DENM).

In combination with the approach from Sect. 3.1, PSC updates can be realized by the proposed mechanism utilizing multi-hop communication.

4 Time and Position Handling

Time and position are fundamental data sets in VANETs across all protocol layers. In regard to security, especially validity restrictions of messages as well as certificates require accurate and secure knowledge about them. Moreover, safety critical collision avoidance applications depend on them.

4.1 Secure Acquisition

Time synchronization among nodes in a VANET and individual node localization are typically achieved using GPS with additional support of local sensors. It has been shown that spoofing of GPS time can lead to massive violation of standardized security requirements by causing manipulation of the internal time of nodes [13]. Thus, secure mechanisms for acquisition of the basic information sets of time and position are required.

A basic mechanism to defend against GPS (or global navigation satellite system (GNSS) in general) spoofing attacks is to equip receivers with the ability to detect such spoofing. Typical civil receivers are not equipped with this capability, as e.g., shown in [13]. However, redundant data source(s) can be used to verify the reference time and location obtained from the GPS signal.

In case an attack gets detected, usage of GPS data can be disabled and local sensors can be used to obtain future estimates about time and position. This will probably lead to a reduced confidence about the obtained values due to a missing reference data source, but the results can be expected to be much more reliable in comparison to results including the spoofed data. Moreover, a confidence value for location accuracy has already been included in data sets [9]. No similar mechanism has been considered for time stamps. Thus, we propose to introduce it. The definition of the security envelope already contains an unused data type for a time stamp with a corresponding confidence interval.

Secure Time Base. Redundant time source(s) can be used for plausibility checks of the reference time obtained from GNSS. Thus, different possibilities to obtain such extra reference times are looked at in the following.

Time synchronization over an internet connection to a NTP (network time protocol) server could be considered for VANETs, e.g., via IPv6 over GeoNetworking [16]. However, NTP has been found to contain various security flaws [21,29]. Moreover, securing of NTP messages via a symmetric key scheme seems infeasible due to the high number of participants. Thus, usage of NTP in its current state is not recommended for safety critical VANET use cases.

Mobile communication networks can optionally provide so called network identity and time zone (NITZ) messages [8]. However, support is optional and the standardized accuracy is in the area of minutes. Thus, this message's content cannot fulfill much stricter time synchronization requirements of VANETs.

802.11p specifies so called time announcement frames for time synchronization among nodes. However, they are generated on the MAC layer without any kind of security mechanism [1]. The standard ETSI ITS and WAVE security mechanisms are not suitable in this case, as they operate on the network layer.

Terrestrial time broadcast is a general alternative to GNSS based time synchronization on land. It typically provides a comparable amount of coverage and accuracy. Various government operated dedicated time senders exist transmitting legal time, e.g., WWVB in the USA [20] and DCF77 in Europe [27].

A drawback of terrestrial time broadcast is that different sender use differing frequencies, data formats and signal shaping schemes. Thus, receivers can typically only obtain data from a single sender. However, regions covered by the individual senders are large (see e.g., [23]). Hence, the complexity of receiver equipment required for large scale mobility of node should be limited.

However, time synchronization messages from terrestrial stations are typically not secured, i.e., they do not contain a digital signature. Thus, their security level is not higher than the one of unsecured GNSS signals in general. Spoofing of terrestrial time broadcast signals has not been looked at in detail. Only the simply resembled amplitude modulated part of the DCF77 signal has been attacked so far [14]. Thus, future work is required to show feasibility of including terrestrial time broadcast as a data source in VANETs.

Moreover, inclusion of digital signatures based on public key cryptography should be considered for terrestrial time broadcast. Low amount of affected and government operated senders in conjunction with expressed interest of governments regarding VANET roll out (see e.g., [18]) make this a promising approach.

Secure Localization. Typical localization systems for nodes rely on GPS for obtaining a global position estimation [13]. This estimation is improved by various kind of locally obtained information, e.g., from acceleration sensors, and by map matching. Various mechanisms for absolute localization within a wireless network have been proposed [17]. However, practical usability is in general limited by a lack of available infrastructure.

Under presence of a mobile phone network, a position estimation can be obtained from it [17]. Such an estimate is typically much less accurate in comparison to one obtained from GNSS. However, large deviations resulting from a spoofing attack can be detected by comparison of both estimates.

Relative localization of nodes is sufficient for some use cases, e.g., longitudinal collision risk warning. Thus, methods like distance estimation based on received signal strength can be used [22,25]. However, use cases like limiting certificate or message validity to geographical areas require absolute localization [12].

In case of successful GPS position spoofing an attacker can force a node to accept messages and certificates outside their limited validity region. This attack becomes especially powerful when it is combined with time spoofing (see above). Thereby, all temporal and spacial validity restrictions of both messages and certificates can be circumvented. Moreover, a major impact on higher layer functionality can be expected, as the attacker can model VANET messages corresponding to arbitrary trajectories. For example, this could be used to cause malfunction of ADAS.

4.2 Mutual Dependency of Time and Location

A time and location entity standard has been started within ETSI ITS, but it is still in a very early stage [6]. The network layer standard [11] states that the time stamp value should be updated every time a new position fix (from GPS with, e.g., 10 Hz typical update rate) is available. Thereby, the time stamp of the location fix is to be used. Moreover, the time stamp within a CAM represents the time of the reference position's fix used in the CAM [10].

Unfortunately, the outlined approach suffers from a major drawback at the network layer. If messages are sent faster than the time (and location) stamp is updated, all receivers accept only the first message after an update. All other messages will be discarded, due to the simple duplicate package detection (DPD) mechanism of the network layer. For single-hop messages (like CAMs), it just uses sender ID and sending time stamp [11]. This behavior leads to packet loss, which can cause various problems within applications relying on the output the network layer. Including the sender's location in DPD does not help, as updates of time and position are coupled. Additional inclusion of a sequence number, as currently only done for multi-hop messages, overcomes the problem. Thus, we propose to also use sequence numbers for single-hop messages.

Within the ETSI ITS protocol stack a multitude of different time stamp formats exist. These include,

- on the facility layer [9,10]
  - "GenerationDeltaTime" (16 bit value) together with various others, e.g., TimestampIts (32 bit value), with at most millisecond accuracy within CAM and DENM,
  - SPAT and TOPO messages use millisecond accuracy (32 bit),
- the network layer uses millisecond accuracy (within the "TST" field) [11],
- the security entity uses [12]

- "Time32" (32 bit) with full second accuracy, and
- "Time64" (64 bit) with microsecond accuracy.

Requirement analysis of VANET security mechanisms shows that there is no need for the standardized microsecond (μs) resolution of sending time stamps within the security envelope of messages [5,12]. This value is used for validation of certificates, whose lifetime limits are specified with full second accuracy. Moreover, [15] suggests that the security entity should accept all incoming messages with time stamps from the last five minutes.

Thus, the 64 bit time value with μs resolution can be substituted in the security envelope by its standardized 32 bit counterpart (full second resolution). Thereby, four bytes of security related overhead can be saved in each message. Moreover, this limits the required time stamp resolution within the protocol stack to millisecond resolution altogether.

Additionally, facility and network layer as well as the security entity use location stamps. No mechanism for obtaining data sets for time and location for the security entity has been standardized, in contrast to network and facility layer (as outlined above). We suggest to use the same mechanisms for the security entity as already defined for the network and facility layer to achieve consistent handling of time and location data throughout the protocol stack. Moreover, no cross layer coordination takes place, i.e., there is no guarantee to have consistent values for time and position on the different layers within a single message. Currently, this is not required by any functionality, but should be taken into regard for future extensions of the system.

Furthermore, the described coupling of time and position is not to be used for RSUs with a fixed location. Strictly following the standards, their time stamp is never updated, as they do not receive a position update. Thus, all their messages receive the same time stamp, which is obviously not the intended system behavior. Moreover, after a short time the security mechanisms of every receiver would discard all messages from such an RSU as being outdated [15]. Hence, a differentiation between mobile nodes and RSUs should be made here, with RSUs always using their current system time to obtain time stamps. As they have a fixed location, there is no need to model a trajectory for them.

5 Conclusions and Future Work

VANETs require a rigid security system to enable their intended usage in safety critical driver assistance systems. Three main design weaknesses of the currently standardized security system within ETSI ITS have been identified. Thereby, the current infeasibility of both encrypted multi-hop communication in general and multi-hop communication for pseudonym certificate updates after vehicle startup have not been identified before. Three main enhancements of current standards are suggested.

At first, the security envelope of messages has to allow signed and encrypted as well as non encrypted (but signed) content within a single message's payload. Thereby, usage of end-to-end encrypted multi-hop communication is enabled.

Secondly, a dedicated pseudonym certificate to send requests for a pseudonym certificate update from a node to its certificate authority should be introduced. This enables usage of multi-hop communication for this important part of the node's start-up process. Moreover, it avoids a significant (D)DOS vulnerability from the pseudonym certificate update mechanism.

Thirdly, a secure and consistent way to obtain both time and position information on the various protocol layers is required. Suggestions for harmonized usage of time and location information are provided. Inclusion of terrestrial time broadcast signals is a promising approach for increased robustness of time synchronization in VANETs against time manipulation attacks. However, future work is required to study this aspect in more detail.

Future work should study advanced secured time synchronization schemes for VANETs, e.g., by enhancing the network time protocol. Moreover, robustness of terrestrial time broadcast against spoofing attacks should be looked at.

References

1. IEEE Standard for Information technology - Telecommunications and information exchange between systems - Local and metropolitan area networks - Specific requirements, Part 11: Wireless LAN Medium Access Control (MAC) and Physical Layer (PHY) Specifications, Amendment 6: Wireless Access in Vehicular Environments, July 2010. Rev. 802.11p-2010
2. IEEE Standard for Wireless Access in Vehicular Environments (WAVE) - Networking Services, December 2010. Rev. P1609.3-2010
3. Memorandum of Understanding for OEMs within the CAR 2 CAR Communication Consortium on Deployment Strategy for cooperative ITS in Europe, June 2011. V 4.0102
4. Intelligent transport systems (its); security; trust and privacy management, June 2012. Rev. 1.1.1
5. IEEE Standard for Wireless Access in Vehicular Environments - Security Services for Applications and Management Messages, April 2013. Rev. P1609.2-2013
6. Intelligent Transport Systems (ITS); Facilities layer function; Facility Position and time management (2013). Rev. 0.0.2
7. Intelligent Transport Systems (ITS); Security; Security header and certificate formats, April 2013. Rev. 1.1.1
8. Digital cellular telecommunications system (Phase 2+); Universal Mobile Telecommunications System (UMTS); LTE; Network Identity and TimeZone (NITZ); Service description; Stage 1 (3GPP TS 22.042 version 12.0.0 Release 12), October 2014
9. Intelligent Transport Systems (ITS); Users and applications requirements; Part2: Applications and facilities layer common data dictionary, September 2014. Rev. 1.2.1
10. Intelligent Transport Systems (ITS); Vehicular Communications; Basic Set of Applications; Part 2: Specification of Cooperative Awareness Basic Service, November 2014. Rev. 1.3.2
11. Intelligent Transport Systems (ITS); Vehicular Communications; GeoNetworking; Part 4: Geographical Addressing and Forwarding for Point-to-Point and Point-to-Multipoint Communications; Sub-part 1: Media-Independent Functionality, July 2014. Rev. 1.2.1

12. Intelligent Transport Systems (ITS); Security; Security header and certificate formats, June 2015. Rev. 1.2.1
13. Bittl, S., Gonzalez, A.A., Myrtus, M., Beckmann, H., Sailer, S., Eissfeller, B.: Emerging Attacks on VANET Security based on GPS Time Spoofing. In: IEEE Ciber and Network Security Conference, September 2015
14. Born, S.: How to manipulate a radio controlled clock via speaker, May 2014. http://bastianborn.de/radio-clock-hack. Accessed March 2016
15. Buburuzan, T., et al.: Draft C2C-CC Standards System Profile. Technical report, CAR 2 CAR Communication Consortium, January 2014. Rev. 1.0.4
16. Campolo, C., Molinaro, A., Scopigno, R. (eds.): Vehicular Ad Hoc Networks - Standards, Solutions, and Research. Springer, Heidelberg (2015)
17. Dardari, D., Falletti, E., Luise, M.: Satellite and Terrestrial Radio Positioning Techniques. Academic Press, Boston (2011)
18. Harding, J., Powell, G.R., Yoon, R., et al.: Vehicle-to-Vehicle Communications: Readiness of V2V Technology for Application. Technical report DOTHS 812 014, Washington, DC: National Highway Traffic Safety Administration, August 2014
19. Khan, S., Mauri, J.L. (eds.): Security for Multihop Wireless Networks, 1st edn. CRC Press, New York (2014)
20. Lombardi, M.A.: NIST Time and Frequency Service, vol. 432. NIST Special Publication, New York (2002)
21. Malhotra, A., Cohen, I., Brakke, E., Goldberg, S.: Attacking the Network Time-Protocol. Technical report, Bosten University (2015)
22. Mao, G., Fidan, B., Anderson, B.D.O.: Wireless sensor network localization techniques. Comput. Netw. **51**(10), 2529–2553 (2007)
23. NIST: WWVB Coverage Area, December 2015. http://www.nist.gov/pml/div688/grp40/vb-coverage.cfm. Accessed March 2016
24. Nowdehi, N., Olovsson, T.: Experiences from implementing the ETSI ITS secured message service. In: IEEE Intelligent Vehicles Symposium, pp. 1055–1060 (2014)
25. Patwari, N., Hero, A.O., Perkins, M., Correal, N.S., O'Dea, R.J.: Relative location estimation in wireless sensor networks. IEEE Trans. Sig. Process. **51**(8), 2137–2148 (2003)
26. Petit, J., Schaub, F., Feiri, M., Kargl, F.: Pseudonym schemes in vehicular networks: a survey. IEEE Commun. Surv. Tutorials **17**(1), 228–255 (2015)
27. Physikalisch-Technische Bundesanstalt (PTB): Dissemination of legal time, August 2011. http://www.ptb.de/cms/en/fachabteilungen/abt4/fb-44/ag-442/dissemination-of-legal-time.html. Accessed March 2016
28. Rasmussen, K.B., Capkun, S., Cagalj, M.: SecNav: secure broadcast localizlocal and time synchronization in wireless networks. In: Proceedings of the 13th Annual ACM International Conference on Mobile Computing and Networking, pp. 310–313, September 2007
29. Röttger, S.: Analysis of the NTP autokey Procedures. Master thesis, Technical University Braunschweig (2012)
30. Schmidt, J., Eckert, K., Schaaf, G., et. al.: Nutzerakzeptanz, IT-Sicherheit, Datenschutz und Schutz der Privatsphäre. Technical report, Sichere Intelligente Mobilität Testfeld Deutschland simTD, June 2013
31. Schütze, T.: Automotive security: cryptography for Car2X communication. In: Embedded World Conference, pp. 1–16, March 2011
32. Scopigno, R., Cozzetti, H.A.: GNSS synchronization in vanets. In: 3rd International Conference on New Technologies, Mobility and Security, pp. 1–5, December 2009
33. Wang, K., Chen, S., Pan, A.: Time and position spoofing with open source projects. In: Black Hat Europe, November 2015

34. Yan, G., Olariu, S., Weigle, M.C.: Providing VANET security through active position detection. Comput. Commun. Mobil. Protoc. ITS/VANET **31**(12), 2883–2897 (2008)
35. Zhang, Z., Trinkle, M., Li, H., Dimitrovski, A.D.: Combating time synchronization attack: a cross layer defense mechanism. In: Proceedings of the ACM/IEEE 4th International Conference on Cyber-Physical Systems, pp. 141–149 (2013)

Modeling of VANET for BSM Safety Messaging at Intersections with Non-homogeneous Node Distribution

Xiaomin Ma[1(✉)], Gregory Butron[1], and Kishor·Trivedi[2]

[1] Deparment of Engineering, Oral Roberts University, Tulsa, OK, USA
{xma, gregory}@oru.edu
[2] Deparment of Electrical and Computer Engineering, Duke University, Durham, NC, USA
kst@ee.duke.edu

Abstract. This paper presents a new analytic model for the performance and reliability of safety-related message broadcast in vehicular ad hoc networks (VANETs) at intersections with non-homogeneous Poisson process (NHPP) for more general road traffic and node distributions. The new analytic model adopts semi-Markov processes (SMP) interacting with M/G/1 queues to characterize the IEEE 802.11p channel behavior of safety message broadcast. Then, the analytic model is applied to derive the MAC-level quality of service (QoS) metrics for safety applications at intersections taking into account impact of hidden terminal problem, *Nakagami* fading with path loss, and concurrent transmissions from different vehicles. The numerical results under various network parameters are cross validated with NS2 simulations. New observations and conclusions are given.

1 Introduction

Vehicular communication systems such as Dedicated Short Range Communication (DSRC) in US and the Conference of Postal and Telecommunications Administrations (CEPT) in Europe have been proposed to support vehicular ad hoc networks (VANETs) for many safety-related applications using one-hop or multi-hop broadcasting to disseminate real-time traffic information or safety-related messages [1, 2]. There are two classes of safety messages that will likely be transmitted for these safety applications: beacon (or basic) safety message (BSM) in US or cooperative awareness message (CAM) in Europe, and event-driven safety message (ESM) in US or decentralized environmental message (DENM) in Europe. We focus on analysis and enhancement of BSM (or CAM) based safety applications in this paper. BSMs, which are periodic ($2 \sim 10$ messages per second), convey state information of the vehicles (*e.g.*, position, speed, direction). These safety applications require highly reliable and timely communications between mobile nodes under adverse environments. According to [3], the worst-case burdens on the vehicular communication channels are likely to occur under the heaviest traffic conditions, when the highest density of vehicles operates in the vicinity of the urban intersections. Several potential BSM based safety applications at

J. Mendizabal et al. (Eds.): Nets4Cars/Nets4Trains/Nets4Aircraft 2016, LNCS 9669, pp. 149–162, 2016.
DOI: 10.1007/978-3-319-38921-9_16

intersections such as cooperative collision avoidance, slow vehicle indication, and rear-end collision avoidance, are likely to be among the most quality of service (QoS) critical applications of vehicular communications [3].

Various relevant QoS metrics and analytic models were proposed to characterize different aspects of safety message broadcast. In [4–7, 10, 12], analytical models were proposed to obtain *PRR* expressions in one-dimensional (1-D) IEEE 802.11 based broadcast VANETs with hidden terminals. Unfortunately, very few of network scenarios in real applications can be abstracted as 1-D models. Recently, performance analysis in a special two-dimensional (2-D) MANET (two parallel lines approximate two opposite roads on highway) [8] as well as intersection with uniform node distribution [9] were conducted. However, the simple assumption of uniform node distributions makes the analytic models fail to characterize realistic traffic situations and uneven node distributions at intersection with traffic lights. To date, there is no analytic model on the performance evaluation (in both MAC and Application level) of IEEE 802.11p broadcast VANETs at intersections with non-homogeneous node distributions. To analyze and examine suitability of the current IEEE 802.11p based VANET for safety applications with stringent QoS requirements under possibly adverse vehicular environments, we propose an analytic model for evaluation of the MAC-level performance and reliability of safety message broadcast VANETs at general 2-D intersections with nonhomogeneous node distributions.

This paper is organized as follows. Section 2 presents an analytic model for evaluating the performance and reliability of IEEE 802.11p based VANET for BSM based safety applications at intersections with nonhomogeneous node distributions. Section 3 verifies the analytic model through extensive simulations and presents some observations acquired from the model. The paper is concluded in Sect. 4.

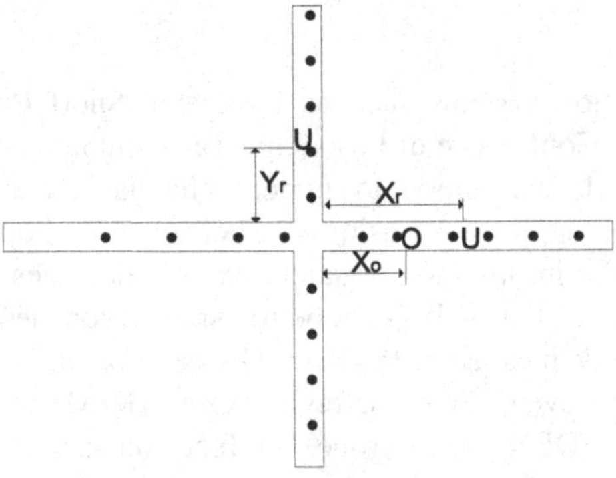

Fig. 1. Abstract of an intersection

2 Assumptions for IEEE 802.11 Broadcast VANET

In the proposed model, we assume that IEEE 802.11 broadcast DCF works under the following scenario.

(1) We consider a VANET with nodes distributed randomly on cross roads at intersections. Assuming width of a road is neglected compared with its length and the common transmission range (300 ~ 1000 meters), it is reasonable to abstract 2-D strip-like multi-lane road to a 1-D single line. Therefore, each intersection can be approximated by two cross lines, as shown in Fig. 1. Nodes in each road are distributed according to a 1-D spatially non-homogeneous Poisson process (NHPP). Assume that $\beta(x)$ is the density of vehicles at a distance x from the center of the intersection as the origin (0, 0) of 2-D coordinate plane, then, the probability of finding i vehicles in a space interval $(x, x + l)$ is given by

$$P[i,(x,x+l)] = \frac{\left(\int_x^{x+l} \beta(y)dy\right)^i e^{-\int_x^{x+l} \beta(y)dy}}{i!} \tag{1}$$

For networks in which transmitters and/or receivers are located or move around randomly at rural or urban intersections where traffic is smooth or uniform over a local area, NHPP is a good approximation to the intersections in the presence of traffic lights and vehicle interaction.

(2) For simplicity of analysis, all nodes are assumed to have the same transmission range, carrier sensing range, and interference range, denoted as R.

(3) At each mobile node, packet arrivals follow a Poisson process with rate λ (in packets per second). In addition to its tractability, the Poisson arrival process is a good approximation of message arrivals of broadcast with deterministic period [12].

(4) Each vehicle has an infinite queue to store the packets at the MAC layer. Hence, each vehicle can be modeled as an M/G/1 queue. The network as a whole is a set of interacting M/G/1 queues.

(5) *Nakagami* fading with distance dependent path loss model is chosen for the impact analysis of vehicular communication channel fading [13].

(6) The intersection under analysis is widely separated from other intersections, so that distance between intersections $D_{in} >> $ node's transmission range (R), which is reasonable because D_{in} is normally bigger than 1 km while $R = 300 \sim 500$ m.

(7) Channel 172 w/o channel switching in DSRC is dedicated to the BSM based safety applications, which is consistent with the new channel deployment option [11]. So, Enhanced Distribution Coordination Function (EDCF) in current IEEE 802.11p is reduced to Distribution Coordination Function (DCF). According to [11], with dual-radio devices in the near future, BSM and other safety messages can be separately transmitted

2.1 Channel Access Performance of IEEE 802.11 Broadcast

Due to the contention medium, the overall channel access can be modeled as a set of interacting M/G/1 queues, one queue for each vehicle. We approach the analysis by adopting a semi-Markov processes (SMP) model developed in [10, 12] for the tagged vehicle that does not directly keep track of the queued requests but captures the channel contention and IEEE 802.11 backoff behavior. This SMP model interacts with the M/G/1 queues of the other vehicles through fixed-point iteration. The reasons that SMP model is adopted to characterize IEEE 802.11 broadcast channel access are: (1) The SMP model can accurately capture the continuous time system behavior beyond the per-slot statistics in the Bianchi's DTMC based models. (2) States for backoff process and states for packet transmissions (collisions) are separated in the SMP model. (3) The transmission probability derived from the SMP model can facilitate precise evaluation of hidden terminal problem influence.

According to the solution to the SMP model [10, 12], the following performance metrics that characterize channel access of IEEE 802.11 broadcast can be derived: (1) π_0: the steady-state probability that the tagged vehicle's backoff counter value is zero. (2) π_{XMT}: the steady-state probability that a node is in the transmission (*XMT*) state. (3) $E[S]$ and $Var[S]$: the mean and variance of service time S for a packet transmission. (4) P_{XMT}: the probability that a neighbor is transmitting in a backoff time slot of the tagged vehicle.

From the tagged vehicle's point of view, p_b is the probability that it senses channel busy during one time slot in the backoff process. Since channel is detected busy if there is at least one neighbor (*i.e.*, a vehicle in the transmission range of the tagged vehicle) transmitting in a backoff time slot of the tagged vehicle on position (x, y), we have

$$p_b(x,y) = 1 - \prod_{i=1}^{\Delta_b} (1 - P_{XMT}(x_i, y_i))^i, \quad |x - x_i|^2 + |y - y_i|^2 \leq R^2 \tag{2}$$

where Δ_b is the average number of vehicles in carrier sensing range of the tagged vehicle covering all lanes at the intersection, which will be derived later in this paper.

2.2 Packet Transmission Delay

As defined in [9], the packet transmission delay is the average delay a packet experiences from the time at which the packet is generated until the time at which the packet is successfully received by all neighbors of the node that generates the packet. The mean transmission delay $E[D]$ includes the queuing delay and medium service time, which can be calculated as [9]:

$$E[D] = E[D_q] + E[S] \tag{3}$$

where

$$E[D_q] = \frac{\lambda Var[S] + \lambda (E[S])^2}{2(1 - \lambda E[S])}$$

Notice that $E[D]$ is a function of p_b and underlying node density that a transmitter senses.

2.3 Packet Reception Probability

Packet reception probability (*PRP*) is defined as the probability that a node within the transmission range of the sender successfully receives a packet from the tagged node (*i.e.*, sender) [9].

Given a transmitting node O placed at coordinates (x_0,0) (see Fig. 2), U is one of the receivers within transmission range R of node O. The position of U is either at (x_r, 0) or at (0, y_r) ($|x_r - x_0| \leq R$, $\left(y_r^2 + x_0^2\right) \leq R^2$). The probability that the node U receives the broadcast message from the tagged node O successfully is denoted as $P_s(x_0, x_r)$ or $P_s(x_0, y_r)$.

There are two factors affecting the performance of packet reception probability: hidden terminal problem and collisions due to concurrent packet transmissions.

Impact of hidden terminals p_b, π_{XMT} can be derived based on the SMP model and its solution in [10, 12]. Note that π_{XMT} for the nodes in hidden terminal areas (denoted as $\pi_{XMT}^{(1)}$) can be calculated assuming all nodes are distributed in a 1-D line.

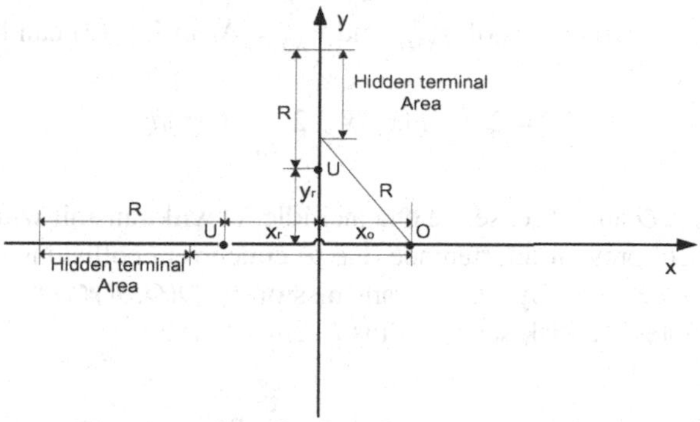

Fig. 2. Impact of hidden terminals at an intersection

In the derivations of $\pi_{XMT}^{(1)}$ and $P_{XMT}^{(1)}$, Δ_b in Eq. (2) is equal to $2R$. It is shown that the time to transmit a packet is *T-DIFS*, where DIFS is IEEE 802.11 DCF Inter-frame Space duration and T is the duration of a packet transmission time plus an idle *DIFS*. Hence, we have the probability that node U's receiving the broadcast message from node O is free from the hidden terminals:

$$P_H(x_o, x_r or\, y_r) = \sum_{i=0}^{\infty} (1 - \pi_{XMT}^{(1)} \frac{2(T - DIFS)}{T})^i \frac{(\Delta)^i}{i!} e^{-\Delta} = e^{-\frac{2(T-DIFS)\pi_{XMT}^{(1)}\Delta}{T}} \quad (4)$$

where Δ is average number of nodes in the hidden terminal area of O's transmission. According to the definition of hidden terminals, the potential hidden terminal area should be area where the nodes are within node U's receiving range but out of O's carrier sensing range on both x-axis and y-axis, as shown in Fig. 2. Thus, denoting $\beta(x)$ and $\beta'(y)$ as vehicle density on x-axis and y-axis, respectively, Δ is expressed as

$$\Delta = \begin{cases} \int_{\min(x_r+R,x_0+R)}^{x_r+R} \beta(x)dx + \int_{\min(x_r-R,x_0-R)}^{x_0-R} \beta(x)dx, \\ \qquad + 2\int_{\sqrt{R^2-x_0^2}}^{\max(\sqrt{R^2-x_0^2},\sqrt{R^2-x_r^2})} \beta'(y)dy, \text{ If } U \text{ in } (x_r,0) \\ \int_{\sqrt{R^2-x_0^2}}^{\max(R+y_r,\sqrt{R^2-x_0^2})} \beta'(y)dy + \int_{\sqrt{R^2-x_0^2}}^{\max(R-y_r,\sqrt{R^2-x_0^2})} \beta'(y)dy \\ \qquad + \int_{\max(x_0-R,-\sqrt{R^2+y_r^2})}^{\max(x_0-R,-\sqrt{R^2+y_r^2})} \beta(x)dx, \text{ If } U \text{ in } (0,y_r) \end{cases}$$

Impact of concurrent collisions. When the tagged node transmits in a slot time, concurrent collisions will take place if any node in the interference range of the tagged node transmits in the same slot. π_0 and P_{XMT} of the transmitting node and concurrently transmitting nodes are the same for all vehicles approaching to the intersection (denoted as $\pi_{XMT}^{(2)}$ and $P_{XMT}^{(2)}$), which can be derived from the solution to the SMP model [10] via setting the tagged node in the center of the intersection. (This approximation is based on the assumption that the transmission range and carrier sensing range are long enough so that all associated nodes closing the intersection can sense each other very well). Therefore, the derivations of $\pi_{XMT}^{(2)}$ and $P_{XMT}^{(2)}$, Δ_b in Eq. (2) can be evaluated as

$$\Delta_b = 2\int_0^R \beta(x)dx + 2\int_0^R \beta'(y)dy$$

Given that both O and U sense the channel idle, O will transmit within the duration of a slot. In order to prevent interference due to concurrent collisions to U's receiving the broadcast message sent by O, no transmission in $D(O, R) \cap D(U, R)$ is allowed, where $D(s, l)$ denotes the disk set of radius l centered at s.

Case 1: U in $(x_r, 0)$

(i) The average number of nodes transmitting in the concurrent slot in area between O and U is

$$\bar{n}_1 = \pi_0^{(2)} \int_{\min(x_r,x_o)}^{\max(x_r,x_o)} \beta(x)dx$$

(ii) Suppose node V is at $(x', 0)$, where $\max(x_r, x_o) - R < x' < \min(x_r, x_o)$, and $\max(x_r, x_o) < x' < \min(x_r, x_o) + R$. The probability that the node V starts transmitting during the slot is the probability that node V intends to transmit and all nodes in $A_c = D(V,R) - D(O,R) - D(U,R)$ are not in transmitting state, which is expressed as

If $\max(x_r, x_o) - R < x' < \min(x_r, x_o)$

$$P'_s(x', x_o, x_r) = \pi_0^{(2)} \sum_{i=0}^{\infty} (1 - P_{XMT}^{(1)})^i \frac{(\Delta_1)^i}{i!} e^{-\Delta_1} = \pi_0^{(2)} e^{-\Delta_1 P_{XMT}^{(1)}}$$

where

$$\Delta_1 = \int_{x'-R}^{\min(x_r, x_0)-R} \beta(x)dx$$

If $\max(x_r, x_o) < x' < \min(x_r, x_o) + R$

$$P_s''(x', x_o, x_r) = \pi_0^{(2)} \sum_{i=0}^{\infty} (1 - P_{XMT}^{(1)})^i \frac{(\Delta_2)^i}{i!} e^{-\Delta_2} = \pi_0^{(2)} e^{-\Delta_2 P_{XMT}}$$

where

$$\Delta_2 = \int_{\max(x_r, x_0)+R}^{x'+R} \beta(x)dx$$

Then, the average number of nodes that start transmission during the slot that collides with the transmission from O is

$$\bar{n}_2 = \int_{\max(x_r, x_o)-R}^{\min(x_r, x_o)} \beta(x) P_s'(x, x_o, x_r)dx + \int_{\max(x_r, x_o)}^{\min(x_r, x_o)+R} \beta(x) P_s''(x, x_o, x_r)dx$$

Suppose node W is at $(0, y')$, where $0 < y' < \min\left(\left(R^2 - x_r^2\right)^{1/2}, \left(R^2 - x_o^2\right)^{1/2}\right)$, and $-\min\left(\left(R^2 - x_r^2\right)^{1/2}, \left(R^2 - x_o^2\right)^{1/2}\right) < y' < 0$. The probability that the node W starts transmitting during the slot is the probability that node W intends to transmit and all nodes in $A_c = D(W,R) - D(O,R) - D(U,R)$ are not in transmitting state, which is expressed as

$$P_s'(y', x_o, x_r) = \pi_0^{(2)} \sum_{i=0}^{\infty} (1 - P_{XMT}^{(1)})^i \frac{(\Delta_3)^i}{i!} e^{-\Delta_3} = \pi_0^{(2)} e^{-P_{XMT}^{(1)} \Delta_3}$$

where

$$\Delta_3 = \int_{\max\left(\sqrt{R^2-x_0^2}, \sqrt{R^2-x_r^2}\right)}^{\max\left(R+y', \sqrt{R^2-x_0^2}, \sqrt{R^2-x_r^2}\right)} \beta'(y)dy + \int_{\max\left(\sqrt{R^2-x_0^2}, \sqrt{R^2-x_r^2}\right)}^{\max\left(R-y', \sqrt{R^2-x_0^2}, \sqrt{R^2-x_r^2}\right)} \beta'(y)dy$$

Then, the average number of nodes that start transmission during the slot that collides with the transmission from O is

$$\bar{n}_3 = 2 \int_0^{\min\left(\sqrt{R^2-x_0^2}, \sqrt{R^2-x_r^2}\right)} P_s'(y, x_0, x_r) \beta'(y)dy$$

Then, the total average number of nodes that may transmit concurrently is

$$\bar{n}_{\Sigma 1} = \bar{n}_1 + \bar{n}_2 + \bar{n}_3$$

Therefore, given a Poisson node distribution, the probability that no nodes within the reception range of U start transmission during the slot that collides with the transmission from O is

$$P_{con}(x_o, x_r) = q_b \frac{(\bar{n}_{\Sigma 1})^0}{0!} \exp(-\bar{n}_{\Sigma 1}) + 1 - q_b = q_b \exp(-\bar{n}_{\Sigma 1}) + 1 - q_b \quad (5)$$

where q_b is the probability that the channel is sensed busy in *DIFS* time by the tagged node, which can be derived in [12].

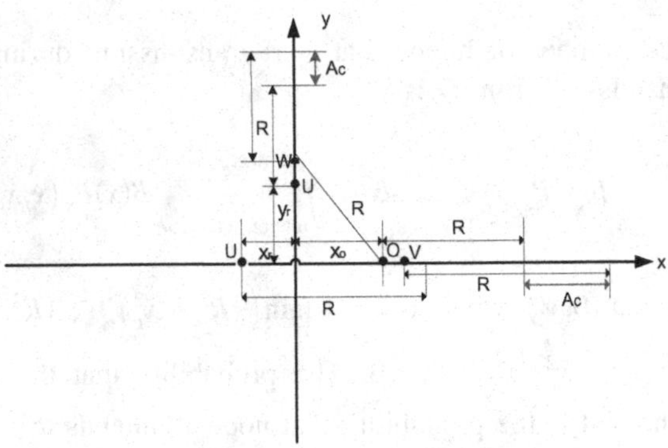

Fig. 3. Impact of concurrent collisions at intersection

Case 2: U in $(0, y_r)$

(i) Suppose node V is at $(x', 0)$, where $\max\left(-(R^2 - y_r^2)^{1/2}, x_o - R\right) < x' < \min\left((R^2 - y_r^2)^{1/2}, x_o + R\right)$. The probability that the node V starts transmitting during the slot is the probability that the node V intends to transmit and all nodes in $A_c = D(V,R) - D(O,R) - D(U,R)$ are not in the transmitting state (See A_c in Fig. 3), which is expressed as:

$$P'_s(x', x_o, y_r) = \pi_0^{(2)} \sum_{i=0}^{\infty} (1 - P_{XMT}^{(1)})^i \frac{(\Delta_4)^i}{i!} e^{-\Delta_4} = \pi_0^{(2)} e^{-P_{XMT}^{(1)} \Delta_4}$$

where

$$\Delta_4 = \int_{x'-R}^{\min\left(\max(R-x_r,\sqrt{R^2-y_r^2}),R-x'\right)} \beta(x)dx + \int_{x'+R}^{\max(R+x_r,R+x')} \beta(x)dx + \int_{\min\left(\min(-\sqrt{R^2-x_o^2},-R+y_r),-\sqrt{R^2-x'^2}\right)}^{-\sqrt{R^2-x'^2}} \beta(x)dx$$

Then, the average number of nodes that start transmission during the slot that collides with the transmission from O is

$$\bar{n}_1 = \int_{\max\left(-\sqrt{R^2-y_r^2},x_o-R\right)}^{\min\left(\sqrt{R^2-y_r^2},x_o+R\right)} \beta(x')P_s(x',x_o,y_r)dx'$$

(ii) Suspose node W is at $(0,y')$, where $\max\left(y_r-R,-\left(R^2-x_o^2\right)^{1/2}\right)<y' <\min\left(y_r+R,\ \left(R^2-x_o^2\right)^{1/2}\right)$. The probability that the node W starts transmitting during the slot is the probability that node W intends to transmit and all nodes in $A_c = D(W,R) - D(O,R) - D(U,R)$ are not in the transmitting state, which is expressed as

$$P_s'(y',x_o,y_r) = \pi_0^{(2)} \sum_{i=0}^{\infty} (1-P_{XMT}^{(1)})^i \frac{(\Delta_5)^i}{i!} e^{-\beta\Delta_5} = \pi_0^{(2)} e^{-P_{XMT}^{(1)}\Delta_5}$$

where

$$\Delta_5 = \int_{\max\left(y_r+R,\sqrt{R^2-x_o^2}\right)}^{\max\left(y'+R,\max(y_r+R,\sqrt{R^2-x_o^2})\right)} \beta'(y)dy + \int_{\min\left(y_r-R,-\sqrt{R^2-x_o^2}\right)}^{\min\left(y'-R,\min(y_r-R,-\sqrt{R^2-x_o^2})\right)} \beta'(y)dy + \int_{-\sqrt{R^2-y'^2}}^{\max\left(-\sqrt{R^2-y'^2},-\sqrt{R^2-y_r^2},x_o-R\right)} \beta'(y)dy$$

Then, the average number of nodes that start transmission during the slot that collides with the transmission from O is

$$\bar{n}_2 = \int_{\max\left(y_r-R,-\sqrt{R^2-x_0^2}\right)}^{\min\left(y_r+R,\sqrt{R^2-x_0^2}\right)} \beta'(y')P_s(y',x_o,y_r)dy'$$

Then, the total average number of nodes that may transmit concurrently is

$$\bar{n}_{\Sigma 2} = \bar{n}_1 + \bar{n}_2$$

Therefore, given Poisson node distribution, the probability that no nodes within the reception range of U start transmission during the slot that collides with the transmission from O is

$$\begin{aligned} P_{con}(x_o, y_r) &= q_b \frac{(\bar{n}_{\Sigma 2})^0}{0!} \exp(-\bar{n}_{\Sigma 2}) + 1 - q_b \\ &= q_b \exp(-\bar{n}_{\Sigma 2}) + 1 - q_b \end{aligned} \tag{6}$$

Impact of fading with path loss. VANET environments present scenarios with unfavorable characteristics to develop wireless communications. The *Nakagami* distribution is believed to fit the amplitude envelope of signal transmitting on DSRC channel well [13]. We obtain the probability of successfully receiving a message at distance r_0 [14]:

$$P_{cf}(r_0) = 1 - \frac{m^m}{\Gamma(m)} \int_0^{(r_0/R)^\gamma} z^{m-1} e^{-mz} dz \tag{7}$$

where $r_0 = |x_r - x_0|$ or $\left|x_0^2 + y_r^2\right|^{1/2}$, m is the fading parameter, and $\Gamma(x) = \int_0^\infty t^{x-1} e^{-t} dt$ is the standard *Gamma* function. γ is the path loss exponent, which is usually empirically determined by field measurements. Normally, γ can be 2 for free space environment, 1.6 ~ 1.8 for line of sight, and 2.7 ~ 5 for a shadowed urban area [13].

Packet Reception Probability. Taking hidden terminal, possible packet collisions, and channel fading into account, and assuming the three probabilities are independent of each other, the *PRP* that the node U receives the broadcast message from the tagged node O is

$$P_s(x_o, x_r\, or\, y_r) = P_H(x_o, x_r\, or\, y_r) P_{con}(x_o, x_r\, or\, y_r) P_{cf}(r_o) \tag{8}$$

2.4 Packet Reception Ratio (PRR)

Packet Reception Ratio (*PRR*) is defined as the percentage of nodes that successfully receive a packet from the tagged node among the receivers that are within the transmission range of the sender at the moment that the packet is sent out.

Since safety applications at intersections are more concerned about *PRR*s over a certain range from the center of intersection, here we focus on *PRR* evaluation over range from $(x_0, 0) = (0, 0)$ to $(x, 0)$ and from (0, 0) to (0, y) (where $|x - x_0| \le R$, and $\left|x_0^2 + y^2\right| \le R^2$). Given the reception probability of each node in Eq. (8), the average number of nodes in dx (or dy) that successfully receive the broadcast message from the tagged node is $P_s(x_o, x)\beta(x)dx$ or $P_s(x_o, y)\beta(y)dy$. For a coverage distance with range x *or* y from the center of the intersection, *PRR* over a coverage range of node O can be found by integrating the probabilities that nodes with distance x or y to the center of the intersection within an incremental range successfully receives the broadcast message from O. Therefore,

$$PRR(x_0, x) = \frac{\int_0^x \beta(x_r) P_s(x_o, x_r) dx_r}{\int_0^x \beta(x_r) dx_r}, \ d(x, x_o) \leq R \tag{9}$$

and

$$PRR(x_0, y) = \frac{\int_0^y \beta'(y_r) P_s(x_o, y_r) dy_r}{\int_0^y \beta'(y_r) dy_r}, \ \sqrt{y^2 + x_0^2} \leq R \tag{10}$$

3 Model Validation and Discussion

In this section, we apply the proposed model to a DSRC communication system for safety message disseminations [1]. In order to validate the proposed analytic model, we extend NS2 simulation program in [9] to 2-D intersection simulations with non-homogeneous node distribution. The communication nodes are Poisson distributed with piecewise constant densities on an intersection with length of 1000 m on each of the crossing roads. The density distributions as function of distances (x or y) to the center of intersection are given by

$$\beta(x) = \begin{cases} 3\beta_{av}/2, & x \leq 50\,\text{m} \\ \beta_{av}/2, & 50m < x \leq 100\,\text{m} \\ \beta_{av}, & x > 100\,\text{m} \end{cases} \quad \beta'(y) = \begin{cases} \beta_{av}/2, & y \leq 50\,\text{m} \\ 3\beta_{av}/2, & 50m < y \leq 100\,\text{m} \\ \beta_{av}, & x > 100\,\text{m} \end{cases}$$

where β_{av} is a constant average road density at intersection during a certain time period. These piecewise constant densities approximate non-uniform vehicle distributions at the urban intersections with traffic lights ($\beta(x)$ for road with red light; $\beta'(y)$ for road with green light). Each node is equipped with IEEE 802.11p based wireless ad hoc network capability with same communication parameters in [9]. DSRC channel 172 is dedicated to three BSM based safety applications. Communication range (transmission/carrier sensing) is R = 500 m. Each node generates periodic broadcast message with rate λ and uniformly distributed message length with mean $E[PA]$ = 200 bytes. Our simulation duration is 10 s and simulation resolution is 1 μs.

Figures 4 and 5 depicts the mean transmission delay and the packet reception ratios for transmissions from (0, 0) to (500, 0) (*i.e.*, *PRR*(0, 500)), respectively, over the average density of nodes (β_{av}) in transmission range of a transmitting (or tagged) node on the center of the intersection. Failure of message delivery is only caused by collisions of messages from concurrent transmissions. As shown in Figs. 4 and 5, analytical results practically coincide with the simulation results (with 95 % confidence interval (CI)), which helps build the proposed intersection model and validation of the approximations (Eq. (4) and (8)) and assumptions (Assumption 2, 3, and 6) made in the analytic model. In addition, we also compare execution time to solve the analytical model with that to run the NS2 simulation code for Figs. 4 and 5. It is measured that the simulation running in a workstation (Dell OptiPlex 790, 3.1 GHz) takes about 45 min to derive 10 points (R_d = 24 Mbps, λ = 10 packets/s) in

Figures 4 and 5, while the analytic model programmed in Matlab for same curve with higher resolution (200 points) can be solved within 3 min.

We also observe from Figs. 4 and 5 that with the same density and communication parameters, the mean transmission delay at the intersection is higher than that in 1-D highway (*e.g.*, for β_{av} = 0.2 vehicles/m, R_d = 24 Mbps, $E[D]_{1\text{-D}}$ = 0.28 ms, $E[D]_{\text{intersection}}$ = 0.4 ms) and *PRR*s at the intersection is lower than that in 1-D highway (*e.g.*, for β_{av} = 0.2 vehicles/m, R_d = 24 Mbps, $PRR_{1\text{-D}}$ = 0.88, $PRR_{\text{intersection}}$ = 0.83). The explanation for the observation is that the number of nodes within carrier sensing/transmission range at the intersection is higher than that in 1-D highway with the same density of nodes on the road.

Figure 6 demonstrates packet reception ratios (PRRs) of vehicles at an intersection with different distances to the intersection center given that a message is sent out at the center of the intersection. The communication environment and network parameters are same as that in [9] plus *Nakagami* channel fading with distance dependent path loss (γ = 2, fading parameter m is 3 for r < 50 m, 1.5 for 50 m ≤ r< 150 m, and 1 for r > 150 m) is considered in the analysis as well as in the simulation. It is seen from Fig. 6 that analytical results practically agree with the simulation results (with 95 % CI). The minor differences between the theoretical distance PRRs and the simulation counterparts may be caused from the approximations in the model. It is intuitively seen that higher average density and longer distance of the nodes to the source nodes degrade PRRs. It is interesting to observe that PRRs are going down nonlinearly with the distance (more rapidly as the distance is bigger than 150 m due to impact of the heavier fading). PRRs are dependent more on average density of the vehicles than on distribution of the nodes at the intersection.

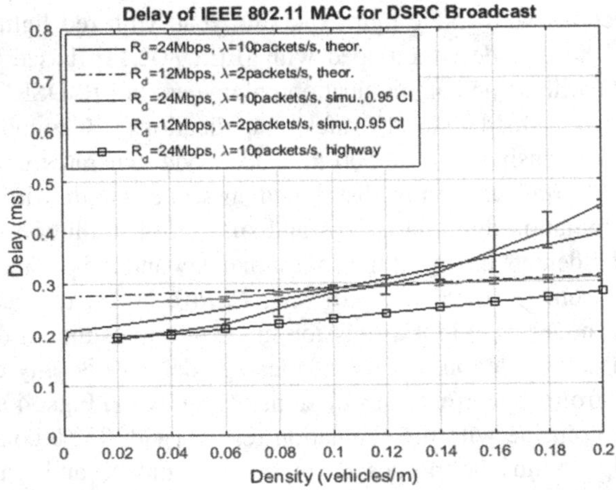

Fig. 4. Mean transmission delay of DSRC broadcast with parameters R = 500 m, W_0 = 15, $E[PA]$ = 200 bytes (Color figure online)

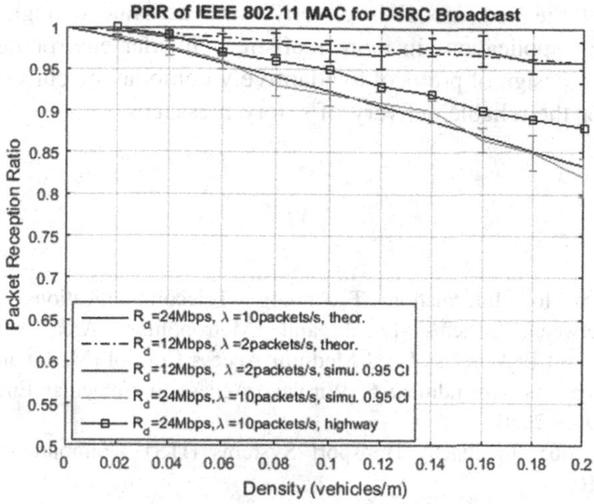

Fig. 5. Packet reception ratio *PRR* (0, 500) of DSRC broadcast with network parameters $R = 500$ m, $W_0 = 15$, $E[PA] = 200$ bytes (Color figure online)

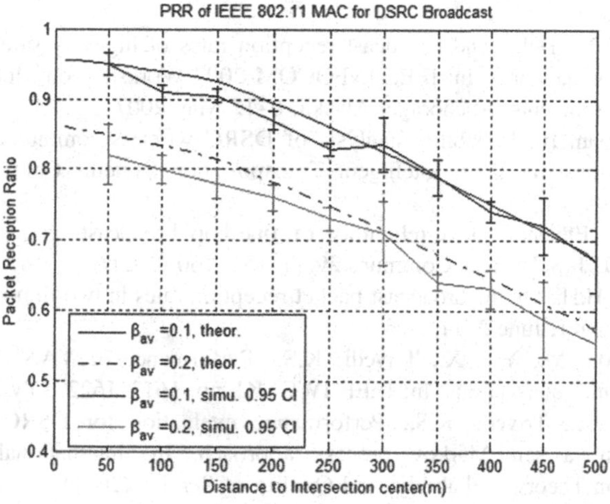

Fig. 6. Packet reception ratios of vehicles as function of distance to the center of intersection with different average densities and network parameters $E[PA] = 200$ bytes, $\lambda = 10$ packets/s, $R_d = 24$ Mbps, $R = 500$ m, $W_0 = 15$ (Color figure online)

4 Conclusions

In this paper, we evaluate the performance and reliability of IEEE 802.11p based broadcast 2-D VANETs at intersections with non-homogeneous node distribution for safety message dissemination. The performance metrics are derived from the analytic models. The analytic model in [9] is a special case of the model proposed in this paper.

We conclude that the new model is effective and accurate enough to characterize VANET for safety applications in more realistic vehicular environments. The future work would be the design of protocol to adaptively combine the current IEEE 802.11p based VANET for the reliable delivery of safety messages.

References

1. IEEE Standard for Information Technology–Telecommunications and Information Exchange Between Systems—Local and Metropolitan Area Networks—Specific Requirements; Part II: Wireless LAN Medium Access Control (MAC) and Physical Layer (PHY) Specifications, Amendment 6: Wireless Access in Vehicular Environments, IEEE Std. 802.11p, July 2010
2. ETSI EN 302 665, Intelligent Transport Systems (ITS), Communication Architecture, September 2010
3. Shladover, S.E.: Effects of traffic density on communication requirements for cooperative intersection collision avoidance system. Technical report UCB-ITS-PWP-2005-1, Institute of Transportation Studies, University of California, Berkeley, March 2005
4. Ma, X., Yin, X., Trivedi, K.S.: On the reliability of safety applications in VANETs. Int. J. Perform. Eng. Spec. Issue Depend. Wirel. Syst. Netw. **8**(2), 115–130 (2012). (Invited Paper)
5. Ma, X., Chen, X.: Delay and broadcast reception rates of highway safety applications in vehicular ad hoc networks. In: IEEE INFOCOM 2007 Workshop on Mobile Networks for Vehicular Environments, Anchorage, Alaska, 6–12 May 2007
6. Bai, F., Krishnan, H.: Reliability analysis of DSRC wireless communication for vehicle safety applications. In: IEEE Intelligent Transportation Systems Conference, September 2006
7. Ye, F., et al.: Efficiency and reliability of one-hop broadcasting in vehicular ad hoc networks. IEEE J. Sel. Areas Commun. **29**(1), 151–160 (2011)
8. Ma, X., Refai, H.H.: On the broadcast packet reception rates in two-dimensional MANETs. In: IEEE ICC 2011, June 2011
9. Ma, X., Wilson, M., Yin, X., Trivedi, K.S.: Performance of VANET safety message broadcast at rural intersections. In: IEEE IWCMC, pp. 1617–1622, July 2013
10. Yin, X., Ma, X., Trivedi, K.S.: Performance evaluation for DSRC vehicular safety communication: a semi-Markov process approach. In: International Conference on Communication Theory, Reliability, and Quality of Service (2011)
11. Campolo, C., Molinaro, A.: Multichannel communication in vehicular ad hoc networks: a survey. IEEE Commun. Mag. **51**, 158–169 (2013)
12. Yin, X., Ma, X., Trivedi, K.S.: An interacting stochastic models approach for the performance evaluation of DSRC vehicular safety communication. IEEE Trans. Comput. **62**(5), 873–885 (2013)
13. Killat, M., Hartenstein, H.: An empirical model for probability of packet reception in vehicular ad hoc networks. EURASIP J. Wirel. Commun. Netw. **2009**, 721301 (2009)
14. Yin, X., Ma, X., Trivedi, K.S.: Channel fading impact on multi-hop DSRC safety communication. In: 16th ACM International Conference on Modeling, Analysis and Simulation of Wireless and Mobile Systems (MSWiM 2013), Barcelona, Spain, November 2013

EPC C1G2 Compliant Batteryless Tire Pressure Monitoring Tag with Pressure and Tire Contact Temperature

Andoni Beriain[1(✉)], Eduardo d'Entremont[2], J. Gonzalez de Chavarri[2], Ibon Zalbide[2], and Roc Berenguer[2]

[1] CEIT and TECNUN, University of Navarra, Donostia - San Sebastián, Spain
aberiain@ceit.es

[2] FARSENS S.L., Donostia - San Sebastián, Spain
http://www.ceit.es, http://www.farsens.com

Abstract. An EPC Class-1 Generation-2 (C1G2) RFID tag based on Farsens' batteryless sensor technology is proposed to build a Tire Pressure Monitoring System (TPMS). Built in a compact printed circuit board format and encapsulated in a cushion gum housing, the tag includes a MS5803-14BA pressure and ambient temperature sensor from Measurements Specialties with an absolute pressure range from 0 bar to 30 bar and ambient temperature range from −40 °C to 85 °C. Additionally, the tag includes a thermistor in the tire contact side for contact temperature monitoring. These RFID sensor tags are compatible with commercial UHF RFID readers (EPC C1G2). The proposed set-up has been successfully installed and tested in cars. With a 2W ERP setup the battery-less temperature and pressure sensor can communicate to over one meter and a half.

Keywords: TPMS · RFID · Tire monitoring

1 Introduction

Tire Pressure Monitoring Systems (TPMS), is an electronic system in charge of the monitoring of the wheels air pressure, providing a real-time information to the driver. This information is very useful in terms of security, but also to reduce gas consumption, and thus reduce air pollution. Besides the intrinsic interest of this system concerning security and environment, it is gradually being mandatory by legislation in many countries, what makes an expected base of vehicles with TPMS in Europe to grow to 36.7 million by 2018. Taking into account 4 devices per vehicle, it turns out in 144 million TPMS units [1].

TPMS are small Printed Circuit Boards (PCB) with small integrated circuits and a small Lithium battery (ER1860), based on the chemical component Li-SOCl2, which are allocated inside the tires. They are designed for a life cycle between 7 and 10 years. In this environment, where high centrifugal forces are experimented and high vibrations suffered, the batteries are usually directly

J. Mendizabal et al. (Eds.): Nets4Cars/Nets4Trains/Nets4Aircraft 2016, LNCS 9669, pp. 163–172, 2016.
DOI: 10.1007/978-3-319-38921-9_17

soldered to the circuit board in order to avoid unfixing. Due to the high volatility of Lithium Ion, the extraction and treatment of the batteries should be done by a specialist. This implies that an in situ replacement of the batteries is not feasible and, instead, all the electronics included in the wheel should be replaced, with the subsequent inherent cost. What is really happening is that, at the end of the life cycle of the wheel or of the vehicle, all those batteries are stored in car cemeteries. The later scrapping of the vehicles and the storing conditions finally drives into an absorption of heavy metals from batteries to the ground [2].

The use of passive sensors instead of the current active solutions would reduce the usage of those 144 million batteries in TPMS systems, with the consequent relief for the environment.

The importance of this objective is not only environmental, but also economical. In terms of cost (and so in price and benefits) the battery costs gets around one third of the total cost of the electronics of the TPMS system.

In this work a EPC Class-1 Generation-2 (C1G2) RFID tag based on Farsens' batteryless sensor technology is proposed. The objective is to develop a RFID passive sensor with small electronic and flexible antenna to be able to embed it into a flat tire patch.

The work is structured as follows. In Sect. 1 the project is introduced. Section 2 presents the tag block diagram and its operation. Section 3 is devoted to the sensor implementation in the tire and the antenna design. In Sect. 4 the measurements results are presented. Last, in Sect. 5 the conclusions and future work are presented.

2 Sensor Tag

2.1 Block Diagram

The proposed sensor tag block diagram is presented in Fig. 1. It consists of a ANDY100 IC for energy harvesting and wireless communication, a start-up circuitry based on a voltage monitor and a voltage regulator, a micro-controller for interface conversion, a NCP18XH103F03RB thermistor and a MS5803-14BA pressure and ambient temperature sensor.

The ANDY100 IC [3] includes a RF frontend for UHF RFID power harvesting and communication, a power supply module to generate the required voltage levels, a EPC C1G2/ISO18000-6C digital processor including a trimmed clock oscillator, a non volatile memory and a SPI master module. The SPI master module can be controlled via EPC C1G2 standard memory access commands.

In order to isolate the supply of the RFID tag from the supply of the rest of the system, the diode D1 is included. The capacitor C1 acts as an energy storage unit to support current peaks of the system during active operation, such as initialization and measurement.

A voltage monitor is included to connect the sensor system only after the energy storage capacitor has been charged. The voltage monitor connects the sensor system when the voltage in the capacitor is over 2.4 V and disconnects

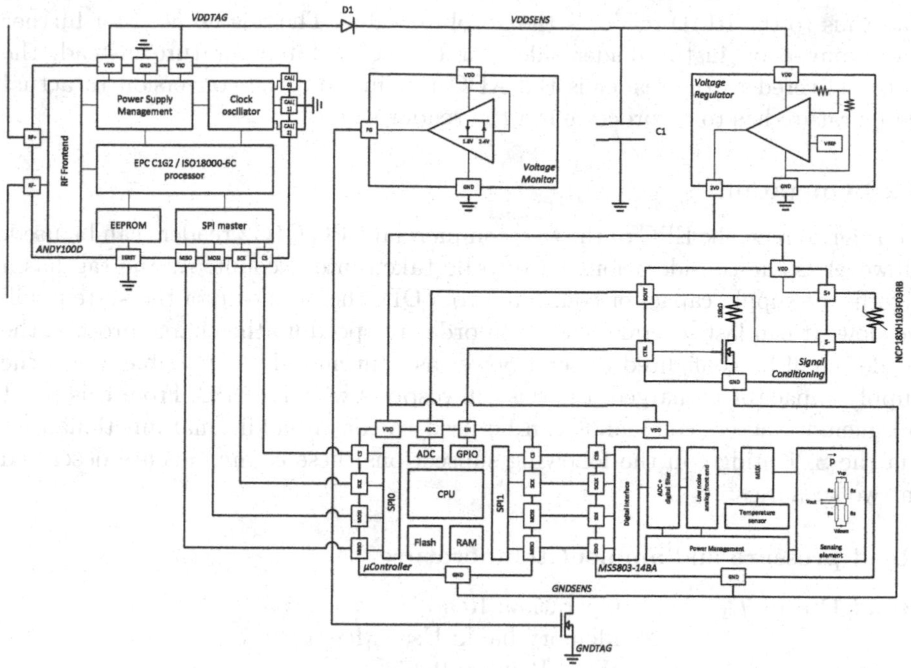

Fig. 1. RFID sensor block diagram.

the sensor system when the voltage falls below 1.8 V. This architecture avoids oscillation of the system during initialization.

The sensor included in this tag is the MS5803-14BA, which contains all the subsystems required to capture pressure and temperature data. The pressure sensing element is based on leading MEMS technology. The outputs of both sensors are multiplexed to the programmable gain amplifier, and the data is digitized with the integrated ADC. The digital interface delivers both, temperature and pressure data, through the SPI interface to the interface conversion micro-controller.

Additionally, this tag includes a NCP18XH103F03RB thermistor for tire contact temperature monitoring. A signal conditioning circuitry allows the thermistor to be powered just during measurement acquisition in order to save power the rest of the time.

The low power micro-controller included int the sensor is an ARM Cortex-M3. Every time a new measurement is triggered, the microcontroller gets digital data from the MS5803-14BA sensor and controls the signal conditioning of the thermistor to get an ADC reading. For the pressure and ambient temperature data, all the calibration parameters are read during start-up, and every time a new measurement is performed, the raw temperature and pressure values are converted to actual physical magnitudes. The temperature compensation of the pressure is also done in this step. This way, the data delivered to the ANDY100, and thus to the RFID reader is the absolute value. There is no need for further data conversion in the reader side. For the contact temperature instead, the data delivered to the reader is the ADC reading and the conversion to actual temperature has to be processed in the reader side.

2.2 Operation

In order to read the EPC of the tag, commercial EPC C1G2 readers can be used. However, some considerations have to be taken into account. As the tag has a significant supply capacitor connected to VDD, the power-up of the system will be slow. It can last several seconds. In order to speed up the charge process, the reader shall be configured to send power as continuously as possible. Once the supply capacitor is charged, the tag will respond with its EPC. From this point on, memory access commands can be used to control additional functionalities via the SPI bridge. In the following subsections these commands are described in two scenarios:

Read pressure and ambient temperature

Read P and T_A Operation: Read
Memory bank: User Memory
Word Pointer: 0x05
Word Count: 6

The answer from the tag to such a request will contain 12 bytes of data. The EPC word size is 16 bits and the SPI word size is 8 bits. The answer received from the SPI interface is right aligned in the EPC words. Assuming that the reader returns the received data in the buffer of bytes *rawdata*, the content of the answer is defined as shown in Fig. 2, where:

- synch: synchronization byte. Default value 0x10.
- P[H:L]: (uint16) absolute pressure value. Resolution of 1 mbar per LSB.
- T[H:L]: (int16) temperature value. Resolution of 0.01 °C per LSB.
- dummy: dummy byte. Default value 0x00.

rawdata	Byte 0	Byte 1	Byte 2	Byte 3	Byte 4	Byte 5	Byte 6	Byte 7	Byte 8	Byte 9	Byte 10	Byte 11
content	0x00	synch 0x10	0x00	P_H	0x00	P_L	0x00	T_H	0x00	T_L	0x00	dummy 0x00

Fig. 2. Pressure and ambient temperature measuring data.

Due to timing issues between the micro-controller and the ANDY100 SPI, sometimes all the data stream is shifted 1 or 2 bits to the right. In order to fix this, the *synch* byte is included. Before extracting the measured values, the synchronization byte has to be found. The following example code shows a simple way to find the *synch* byte and extract sensor data.

```
// Find sync 0x10
while (!(rawdata[1] & 0x10))
{
// Shift one bit to the left
for (int i = 0; i < 12; i++)
{
rawdata[i] = (byte)(((byte)rawdata[i] << 1) |
 (byte)(rawdata[i + 1] >> 7));
}
}
// Extract sensor data
uint16 pressure = (uint16)((data[3] << 8) | data[5]);
int16 ambient_temperature = ((data[7] << 8) | data[9]);

// Set correct scale
double pressure_bar = pressure/1000.0;
double ambient_temperature_C = ambient_temperature/100.0;
```

Read pressure and contact temperature

Read P and T_C   Operation: Read
Memory bank: User Memory
Word Pointer: 0x0F
Word Count: 6

The answer from the tag to such a request will contain 12 bytes of data. The EPC word size is 16 bits and the SPI word size is 8 bits. The answer received from the SPI interface is right aligned in the EPC words. Assuming that the reader returns the received data in the buffer of bytes *rawdata*, the content of the answer is defined as shown in Fig. 3, where:

- synch: synchronization byte. Default value 0x10.
- P[H:L]: (uint16) absolute pressure value. Resolution of 1mbar per LSB.
- T[H:L]: (int16) ADC reading.
- dummy: dummy byte. Default value 0x00.

Same timing issues must be considered in this reading mode.

rawdata	Byte 0	Byte 1	Byte 2	Byte 3	Byte 4	Byte 5	Byte 6	Byte 7	Byte 8	Byte 9	Byte 10	Byte 11
content	0x00	synch 0x10	0x00	P_H	0x00	P_L	0x00	T_H	0x00	T_L	0x00	dummy 0x00

Fig. 3. Pressure and contact temperature measuring data.

3 Implementation

In order to be able to introduce the sensor tag into the wheel the traditional Farsens' sensor presentation method, with a rigid antenna, has been substituted by a flexible wire antenna (Fig. 4).

3.1 Casing

Cushion gum is, very flexible, easy to mechanize, extremely sticky with other strips of cushion gum and cheap material. Therefore it was selected to make the sensor casing, embedding the sensor electronics between two strips of cushion gum. The resultant casing is presented in Fig. 5. The yellow surface is only a protective strip. Removing the yellow strip a black sticky material can be found which is the gum, easily attachable to the tire.

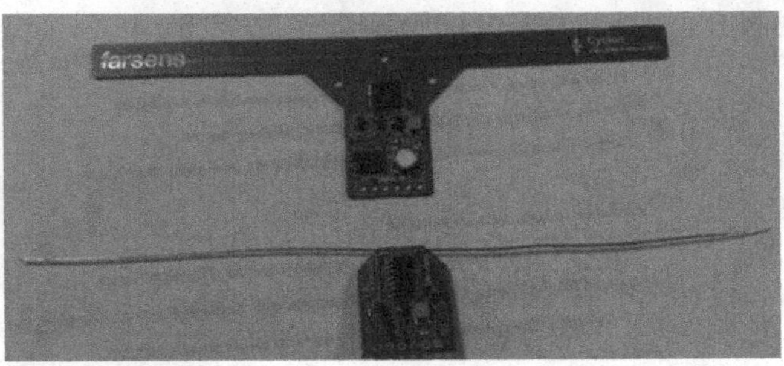

Fig. 4. Farsens' traditional pressure sensor with rigid antenna and modified version.

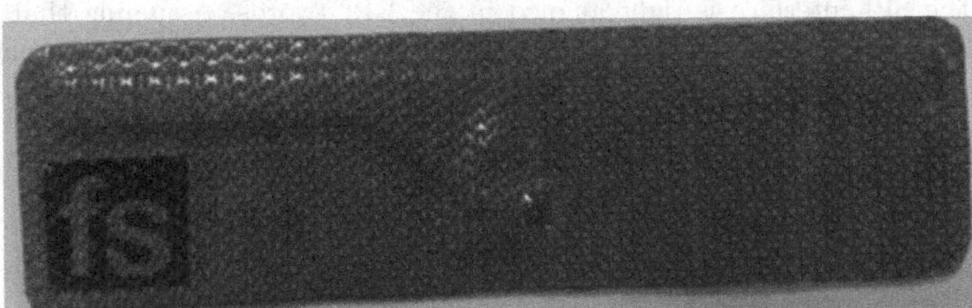

Fig. 5. Sensor casing.

3.2 Antenna Design and Matching

The designed antenna is a pure landa-half dipole designed for open air environment. In order to cover both RFID UHF frequencies (868 MHz and 915 MHz) with a unique length the antenna has been designed for 890 MHz. Each antenna arm has 8 cm length of a solid state wire (REF NTE electronics: WHS24-00-100).

Several tests were done to match the antenna and IC according to the surrounding material using a matching network. A nude PCB with the antenna was embedded into the cushion gum stuck to the tire. A little UFL wire soldered to the matching network (Fig. 6) made possible the antenna impedance measurements.

Fig. 6. UFL wire in soldered to matching network.

A iterative method using a VNA to match the antenna to FARSENSs tag was used. For each iteration it was required to take off the prototype from the tire.

The methodology used was:

1. Calibrate VNA with the UFL kit.
2. Measure FARSENS's IC impedance @ VDD = 2.6 V
3. Measure antenna impedance without matching network (0R in the LC footprints).
4. Calculate the theoretical matching network to obtain a first approximation to the optimal tuning.
5. Iterate with the commercial inductors and capacitors to fit the antenna impedance.
6. Calculate the return loss.

The antenna and tag follows different trends in their impedances (one increases and the other decreases with the frequency) so it was extremely hard to make a proper tuning to obtain a wideband antenna. Therefore, two different matching networks were calculated.

868 MHz Matching network:

1. 868 MHz: Z = 19 + 43j; RL = 15.79 dB
2. 915 MHz: Z = 21 + 63j; RL = 5.9 dB

915 MHz Matching network:

1. 868 MHz: = 11 + 22j; RL = 2.91 dB
2. 915 MHz: = 15 + 39j; RL = 20 dB

3.3 Tag to Tire Attachment

Different glues and methods were tested to attach the prototype to the tire. As a result of this study it was concluded that best way to fix the prototype to the tire was using the same methods they use in the automotive repair industry: Vulcanizing. There are two ways of vulcanizing, cold and hot. In both cases the tire surface must be extremely clean to obtain a good bonding to the tire. The tag must be placed inside the tire with the pressure sensor pointing inside the wheel and must be located in the side wall, avoiding the metal parts of the tire.

Hot vulcanization is expected to have better characteristics than cold vulcanization. However, in this work cold vulcanization has been selected due to the its easier application (Fig. 7).

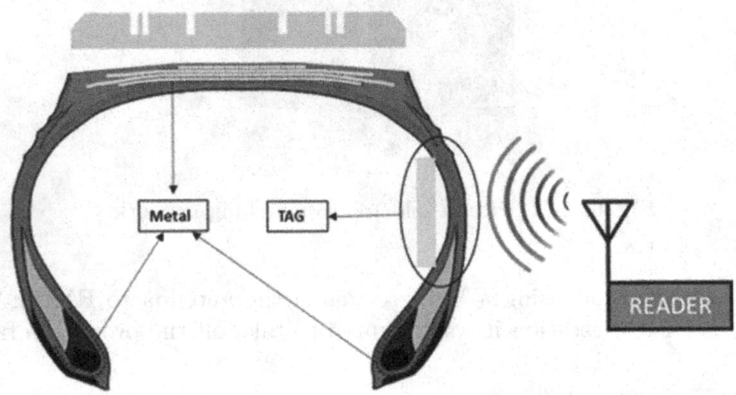

Fig. 7. RFID sensor placement.

4 Test and Results

In order to evaluate the feasibility of the proposed technology it was attached to the wheel of a real car. The purpose of the test was to evaluate the prototype under real conditions of pressure, temperature and motion. Two scenarios were planned:

In the first scenario the car is in motion. A fixed reader was mounted into the car and 3 antennas were attached in the wheel cavity as we can see in Fig. 8. The test was done with the car in movement at different speeds. A RF splitter was used with the antennas to cover a bigger read range with the cost of losing power transmission. Without the splitter, the reader would multiplex the readings between the three antennas reducing the coverage area.

In the second scenario (Fig. 9), without motion, a handheld reader was used to obtain data from the tag.

In both cases, data obtained from the tags was compared with the results obtained with an analog pressure meter in motionless state. Only pressure could be compared as there was no way to measure temperature with a meter inside the wheel.

Fig. 8. Motion test set-up.

Fig. 9. Stationary test scenario.

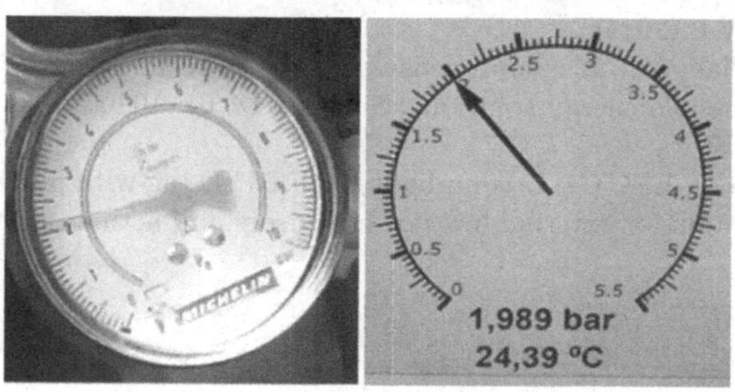

Fig. 10. Reference results and proposed sensor results.

The quality of the measurements, was very high (See Fig. 10). A constant offset of 0.1 bar was reported between the analog meter and the tag. Probably caused by the analog reference pressure meter and enough accurate for TPMS applications.

Regarding the data communication, the results obtained in the motion test were not satisfactory. The measurement at high speed were inconsistent and the tag alignment towards the middle antenna was determinant. Anyway the tag survived pressure, temperature and motion which is considered a good feedback for the first motion trials.

However, in the stationary test a successful ID and measurement communication was reported at an average distance of a meter and half.

5 Conclusions and Future Work

Due to the growing TPMS market there is a great interest on the development of passive pressure sensors that could reduce the cost and environmental impact of current active TPMS sensors. In this work a UHF passive RFID pressure sensor has been proposed, based on Farsens' ANDY 100 RFID tag. The tag, a commercial sensor and the required electronics have been implemented, inserted into a cushion gum and attached inside a tire. The implemented TPMS prototype has worked properly in terms of measurement and communication when the car is not moving, being possible to read the measurements with a distance of a meter and half. This way, the suitability of the proposed technology for TPMS applications has been demonstrated. However the system has not been capable of transmitting the measurements when the car is moving. A better antenna design and set-up specific for the application has to be found in order to keep the tag inside the coverage area of the reader even in motion and be able to substitute with full functionality current TPMS systems.

References

1. Freescale Whitepaper: A Global Solution for Tire Pressure Monitoring Systems. N: TPMSWP REV 2 (2014)
2. Kubba, A.E., Jiang, K.: A comprehensive study on technologies of tyre monitoring systems and possible energy solutions. Sensors **14**(6), 10306–10345 (2014). doi:10.3390/s140610306
3. Datasheet Farsens: EPC C1G2 compliant UHF RFID tag with power harvesting and SPI communication for external low power sensors and actuators. N DS-ANDY100-V08 (2015)

Nets4aircraft

Performance Analysis of Routing Algorithms in AANET with Realistic Access Layer

Quentin Vey[1,2](✉), Alain Pirovano[1,2], and José Radzik[3]

[1] ENAC, TELECOM/Resco, 31055 Toulouse, France
vey@recherche.enac.fr
[2] Univ de Toulouse, 31400 Toulouse, France
[3] Université de Toulouse/ISAE, 10 Avenue Édouard Belin, BP 54032, 31055 Toulouse Cedex 4, France

Abstract. Aeronautical Ad-hoc NETworks (AANETs) have been studied and could be proposed as an complementary communication system for civil aviation. Several routing algorithm have been proposed and assessed through simulation, but there is a lack of evaluation in realistic conditions, especially regarding the access layer. In this paper we propose to use Random Packet CDMA (RP-CDMA) as a MAC layer protocol for AANETs. We then present the results of simulations with actual aircraft trajectories considering successively three well-known routing algorithm (namely AODV, DYMO and BATMAN). We conclude from these simulations that AODV has the best performances, but also that the realistic access layer is quickly saturated by the mere signalization traffic. This calls for improvements in both routing algorithms and access layer.

Keywords: AANET · Ad-hoc · Network · Routing · RP-CDMA

1 Introduction

AANETs are ad-hoc networks in which the nodes are civil aircraft in flight. They are a subset of Mobile Ad-hoc NETworks (MANETs) and share properties with the Vehicular Ad-hoc NETworks (VANETs) [1].

In the future, AANETs could enable new peer-to-peer services for en-route aircraft such as wind-networking [2] or automatic conflict resolution [3].

In the short term however, only traditional communication systems such as satellite links and HFDL (High Frequency Data Link) are available to commercial aviation in oceanic and remote areas. Because of this, most of the currently used services are designed to use a air-ground communication system, as in [4]. In consequence, AANETs are considered in the middle term as a complementary solution to air-ground communication systems [5], and this paper will focus on air-ground communications.

As in any multihop network, a routing algorithm is required to determine the end to end path for each packet. Numerous protocols have been proposed for AANETs (e.g. ARPAM [6], AeroRP [7], greedy forwarding [8] ...), and they

J. Mendizabal et al. (Eds.): Nets4Cars/Nets4Trains/Nets4Aircraft 2016, LNCS 9669, pp. 175–186, 2016.
DOI: 10.1007/978-3-319-38921-9_18

have been evaluated against classical routing algorithms in simulations (AODV for the two given examples). However, to our knowledge, none of these protocols was assessed against real aircraft trajectories with an appropriate and realistic access layer model. The goal of this paper is to present the results of simulations of selected classical routing algorithms on replayed aircraft trajectories, with a realistic access layer model. These algorithms have been well studied, and are often used as a reference to compare the performances of other routing algorithms. We want here to explore their performances in realistic AANET simulations.

This paper is organized as follow: related work is presented in Sect. 2, the protocols and their adaptation to our case are described in Sect. 3. The experimental settings are described in Sect. 4 and the results are presented in Sect. 5 then discussed in Sect. 6. Our conclusion (Sect. 7) summarizes our findings, and future works are described in Sect. 8.

2 Related Work

Most of VANETs studies rely on the use of either 802.11 access layer or an ideal access layer. Simulations with an ideal access lack of realism, and 802.11 link layer was not primarily designed for ad-hoc networks, especially when ranges exceed 300 km [9]. The access layer used in this paper is based on the following work, specifically tuned for AANETs.

In [9], the author advocates for the use of Code Division Multiple Access (CDMA), but uses a static code allocation, under the hypothesis that enough codes are available to give one to each aircraft. This solution was tested for AANETs, with real aircraft trajectory but an ideal routing module.

RP-CDMA is a code allocation mechanism proposed in [10], in which the spreading codes are randomly selected for each transmission (see Description in Sect. 3.1). RP-CDMA offers the best performances when used with partitioned spreading, an interference cancellation method.

RP-CDMA has been augmented with link layer functionalities in [11], and tested in an ad-hoc environment.

3 Protocols Used

3.1 Access Layers

Description. RP-CDMA solves the problem of code attribution inherent to CDMA access layer in an elegant and simple way. The payload of an RP-CDMA frame is spread with a randomly chosen code, and an identifier for this code is included in the header. The header contains a preamble in order to improve packet detection and synchronization, and the code ID is spread with a code, common to every header (cf. Fig. 1).

This frame structure provides channel separation between signalization (headers) and the data (payload). If the pool of payload codes is big enough, RP-CDMA is mainly limited by header collisions.

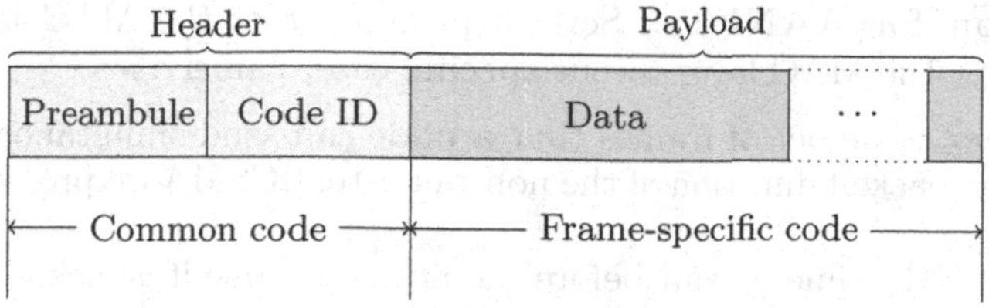

Fig. 1. Base structure of a RP-CDMA frame.

Several techniques are available to detect the payload and recover their collisions. Amongst them, Partitioned Spreading (PS) offers the best performances [10]. PS is also resistant to the near-far effect, one of the biggest limitations to other CDMA systems. Near-far situations are encountered when the difference in received power between two colliding frames is so high that the processing gain isn't enough to decode both frames.

In [11], the authors add MAC and LLC functionalities to the base RP-CDMA. Access control is performed in a way similar to non-persistent CSMA, with the addition that several messages can be transmitted at the same time.

The added LLC services are acknowledgement, automatic retransmissions and integrity control. These requires to add some fields to the base RP-CDMA frame: sender and destination addresses, CRC and frame ID. In order to reduce header collision probability, these fields are added to the section of the frame spread with the frame-specific code. Payload length and coding rate are also added to the header in [11].

Modelisation. We modeled RP-CDMA with the following assumptions:

- When two header collide, both frames are considered unrecoverable.
- If there are less than $maxPayload_{rx} - 1$ other frames colliding simultaneously with a given payload, this payload can be decoded. Otherwise, it is not recoverable [10].
- If the distance between a sender and a receiver is above *range*, the frame is not taken into account.

In [9], the author demonstrate that a radio range of 350 Km is enough to have an average connectivity over 90 % and provides a link budget for this range. Based on this publication and on results in [10], we have used the following values: $maxPayload_{rx} = 25$, $range = 350$ km and $bitrate = 800$ kb/s.

After an adaptation of the work presented in [10] to the context of AANETs, the header length of the RP-CDMA frame header was set to 80 bits, and the RP-CDMA fields spread with the specific code use to 102 bits.

The access layer modules uses FIFO queues to store pending packets. These queues can hold 100 packets, and they drop any new packet received from upper layer when this limit is reached.

Optimization for AANETs. Several parameter of the MAC layer can be tuned to adapt the MAC layer to our specific case, namely:

- $maxFrame_{tx}$: number of frames that a node can send simultaneously.
- $backoff$: the backoff duration of the non-persistent CSMA (expressed in header duration).
- $ackTimeout$: the time to wait before resending a frame if no acknowledgement is received.

These parameters have been optimized through simulations, the metrics, observed at the link layer, were:

- Success ratio: ratio of the volume of data passed to upper layer to the volume of data received from upper layer.
- Delay: delay between the queuing of a packet in a MAC module and its reception by the receiver's MAC module.
- Efficiency: ratio of the volume of data passed to upper layer to the volume of data sent by the radio module.

In the simulations, 53 nodes (the maximum number of neighbors in 99 % of the time in real aircraft trajectories) are randomly positioned in a 350 Km radius disk, each node generating a constant bit rate UDP traffic toward a center node, and the center node generating a similar traffic toward each node.

Several batches of simulation were run, modifying only one of the three parameter at a time. After each batch, the best value for this parameter is kept and used in the next batch of simulation. The independence of each factor is checked by the absence of influence between the behavior of one parameter and the value of the others. The following values have been obtained after this campaign of simulation: $maxFrame_{tx} = 1$, $backoff = 100$, $ackTimeout = 50$ ms. The success ratio obtained with these values is presented in Fig. 2.

3.2 Routing

The routing protocols used in this paper were chosen because they are typical examples of two families of routing protocols: reactive protocols with AODV and DYMO, and proactive protocols with BATMAN.

Because of the profile of the traffic and the positions of the nodes, we expect to see data traveling along long routes toward and from ground stations. AODV and DYMO seems both well suited this setting because they let intermediary node construct routing table toward both ends of a route during route resolution, which renders unnecessary any later route resolution between the intermediary node and the ground station. DYMO, with its path accumulation, is expected to reduce even more the required route resolutions.

BATMAN is an effective proactive routing algorithm. It has been preferred over OLSR because of its better scalability [12].

We have selected these classic routing algorithms because their performances have been widely studied in a variety of networks, and we want to extend this knowledge in the context of AANETs with realistic conditions. We describe in this section the general working principle of each of these routing protocols.

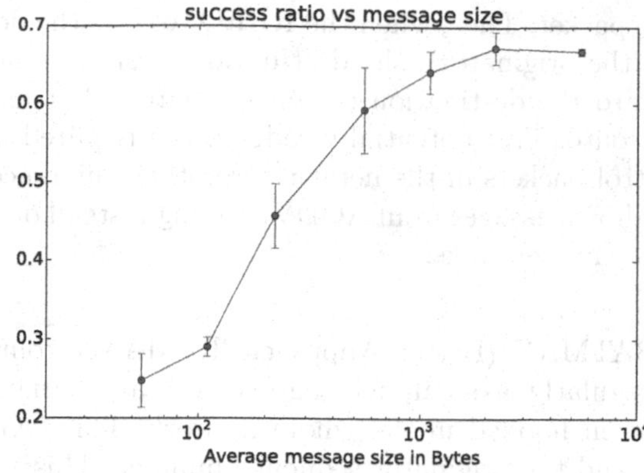

Fig. 2. Success ratio of the MAC layer after optimization campaign (generated load: 0.5 × channel capacity)

AODV. Ad-hoc On demand Distance Vector (AODV [13]) is a reactive routing algorithm which performs route discovery on demand, and handles route maintenance while they are in use.

Route discovery is performed when a packet is generated and there is no route entry toward its destination. A "route request" packets (RREQ) is broadcasted to the whole network, in a flood-like manner. Any node records from which neighbor this request was received and, if it has a fresh route entry toward this destination, sends a "route reply" packet (RREP) to the originator of the request. Nodes which are relaying this RREP learns by the way a route toward the destination. Because AODV uses symmetric links (e.g. to transmit RREP), a mechanism involving periodic "hello" messages is used to detect neighbors reachable through a symmetric link. Broken links are detected in the same way, and they trigger the sending of a route error message (RERR).

AODV features a rate limitation for control messages: no more than 10 control messages can be sent per second. However, given the geographic positions of the aircraft in our scenario, there is sometimes a significant amount of aircraft that could not be reached (e.g. flying alone on a remote route). In consequence, if the ground station tries to reach every aircraft, it will keep sending RREQ even though they are doomed to fail, these request being repeated while there are messages to send. This constant flow of control messages can reach the rate limit in the nodes close to ground stations, so any further control message is dropped, including RREQ which could succeed. In order to mitigate this issue, the traffic generation is initiated by aircraft, and ground stations only replies to it, thus preventing the constant flow of RREQ from the ground station.

DYMO. The Dynamic MANET On-demand routing protocol (DYMO, [14]), also called AODVv2, is a derivative of AODV. It uses the same mechanism of RREQ and RREP. The main difference is that DYMO implements a "path accumulation" feature: each node forwarding a RREQ/RREP can add its own address in the header of the packet. Thus, when the RREQ reaches the destination (resp, the RREP reaches the originator), the destination (resp. originator) learns not only the route toward the destination (resp. originator), but also toward every other node on the route. This potentially reduces the required number of route resolution and control packets in the network. Another difference is that it does also not use the "hello" messages from AODV, relying instead on received RREQ and RREP to detect broken links.

BATMAN. In BATMAN (Better Approach To MANet routing, [12]), each node broadcasts regularly a small message, called an "Originator Message" (OGM), which is then flooded in the whole network. This OGM contains the originator address, and the originator sequence number. This sequence number is increased after each sending of an OGM, and is used by the nodes receiving this OGM to keep track of already received OGMs.

Each node receiving the OGM records its sequence number, originator address, and the address of the neighbor node that just sent it. It then uses a ranking procedure to give a rank to this neighbor as a next-hop toward this originator, then uses the highest-ranked neighbor to define the route toward this originator.

The period of sending of the OGMs is a critical parameter, as it controls the refresh rate of the routing information, but also the amount of signaling data generated. If it is low few control packets will be generated, so the network consumption will be low, but the routes will take time to be refreshed, leading to more routing errors. A faster sending rate will keep the routes more up to date, but will increase signaling.

This value was optimized for case of AANETs. Several simulations have been run for different values of this period under a low aircraft density scenario. The value of 5 s minimized the delay and reachability, and is used in the simulations presented in this paper.

4 Experimental Setting

4.1 Simulation Environment

The simulations were conducted in the simulator OMNeT++ [15], based on the INET framework [16]. The model nodes were using INET's module for the protocols AODV, DYMO, BATMAN [17], UDP and IP, and custom modules for the traffic generation and node mobility.

4.2 Node Positions

In our study, we focused on the North Atlantic Tracks (NAT) [5] as an example of structured air traffic. We used real aircraft position data from Eurocontrol historical traffic repository, tailored to our study case, as an input to our simulations [18].

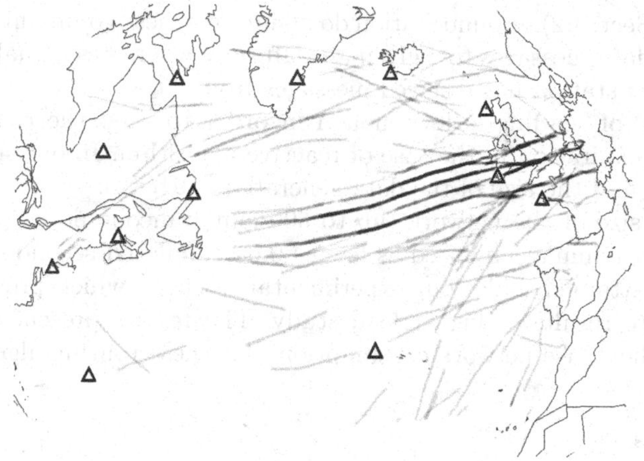

Fig. 3. Aircraft density on the 2014-05-02, 8 h to 9 h time slot (greyscale). Ground station are presented as black triangles.

In MANET, protocol performances does not depend only on node density, but also on node spatial distribution [19]. In order to take this into account, we used real traffic data. Several different days were re-played to add statistic diversity to the aircraft positions while using real geographic data.

Because of the computational cost of the simulation, we had to restrict the simulations to a set of representative time slots. In this paper, we present the results of simulation conducted on the 8 h to 9 h time slot, for the 2013-09-14, 2014-05-02 and 2015-05-15. These dates present the median number of aircraft per day for their year, and the 8 h to 9 h time slot corresponds to a medium Instantaneous Aircraft Count (IAC) during the day. Furthermore, this time slot correspond to the end of the eastbound traffic flow, and the beginning of the westbound flow, which is the time of the day during which the topology of the network seems to vary the most.

In order to match the different possible air routes and hence maximize the probability of delivery, twelve ground stations were placed on land masses around the area of interest (see Fig. 3).

4.3 Traffic Generation

The traffic generation is designed to trigger a minimum response from the reactive routing algorithms, and acts also as a probe to measure several metrics. It mimics the communication between inflight aircraft and air traffic management authorities on the ground. Because one of our goals is to assess the "base" network consumption for each algorithm, this traffic is kept as low as possible.

It consists in periodic UDP message (data messages) exchanged between aircraft and ground. When a data message is received, an acknowledgement is sent (another UDP message). In order to handle the rate limit problem of AODV (cf. AODV in Sect. 3.2), ground station do no initiate these communications, they start sending data messages to a given aircraft only when it is actually reachable (i.e. the ground station has received messages from it).

The period of sending is low enough in order to keep the route active to prevent route expiration in the case of reactive algorithm. In our simulations it was set to 1 s, and the size of the data generated is 9 bytes.

Given the size of the network (up to 600 simultaneous nodes), the computation are slow (simulation speed as low as 0.01 simulated seconds per runtime seconds were attained under our experimental setting), which prevent us from publishing here results of higher load study. The results presented here show nevertheless the "base network consumption" for these routing algorithm.

4.4 Metrics

Delay. The one way end to end transmission delay is measured with the UDP packets, and recorded in an histogram.

Reachability. We define reachability as the ability to exchange messages bidirectionally between a host and a ground station. It is measured by sending a probe packet and waiting for its acknowledgement. If this acknowledgement is received within a given time (*ackTime*), the node is considered reachable. The node is considered unreachable when no acknowledgment packet is received in time. This is measured with the probe packets sent by the traffic generator module and their acknowledgements. Previous simulation with and ideal access model (i.e. without loss, and with a delay equal to the sum of propagation and transmission delays) have shown that the one-way delay was lower than 1 s for 98 % of the packets. We thus set *ackTime* to 3 s in this study, large enough to ensure that the measured losses of reachability do not correspond to the "ideal" delay, and small enough to provide a sensible value in regard of the requirements of actual services [4].

In the actual topology of our network, some subset of the nodes can not be reached because they are too far from any other nodes, however good the routing algorithm is. In order to take this into account and remove this bias from the measure, the reachability values are normalized against the "connectivity to the ground" (connectivity has here the meaning used in graph theory).

Let $\mathbf{G} = (\mathbf{A} \cup \mathbf{S}, \mathbf{E})$ be the graph representing our network. The vertices $\mathbf{A}$ are the inflight aircraft and $\mathbf{S}$ the ground stations, and the edges $\mathbf{E}$ are the possible ideal links (i.e. there exist a link when two aircraft are closer than 350 Km in our case). Let N_p be the number of aircraft in $\mathbf{A}$ for which there exist a path to a ground station. We define the "connectivity to the ground" as $C = \frac{N_p}{|A|}$.

Network Routing Load. The network load due to the routing signalization is measured by counting routing packets passed from IP modules to MAC modules.

5 Results

On every graph in this paper, error bars represent 95 % confidence interval.

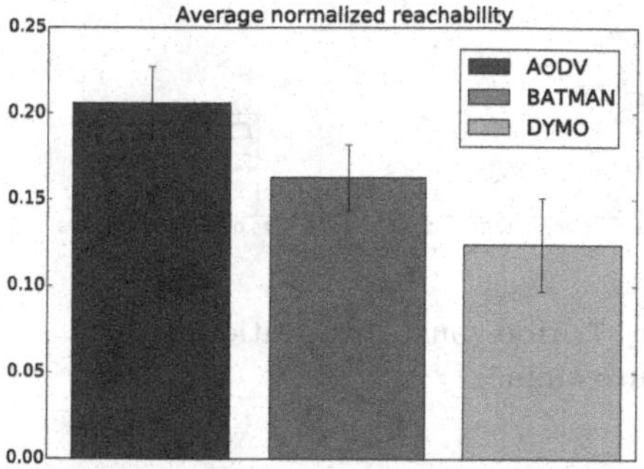

Fig. 4. Average normalized reachability. (Color figure online)

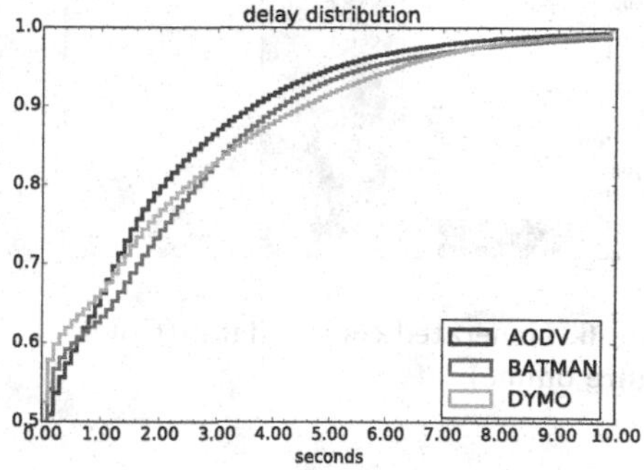

Fig. 5. Cumulative density function of end to end delay. (Color figure online)

The average normalized reachability is presented in Fig. 4. From this graph, we can conclude that AODV performs significantly better than DYMO. Given the uncertainty associated to BATMAN, we can say that the latter performs between AODV and DYMO with respect to reachability.

The Fig. 5 represents the histogram of one-way end to end delay for each protocol. The delay obtained for AODV is the lowest for the last 30 % of the distribution.

The amount of signalization generated by each protocol, presented in Fig. 6, follows the expected pattern. BATMAN generates significantly more routing control messages than AODV, which generates significantly more signalization than DYMO. This graph shows only the generated signalization volume, the data rate measured at the MAC layer ranges from 54 kB/s (DYMO) to 70 kB/s (AODV).

The packet hop count histogram, presented in Fig. 7, shows AODV carries a higher ratio of packets on longer routes.

6 Discussion

The low values of reachability in the Fig. 4 can be explained by the high delays observed in Fig. 5: roughly 28 % of the packet takes more than 1.5 s to reach their destination. This very high delay is due to the congestion of the access layer queues in the vicinity of the ground stations. This congestion also leads to packet drops when the queues are full, which further decrease the probability that a probe packet (or its response) reaches its destination.

BATMAN signalization is one order of magnitude above AODV and DYMO because, as a proactive protocol, it maintains routing information toward every node in the network. With BATMAN, the load generated by each node is proportional to the square of the number of node in the same connected subnet

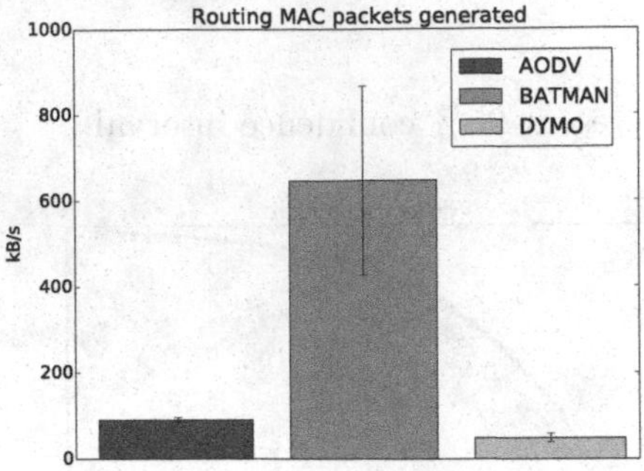

Fig. 6. Generated control data. (Color figure online)

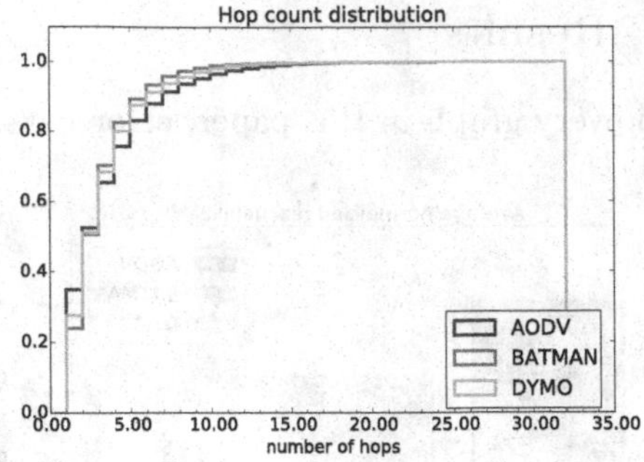

Fig. 7. Hop count distribution. (Color figure online)

(connected as in graph theory) because it rebroadcasts every OGM it receives. So when the network is partitioned, the amount of signaling packets sent by each node is reduced by the square of the size reduction of each subnet, which leads to a great variation in the load generated by BATMAN, hence the wide confidence interval. The reactive protocols generate less signalization than BATMAN and, as expected, DYMO generates less control packet than AODV.

The data in Fig. 7 also explain the better results of AODV in terms of reachability, because it allows further nodes to be reached. Compared to DYMO, AODV features indeed an active broken link detection mechanism ("hello" messages), which leads to faster route error detection and repair. On a long route, a broken link is more likely to occur, so the speed of its detection has more impact on the average success ratio of packets on this route. If this error is detected quickly, packets arriving from far nodes suffer less from this effect. This explains why AODV shows a higher proportion of large hop counts than DYMO. The same "long route" effect explains also why AODV has a higher hop count than BATMAN. Because BATMAN generates a higher MAC load in the whole network, the probability of loss because of MAC congestion is higher in overall, and it is more detrimental if the route is longer.

The poor absolute performance of the network presented here, must be considered with respect to the success ratio of the MAC layer presented in Fig. 2. Because the generated network traffic consists of small probe and signalization packets (on average less than 110 bytes), the MAC layer operates where it is less effective. In consequence, these results encourage for performing aggregation in the link layer in order to increase the size of the frames. Because the generated traffic was only made of probe packets, it is not meaningful to compare these absolute performances to classic communications systems such as satellite links and HFDL.

Independently of the absolute performances, these results show that AODV performs better than BATMAN and DYMO in terms of reachability. Even though AODV has a bigger overhead cost than DYMO, the reachability gain offsets this weakness.

Furthermore, we have also conducted simulations based on an ideal access layer, and their results confirm this trend (AODV performs better than BATMAN and DYMO).

7 Conclusion

We have assessed the behavior of three well-known routing algorithms dedicated to MANET in AANET simulations, with both a realistic access layer based on RP-CDMA and actual aircraft trajectories. Simulation results show that AODV is the best suited routing algorithms for our air-ground communication system based on an AANET. The changes to AODV brought by DYMO are detrimental in terms of reachability. And BATMAN is already overloading the access layers with the signalization traffic it generates, so it will not be scalable to a situation with more load or more nodes.

Even if AODV shows the best performances in term of reachability, delay and route length, this study confirms that, as the resources are scarce in AANETs, the development of frugal routing algorithms has to be considered.

8 Perspectives

We will address the problems illustrated in this paper in the following ways:

The RP-CDMA model will be improved by adding aggregation to the current MAC model to use it layer in its optimal performance domain.

Because considered routing algorithms signalization already overloads the access layers, the development a new frugal routing algorithm seems necessary. Geographic routing algorithm can make use of already existing system aboard aircraft (GPS positioning, ADS-B traffic monitoring...) in order to reduce the required signalization. We are currently validating and assessing an innovative routing algorithm derived from trajectory based forwarding [20], taking into account the actual aircraft density to create sensible packet trajectories without requiring exact route resolution.

References

1. Garcia, F., Pirovano, A., Royer, M., Vey, Q.: Aeronautical air-ground data communications: current and future trends. In: Fiorini, M., Lin, J.-C. (eds.) Clean Mobility and Intelligent Transport Systems, pp. 401–416. IET, Xi'an (2015)
2. Rodionova, O., Delahaye, D., Sbihi, M., Mongeau, M.: Trajectory prediction in north atlantic oceanic airspace by wind networking. In: 2014 IEEE/AIAA 33rd Digital Avionics Systems Conference (DASC), October 2014, pp. 7A3-1–7A3-15 (2014)
3. Guys, L., Puechmorel, S., Lapasset, L.: Automatic conflict solving using biharmonic navigation functions. Procedia Soc. Behav. Sci. **54**, 1378–1387 (2012). Proceedings of EWGT2012 - 15th Meeting of the EURO Working Group on Transportation, Paris, September 2012

4. EUROCONTROL and the Federal Aviation Administration (FAA). COCR: Communications operating concept and requirements for the future radio system - version 2.0 (2006)
5. Vey, Q., Pirovano, A., Radzik, J., Garcia, F.: Aeronautical ad hoc network for civil aviation. In: Sikora, A., Berbineau, M., Vinel, A., Jonsson, M., Pirovano, A., Aguado, M. (eds.) Nets4Cars/Nets4Trains 2014. LNCS, vol. 8435, pp. 81–93. Springer, Heidelberg (2014)
6. Iordanakis, M., Yannis, D., Karras, K., Bogdos, G., Dilintas, G., Amirfeiz, M., Colangelo, G., Baiotti, S.: Ad-hoc routing protocol for aeronautical mobile ad-hoc networks. In: Fifth International Symposium on Communication Systems, Networks and Digital Signal Processing (CSNDSP), Citeseer (2006)
7. Jabbar, A., Sterbenz, J.P.: AeroRP: a geolocation assisted aeronautical routing protocol for highly dynamic telemetry environments. In: International Telemetering Conference (ITC 2009) (2009)
8. Medina, D., Hoffmann, F., Ayaz, S., Rokitansky, C.-H.: Feasibility of an aeronautical mobile ad hoc network over the north atlantic corridor. In: 5th Annual IEEE Communications Society Conference on Sensor, Mesh and Ad Hoc Communications and Networks, 2008, SECON 2008, June 2008, pp. 109–116 (2008)
9. Besse, F.: Reseaux ad hoc aeronautiques. Ph.D. thesis, ISAE, Toulouse, February 2013
10. Kempter, R.: Modeling and evaluation of throughput, stability and coverage of RP-CDMA in wireless networks. Ph.D. thesis, University of Utah (2006)
11. Mortimer, T.: A MAC protocol for multihop RP-CDMA ad-hoc wireless networks. Master's thesis, University of Alberta, Edmonton, Fall 2012
12. Johnson, D., Ntlatlapa, N., Aichele, C.: A simple pragmatic approach to mesh routing using batman. In: 2nd IFIP International Symposium on Wireless Communications and Information Technology in Developing Countries, October 2008, p. 10. CSIR, Pretoria (2008)
13. Perkins, C., Belding-Royer, E., Das, S.: Ad hoc on-demand distance vector (AODV) routing (RFC3561) (2003)
14. Thorup, R.E.: Implementing and evaluating the dymo routing protocol. Master's thesis, University of Aarhus (2007)
15. OMNeT++ (2013). http://www.omnetpp.org/
16. INET (2014). http://inet.omnetpp.org/
17. Ariza-Quintana, A. Casilari, E., Trivino Cabrera, A.: Implementation of manet routing protocols on OMNeT++. In: Proceedings of the 1st International Conference on SimulationTools and Techniques for Communications, Networks and Systems & Workshops, Simutools 2008, pp. 80:1–80:4. ICST (Institute for Computer Sciences, Social-Informatics and Telecommunications Engineering), Brussels (2008)
18. EUROCONTROL. Data demand repository, 2 September 2015
19. Garcia de la Fuente, M., Ladiod, H.: A performance comparison of position-based routing approaches for mobile ad hoc networks. In: 2007 IEEE 66th Vehicular Technology Conference, VTC 2007 Fall, September 2007, pp. 1–5 (2007)
20. Niculescu, D., Nath, B.: Trajectory based forwarding and its applications. In: Proceedings of the 9th Annual International Conference on Mobile Computing and Networking, MobiCom 2003, pp. 260–272. ACM, New York (2003)

Author Index

Printed in the United States
By Bookmasters